D1025148

RENEWALS 458-4574

## DATE DUE

| | | | |
|---|---|---|---|
| | | | |
| | | | |
| | | | |
| | | | |
| | | | |
| | | | |
| | | | |
| | | | |
| | | | |
| | | | |
| | | | |
| | | | |
| | | | |
| | | | |
| | | | |
| | | | |
| | | | |

*American Babel*

# American Babel

## Rogue Radio Broadcasters of the Jazz Age

CLIFFORD J. DOERKSEN

**PENN**

University of Pennsylvania Press

Philadelphia

10  9  8  7  6  5  4  3  2  1

Published by
University of Pennsylvania Press
Philadelphia, Pennsylvania 19104-4011

Library of Congress Cataloging-in-Publication Data

Doerksen, Clifford John, 1963–
    American Babel : rogue radio broadcasters of the jazz age / Clifford J. Doerksen.
        p. cm.
    Includes bibliographical references and index.
    ISBN 0-8122-3871-0 (cloth : alk. paper)
    1. Radio broadcasting—United States—History.    2. Radio broadcasters—United
States—Biography.    I. Title.

PN1991.3.U6D64    2005
384.54′0973′09042—dc22                                                    2004061240

# Contents

# Preface

When I began the research that led to the writing of this book, my intent was to write about border radio stations, the high-powered pirates that cropped up on the southern side of the Texas-Mexico border in the 1930s to bombard the United States and Canada with hillbilly music, fundamentalist preaching, populist politics, seedy mail-order merchandising, and advertisements for quack medical treatments. The border-blasting tradition was started by Dr. John Romulus Brinkley of Kansas and Norman Baker of Iowa, pioneer broadcasters whose licenses were among the first to be revoked by the Federal Radio Commission on the grounds that the programs their stations provided were at odds with "the public interest, convenience, and necessity." I came to this subject as a fan of the Carter Family, the seminal proto-country-music act who spent much of the 1930s making prerecorded programs to be broadcast by Brinkley's ultrapowerful border station, XERA.

As I traced the careers of Baker and Brinkley back to the days before they were pushed off the airwaves by federal regulators, however, I lost interest in the border blasters in favor of a general study of independent radio broadcasters in the 1920s, some of whom made the border pirates look fairly staid. The field, I was happy to discover, was seriously underdeveloped. Almost all of the scholarship on early broadcasting was narrowly focused on the "Big Four" corporate players: Westinghouse, General Electric (GE), American Telephone & Telegraph (AT&T), and the Radio Corporation of America (RCA). By and large the early 1920s were treated as a messy prelude to the rise and consolidation of the tidy network systems: it was a period of undifferentiated chaos to be covered as quickly and efficiently as possible in order to get to the big players and the main events in which they starred. The five hundred or so independent stations on the air at the time were generally treated as bit players, if not mere background scenery. To me, they soon came to represent something more significant.

An apocryphal tradition has it that when asked why he robbed banks, the bandit Willie Sutton answered, "Because that's where the money is." Historians operate on similar principles: they gravitate toward the largest available troves of documents. As Michele Hilmes acknowledges in her *Radio Voices: American Broadcasting, 1922–1952*, there are draw-backs to this approach. Hilmes writes:

Many—the vast majority—of broadcast hours are lost forever. What does exist tends to privilege the dominant and centralized sources. I have drawn heavily on NBC records for this study because they make up a very large proportion of what has been preserved and is accessible to the historian. Records and accounts of the larger and more successful stations, programs, and performers are more likely to survive than those that actually may be of more interest to the post-structuralist scholar: those small stations providing a different service to a more marginalized audience, those programs deemed of specialized interest or least appeal whose scripts and records have long been destroyed, limited regional and local broadcasts, those efforts that never made it to realization precisely because they went against the grain of dominant practice. Much research needs to be done in these lesser-known areas to bring them to other scholars' attention and to reflect more fully our diverse and conflicted media heritage.[1]

In a sense, this book is my attempt to fulfill the research mandate pro-posed by Hilmes—except that I am not a poststructuralist and I take issue with her assumption that small stations were necessarily marginal. I have found, to the contrary, that many of these were among the most successful and popular stations of the day, and that many of the com-mercial and cultural practices that eventually came to dominate and define American broadcasting originated among them.

Obviously the profiles of independent broadcast pioneers in this book are just as dependent on documentary sources as any previous history was (I have heard the recorded voice of just one of the broadcasters pro-filed here, William K. Henderson of station KWKH, Shreveport, Louisi-ana). Turning up information on these largely neglected stations was partly a matter of persistence and partly one of dumb luck. Had I not spent a week in the basement of Christ Community Church in Zion, Illi-nois, I could not have reconstructed the story of WCBD, a phenomenally popular midwestern station dedicated to gospel music and flat-earth geophysics. But I also got luckier than any historian can reasonably hope to be when I met Maureen Walthers, editor and publisher of the *Times Newsweekly*, a neighborhood newspaper in Queens, New York, formerly known as the *Ridgewood Times*. I telephoned Ms. Walthers in 2001 to ask her if she knew where I might look for papers relating to WHN, a hugely influential vaudevillian radio station founded eighty years earlier by her predecessor at the helm of the *Ridgewood Times*, George Schubel. "Oh, I've got a whole box of papers from the radio station," she told me. "I was going to throw them out the last time we moved our offices, but I said to myself, 'No, you should hang on to this because someday a histo-rian is going to come looking for them.'"

The box she saved included documents that provided invaluable insight into the minds and motives of key but forgotten contributors to the commercialization of the American airwaves. Most of the papers inside were about eighty years old, but one was dated 1980. It was a short but highly informative memoir typewritten by WHN's original engineer, William Boettcher, who was just a few years out of his teens when the station took to the air in 1921. In 1980 the octogenarian Boettcher apparently felt a need to record and register his participation in what he correctly saw as unheralded historic events. Walthers was unable to tell me how Boettcher's brief testament found its way into the business papers of George Schubel. Probably, she reckoned, he simply mailed it to the *Times Newsweekly* office and some thoughtful person dropped it into the box.

The flipside to the story of the fluke preservation of George Schubel's papers and Boettcher's memoir is my distant brush with the recovery of equivalent files of another New York station, WHAP, which in 1925 presented itself to the city as a nonprofit broadcaster dedicated to the highest cultural and civic values, but which was actually a propaganda front for a rich, racist, ultraconservative cult of heretical Christian Scientists. In 1998 I met the daughter of WHAP's primary announcer, Franklin Ford. It turned out that I had discovered a lot about her father's life that she had never known. "He was known as 'the Strange One' in our family," she told me. "He was always very secretive. We knew he had some sort of background in radio, but that was all. Although as I grew older I did learn enough about his politics to think they were repugnant—he was a big admirer of Joe McCarthy, for instance." She further recalled that a filing cabinet full of her father's radio-related papers had sat unopened for decades at an industrial plant owned by her family, but that it had been hauled away to the dump some eight or ten years earlier. Finding that filing cabinet became the subject of a recurring dream that still visits me from time to time.

The first purpose of this book is to provide a sense of what these forgotten radio stations were like and what they meant to the people who listened to them. But in the course of my research, I kept bumping into material relating to the issue of broadcast advertising that seemed at odds with a premise common to several recent contributions to the historiography of early radio. Much of this literature treats the commercialization of the American airwaves as something engineered from above by corporate interests and consolidated in the face of universal public resistance. But the longer I looked at the independent stations and their audiences, the clearer it became that attitudes toward broadcast advertising were strongly conditioned by socioeconomic standing. Antipathy toward commercialization was strongest among the well off and well educated. People lower down the economic scale minded it less or even liked it. It was the latter class of listener that was served by the independent stations, who were thoroughly and brazenly commercialized at a time when corporate broadcasters were eschewing advertising in the name of good taste and high cultural ideals. In other words, commercial broadcasting originated at a grassroots level, as a populist deviation from polite corporate practice.

In airing this thesis in various forums over the years, I have found that it strikes different people in different ways. A minority embraces the idea that hostility to broadcast advertising was essentially bourgeois as intuitively—even self-evidently—correct; another minority vehemently rejects it as a slur on the virtue of the working classes and a justification of the cultural crimes of present-day media conglomerates. I hope that readers belonging to the first category will not find my frequent returns to matters of class redundant, and that those belonging to the second will keep an open mind in relation to all the various proofs I have piled up.

In writing this book I have been aided and sustained by a legion of advisers, friends, kin, and obliging strangers. I thank Professors Dan Rodgers, Dirk Hartog, Sean Wilentz, Dan Czitrom, John Wilson, David Como, Michael Gill, Johannes Wolfart, Andrew Shankman, Brad Verter, Richard John, Frank Chorba, Peter Lake, Bruce Carruthers, and Wendy Espeland. I also owe debts of gratitude to Mitzi Baryla, Kiki Yablon, Julian Breen, Thomas H. White, Virginia Fletcher, Mick Letourneaux, Maria Evans, Maureen Walthers, Anaheed Alani, and Ira Glass.

Thanks to the administrative staff of the Princeton History Department, especially Kathy Baima, Peggy Reilly, Melanie Bremer, Leah Kopscandy, Vicky Glosson, and Pamela Long.

I thank my editor, Robert Lockhart, for his encouragement and intelligent guidance.

Prototypes of these chapters were tested in a variety of forums: the Graduate Seminar of the Wilson Society of Fellows at Princeton University; the Workshop in the History of Technology, Medicine and Science at Rutgers University; a panel discussion at the twentieth annual conference of the Popular Culture Association and American Culture Association; the Conference on Technology and Culture at the Newberry Library in Chicago; the Wednesday afternoon Brown Bag Seminar of the University of Illinois-Chicago Department of History; and in the pages of *The Journal of Radio Studies* and the *Chicago Reader*. Each occasion yielded valuable criticism, insights, information, and advice from interlocutors, editors, and readers.

I am deeply indebted to the staff of the Firestone and Mudd Libraries at Princeton University; the U.S. National Archives I and II; the Zion Historical Society; the History Office of the Christian Science Mother

Church; the Smithsonian Institution; the AT&T Archives; and the Broadcast Pioneers Collection at the University of Maryland's Hornbake Library. Despite the fact that it is not a research institution, the Christ Community Church of Zion, Illinois, afforded me every courtesy that a visiting scholar could desire.

The research and writing of this book were financially supported by the Princeton University Department of History, the Princeton Society of Fellows of the Woodrow Wilson Foundation, and the Mellon Foundation.

Thanks to my parents, Pat and Bill Doerksen, and my brothers, Mark and Mike, for their solid love and support.

Thanks especially to my wife, Elspeth Carruthers, for absolutely everything and above all for Gladys Wilhelmina Doerksen Carruthers. With love, I dedicate this book to them.

# Prelude

In late December 1921 a farewell reception was held in New York City for the Viennese composer Richard Strauss, who had been touring America. A novel entertainment had been arranged for the occasion: three piano rolls recorded by the composer were to be "shot from" the experimental transmitting station WDY, maintained by the Radio Corporation of America in nearby Roselle Park, New Jersey. At precisely half past four Mme. Elizabeth Schumann, soprano, was to rise, stand beside a radio receiver, and sing along to the transmission of Strauss's prerecorded piano accompaniment before the guest of honor and a gathering of the New York classical music elite. At the appointed hour, however, the engineer in charge could bring in nothing but static. A decision was made to proceed with tea while technicians worked on the problem. After the tea service had been cleared away, the experiment was tried again. This time the hapless engineer tuned in the strains of a popular air called "The Jazz Baby," followed by "The Alcoholic Blues." The fillip of wireless technology was hastily abandoned, and Herr Strauss graciously sat down at the keyboard and accompanied Mme. Schumann himself. Reported in the *New York Herald* as an amusing curiosity, in retrospect the incident takes on an emblematic aspect as a warning skirmish in the coming struggle over the correct cultural uses of radio.[1]

*Chapter 1*
# The Education of Frank Bannister

It is an interesting fact that the ideals of the owners of a station are bound to creep in and be reflected in the output from that station. Water seeks its own level. Listeners, likewise, seek their own level.

—*Chicago journalist, 1928* [1]

The year 1930 was a bad time to be a commercial traveler, and Frank Bannister, a midwestern sales agent for a New York pharmaceutical concern, was facing both middle age and hard times, his drugstore commissions dwindling to nothing in the worsening Depression. The Detroit-based salesman was seeking temporary solace in a Toledo speakeasy when he fell into conversation with a fellow "drummer" working a different line, that of selling commercial broadcasting time. "Selling broadcasting time sounded good to me," recalled Bannister; "I made a mental note to look into it as soon as I got home to Detroit." On returning home, Bannister applied for a sales job at WJR, a five-thousand-watt commercial station, only to be rebuffed by its sales manager, Lou Cavanaugh, who told him that if he wanted to break into time sales, he would have to start at the bottom of the ladder: "Go over to one of the small stations—like WMBC. . . . They'll hire you, because they'll hire anyone. . . . Stick it out for six months, learn the broadcasting business, then come back here. I'll give you a job, if you're still alive." The next day, Bannister found that Cavanaugh had been right about his chances at WMBC, "a 100-watt station with studios in a second-rate hotel on the edge of a garish nightlife district." Upon applying there, he was immediately put to work on a straight commission basis. [2]

Although he was glad to be working, Bannister felt no respect for his new employer and no affinity with the station's clients. "The audience for this small independent station was minimal," he wrote, "and the quality of its advertisers reflected the size and type of its audience—shoe repair shops, beauty parlors, advertising dentists and dollar-down-and-dollar-a-week credit houses." His response to his downmarket milieu was to act as if he were already working in a better one. "I decided," he wrote, "to stay away from the type of advertisers then using WMBC and go across the railroad tracks to solicit only the best advertisers in town, those whom no previous salesman from WMBC had dared to call on." The initiative paid off: in short order Bannister landed a substantial account with Chevrolet Motors, whose advertising office agreed to sponsor thirty-nine episodes of a historical program detailing American battle exploits in World War I, to be called *The Chevrolet Chronicles*. With this and other solid accounts under his belt, Bannister returned to see Cavanaugh at WJR just one week after their initial interview. Impressed, Cavanaugh gave Bannister his second job in radio.[3]

Although the new position was an improvement over WMBC, Bannister still felt as though he were slumming. The mercenary ethos of WJR, as laid out for him by Cavanaugh, violated Bannister's sense of what broadcasting could and should be. "Neophyte though I was," he wrote, "it was apparent to me that my new boss had no interest in programming and regarded everything as something on which to hang a commercial. He made no serious reference to any broadcasting function other than sales. . . . He impugned the character, integrity and motives of all who sought to interfere with 100 per cent commercial operation. It was quite an education."[4]

Again turning his gaze upward, Bannister determined to make one more jump up the ladder, this time to WWJ, "the class station of Detroit." WWJ's aura of class derived from the fact that it was owned and operated by the *Detroit News*, the city's leading broadsheet newspaper. The station also enjoyed a special relationship with the Detroit Symphony Orchestra; in fact, the business manager of the orchestra was also general manager of WWJ. Equally important to Bannister was the fact that the station maintained strict standards of discretion in its advertising practices. In the view of WWJ's management, he wrote,

a good radio station had to be run at a loss. Commercialism, they believed, would impair the entertainment value of programs and lose audiences. Naturally, WWJ's standards were higher than those of other Detroit stations, and perhaps even the highest in the country. Sponsorship of the news was not permitted. . . . No pharmaceutical advertising was permitted; no comparison-price advertising permitted. . . . There were many other taboos which did not win business for the station. This was ethical and principled broadcasting at its most illustrious."[5]

A crowning feather in WWJ's cap was its status as an affiliate of the National Broadcasting Company from the time of that network's creation in 1926.

In January 1931 Bannister realized his ambition of moving up to WWJ, a promotion that proved as satisfying as he had hoped it would. "For one thing," he wrote, "I could earn my living without shutting my eyes to many things I didn't like to do. For another, I saw in WWJ an instrument for practical altruism, a symbol of capitalism at its best, an organization that earned substantial profits while benefiting millions of people." Bannister soon discovered, however, that maintaining the standards of "ethical and principled broadcasting" at WWJ required vigilant resistance to downward pressures brought to bear by his clients. Soon after joining the station, Bannister found himself at loggerheads with Sam Osnos, proprietor of Sam's Inc., a cut-price retail outlet "on the shoddy fringe of the downtown shopping area" that specialized in work clothes and various other lines of goods "appealing to the masses rather than the classes." As Bannister relates, Osnos had begun his activities as a radio sponsor "using the small 100-watt stations with transcribed announcements [featuring] loud, insistent, repetitive, hard-sell copy." Having initially turned him down as a sponsor ill-suited to WWJ, Bannister was eventually obliged by the station's management to take on the Osnos account, only to regret the resulting program and its accompanying advertising as a betrayal of WWJ's standards. Unable to contain his irritation at this blot on the station's reputation, Bannister finally boiled over at Osnos. "You have failed utterly to understand the function that WWJ can fulfill for you better than any other vehicle," he recalled lecturing his crass client. "It can endow your business with respectability and upgrade your clientele so that my wife and your wife or your wife's friends will shop there. . . . Go up to Ann Arbor and get a professor of political science and put him on the air discussing world affairs. . . . Sponsor a symphony orchestra. That's what you should be doing!"

Duly chastened, according to Bannister, Osnos proceeded to clean up his act as a sponsor, signing a five-year contract to underwrite broadcasts of "the 100-piece Detroit symphony orchestra for one hour, every Sunday night, with known conductors as guests, and with no commercials of any kind." The time salesman boasted, "This was clearly the most ambitious, most expensive, most cultural single program ever to be scheduled on any single radio station." Whether or not the promised social upgrade of Osnos's clientele ever materialized, Bannister did not say.[6]

This anecdote, taken from Bannister's 1965 memoir, *The Education of a Broadcaster*, touches on a variety of interesting features of the early American broadcasting scene. Most obviously, it traces the contours of a pyramid of prestige, such that certain stations counted as "cheap" while others were "high class." To date, this hierarchy of status has received little attention from historians and media scholars, who have given most of their attention to corporate-owned stations at the top of the pyramid while all but ignoring small, independent stations such as WMBC. Neglect of the cheap stations has distorted the historiography of early broadcasting in a variety of ways. The high- class character of the corporate stations, for instance, tends to fade when they are studied in isolation from their social inferiors. But the independent stations are also significant and interesting in their own right—as is the fact of their disappearance from the standard narrative accounts of the evolution of the American broadcasting system.

Maybe Bannister included WMBC in his memoir only because it fulfilled an important convention of the businessman's memoir, the start at the ladder's lowest rung in relation to which the subject's rise in the world—in Bannister's case, to the office of vice president of the NBC television network—can be measured and fully appreciated. The publication date of Bannister's memoir, however, hints at an additional motive. In 1965 the American broadcasting industry was still reeling from an attack from an unexpected quarter: the chair of the Federal Communications Commission. Historically, the FCC and its predecessor, the Federal Radio Commission, had been most amiable confreres to the network interests. In the early 1960s, however, the FCC chair was held by a maverick, Newton Minow. In the course of an address to the thirty-ninth annual convention of the National Association of Broadcasters in May 1961, Minow had made national headlines by lambasting the broadcasting industry for having reduced the airwaves to the cultural condition of a "vast wasteland" in pursuit of commercial profits.[7]

The closing pages of the *Education*, in which Bannister confronts the "vast wasteland" charge head-on, confirm that he had Minow very much in mind. Given the reservations Bannister expressed about broadcast commercialism in the early pages of the book, a reader might expect Bannister to deliver a reasoned, perhaps rueful consideration of the justice of Minow's critique. Instead, he performed a curious reversal. Unconsciously replicating the performance of station manager Lou Cavanaugh thirty-five years earlier, Bannister now impugned the motives of commercialism's critics. The "vast wasteland" slur, Bannister angrily asserted, represented the cavils of a small claque of "eggheads, bluenoses, and critics" who presumed to "do the thinking and planning" for the rest of the world. "Those who don't like television," concluded the erstwhile champion of ethical and principled broadcasting, "seldom if ever watch it. Those who watch it think it's swell."[8]

As if the conflicted condition of Bannister's mind were not evident enough, he confesses elsewhere in *The Education* to having "a split personality" and harboring "schizophrenic" attitudes in relation to the system of broadcasting to which he had devoted the better part of his professional life.[9] Bannister's confusion about matters of value, however, should not be allowed to impeach his factual testimony about the condition of the radio business as he found it in 1930. We can take the salesman at his word when he states that "the use of radio advertising started at the lower levels of business and worked its way up"[10]—started, in other words, at a local level for local sponsors at local cheap stations such as WMBC, only later to work its way up to the national level on national network stations. Evidence on this count abounds. In his pioneering 1927 study of the feasibility of broadcast advertising, for instance, the journalist Edgar H. Felix referred to a ubiquitous class of broadcaster he termed "the station of local interest,"

a description of which will instantly call to the mind of the reader, familiar with broadcasting conditions in his district, one or more stations which serve his area. This is the popular local station with its chatty announcers. . . . [who] introduce their artists with elaborate words of praise, not always justified. They feature local talent, refer glibly to their "dear friends, the radio audience," and speak of artists as "this little girl" and "this grand old man." There is ample evidence that such stations have faithful audiences. Local merchants use them effectively and trace results. Usually, the commercial broadcasting they offer is unconcealed direct advertising, spiced with a little vaudeville entertainment. Such stations are useful to the small merchant and the local advertiser. Their rates are naturally low because they appeal to a limited class of the radio audience. Nevertheless, they are not to be dismissed from consideration merely on the ground that they do not hold the more discriminating class of radio listener. The rise of the confession type of magazine is evidence of the numerical and buying power of this group.[11]

In 1926 the New York-based magazine *Radio Broadcast* referred to the same class of broadcaster more bluntly as "the smaller and irresponsible stations." While lamenting the "blatant advertising" of the latter, *Radio Broadcast* also extended blame to the small businesses that purchased their time: "Unfortunately it is a fact that only the largest concerns can see the value of genteel publicity, while the smaller firms will insist on inserting everything even down to the names of the firm members, where they were born, the size of the plant, the amount of business done, and other details of interest to no one but themselves."[12]

Recognition of the ubiquity of such stations on the early airwaves helps to bring into sharper focus some blurry details of radio history. Take, for example, the confusion surrounding airborne advertising and its moment of origin. According to the media critic Robert W. McChesney, "commercial advertising [on radio] in the modern sense of the term was almost nonexistent prior to 1928."[13] "Never," counters the cultural historian Michele Hilmes, "was there a time in the development of broadcasting when commercialism, and its avenue of access to the popular, did not form a central core of the listening experience. . . . Many accounts testify to the pervasiveness of commercial announcements on the air from the earliest days."[14] If we broaden our scope of inquiry beyond the large corporate broadcasting interests, what looks like a stalemate of expert opinion becomes a simple difference of perspective. McChesney is correct in regard to the early "high class" metropolitan stations such as WWJ; Hilmes is sustained in relation to the global field of broadcasters—provided, that is, that cheap stations are recognized and taken seriously.

But how much attention do these footling "stations of local interest" merit? In the case of WMBC of Detroit, the answer is clear: a lot more than has yet been accorded it. Consider, in this regard, a passing allusion that Bannister makes to the funeral of WMBC's announcer Jerry Buckley, an event that took place on 26 July 1930, the day before Bannister first reported to work at the station. "There were 50,000 uninvited mourners at his funeral," wrote Bannister, "which was held in a pelting rainstorm."[15]

Fifty thousand is a figure that accords poorly with Bannister's contention that WMBC's audience was "minimal"—unless, as I suspect, he was using that term as a social rather than a numerical descriptor. But some eyewitness accounts of this event put the toll of mourners far higher. Calling it "the greatest throng that ever gathered in Detroit to attend the funeral of a private citizen," the *New York Times* reported that one hundred thousand Detroiters—"persons in humble circumstances, who had listened to Buckley's voice but had never seen him personally"— braved the driving rain to file past the closed casket that held the announcer's bullet-torn body.[16]

Who was Buckley to draw such a throng? The answer will forever remain a matter of opinion. Cut down by three gunmen as he left the WMBC studio on 23 July, Gerald Emmett Buckley had been a popular fixture of the Detroit airwaves since 1928. To the admiring multitude of listeners he addressed as "The Great Common Herd," he was a courageous muckraker who used his microphone to expose graft and corruption in Detroit's municipal government. To his detractors, he was an unprincipled racketeer who abused his charismatic sway over an immense, credulous, primarily working-class radio audience in order to extort tribute from the city's politicians, law enforcement officials, and gangland chieftains. In either case, Buckley's voice was widely acknowledged to have been the primary impetus behind the 1930 recall of Detroit mayor Charles Bowes and his subsequent replacement by the reform candidate Frank Murphy.[17]

A lesson of the Buckley story is that early "local-interest" stations are not to be judged by the meagerness of their signal strength or their remoteness from the allegedly dominant corporate nexus. By any reasonable standard WMBC was the most important radio station of its region and moment, and yet it has tumbled into historical oblivion, overlooked (with a single and marginal exception) even by the many biographers of Detroit's second great radio demagogue, Father Charles Coughlin.[18]

Of course, not every low-watt station of the day served as a base of operations to a charismatic firebrand like Buckley. But if political meteors like Buckley were a minority among independent broadcasters, independent broadcasters vastly outnumbered high-class corporate stations throughout the 1920s—and many of these stations enjoyed popularity comparable to that of WMBC.

It was axiomatic among contemporary observers of the broadcasting scene that fans of these cheap stations came from the lower end of the socioeconomic ladder. In the case of WMBC and Buckley, the evidence is clear enough on this point. Covering the Buckley funeral for *Radio Digest*, the reporter Robert L. Kent recorded a homogenous procession of Detroit's laboring classes: "trucks, delivery wagons, a coal cart, patient children, overalled men who were tired from long walks across the city. . . . more hands blackened by toil than fresh with leisure."[19]

Regrettably, moments like this, in which the audience of a given station obligingly turned out in the streets to be counted and categorized, were rare. Worse, there are no demographically predigested broadcast ratings data available for the 1920s, nor is there much in the way of reliable survey data. There does exist, however, a wealth of data concerning the social stratification of the radio audience from the subsequent two decades, and on this some inferences may be grounded.[20]

In 1933 Clifford Kilpatrick, a sociologist at the University of Minnesota, found that principled disapproval of broadcast advertising was very much a class attribute, strongly correlated to economic and educational status, a finding subsequently affirmed by many other studies.[21] In one such work the Columbia University sociologist Paul Lazarsfeld found that a good portion of lower-income listeners actually *enjoyed* radio advertising. "It is quite startling," wrote Lazarsfeld, "to see how consistently dissatisfaction becomes higher as education increases."[22]

An equally consistent feature of these surveys is the finding that lower-class radio listeners overwhelmingly preferred popular entertainments to "cultural" programs. "When the audience of a serious musical program is analyzed," reported H. M. Beville Jr. of the 1939 Princeton Radio Research Project, "good music is shown to be the monopoly of the upper income classes."[23] In 1946, Lazarsfeld confirmed Beville's findings, noting that "the program types which reveal most marked differences in taste are those which have come to symbolize radio's cultural or educational mission. They are favorites of highly educated listeners, but they hold relatively little appeal for listeners on the lower strata."[24]

Not only was class a powerful determinant of program preference, but it also strongly influenced listener choice among available stations. Such was the conclusion of Alvin Meyrowitz and Marjorie Fiske of the Princeton Radio Research Project, whose survey data showed "quite clearly that as economic level decreases the proportion of small stations listened to regularly increases," a pattern that was made even clearer "if the respondents are classified by educational level." These findings, noted the authors, corroborated the assumption, widely held among small business advertisers, "that 'the little fellow likes the little station.'" The researchers elaborated: "Merchants selling low-priced merchandise and credit-store merchants in the metropolitan area . . . claim that they reach their public better over small stations, and would use them even if they could afford to advertise over the big stations."[25]

In sum, survey data from the 1930s and 1940s reveal lower-class radio listeners to have been tolerant of broadcast advertising, indifferent to "good music" and "cultural or educational" programs, fond of popular entertainment, and inclined to favor small local stations over "big" ones. These are suggestive findings, in that they correspond closely to the distinctions separating high-class from cheap stations in the 1920s. The former aspired to tact in their advertising practices, aimed at cultural gentility in their programming, and were cosmopolitan in outlook, which is to say that they interpreted their service mission to be national in scope. Cheap stations, on the other hand, were locally oriented, candidly commercial, and unapologetically populist—"lowbrow"—in their cultural agenda.

How highbrow, then, was corporate broadcasting? In their own estimate, the corporate broadcasters in the 1920s were as genteel as could be. The cultural template for corporate broadcasting was set early on by KDKA, the Pittsburgh station established by the Westinghouse Corporation in 1920. As the RCA-backed magazine *The Wireless Age* noted approvingly in 1922, KDKA from the start eschewed popular music of the kind "being played in every cabaret and theatre" and instead "gave the public the best class of music, even if this did not meet with immediate popular demand."[26] Such responsible policies of uplift, explained the music writer Charles Isaacson in a later issue, were part of "the special wonder of radio": "The broadcasting executives are particular not to send out anything which lowers tastes and so the inevitable effect of radio is to raise taste, appreciation, culture, understanding, intelligence, everywhere."[27]

In actual practice, corporate stations perhaps fell short what a discriminating audience today would honor as a highbrow profile from week to week. In describing the average aesthetic tone of American broadcasting in the 1920s, the historian Erik Barnouw influentially dubbed the decade "the era of the potted palm," a coinage referring to the flora found in the ballrooms of big metropolitan hotels and evocative of the music played there by house orchestras. "Potted palm music," elaborates Barnouw, was "recital music . . . European in origin, it was 'culture' to many Americans. . . . This music completely dominated radio in its first years and retained a leading role throughout the 1920s."[28]

The phrase "completely dominated" is, again, a corporate-centered overgeneralization. The "potted palm" metonymy is valid enough for the corporate stations at the top of the heap but not at all applicable to urban independents such as WMBC, whose musical fare was a mix of Tin Pan Alley pop and jazz. Nor does it apply to the rural independents known as "farmer stations," which broadcast Protestant hymns and old-time music, the folkish progenitor of the country-and-western genre.

It is out in the countryside that the socially partitioned character of early radio becomes most obvious. Consider the attitudinal split between the two leading radio periodicals of the day, *Radio Digest* and *Radio Broadcast*. The former was a program schedule and fan forum published out of Chicago and catering to a predominantly rural midwestern readership; the latter was a slick national periodical published out of New York. Each publication had a fixed editorial vision as to what good broadcasting sounded like, but these visions were antithetical. *Radio Broadcast* rarely acknowledged the existence of the rural farmer stations favored by *Radio Digest* except to denounce them as violators of the unwritten codes of commercial decency in broadcasting, and therefore as candidates for suppression. Conversely, the high-class corporate stations upheld by *Radio Broadcast* as reflecting broadcasting's best hope were assailed as overbearing pests of the air by *Radio Digest*. "Will the Westinghouse company, the General Electric company, the American Telephone and Telegraph company through their subsidiary, the Radio Corporation of America, and its new baby, the National Broadcasting Company, control the majority of time on thirty-seven wave bands with the plea that the public be served?" demanded an editorialist for the paper in April 1927. The writer continued, "Also under the persuasion that the chain programs are the ultimate in achievement and that the overwhelming majority of listeners prefer the opera, high-brow orchestras and Princeton-student-with-the-Harvard-accent announcers, will these Five Horsemen monopolize the choicest wavelengths?"[29]

Only occasionally was there something resembling dialogue between these segregated listening publics. In June 1927, for example, Russell Ryan of Kansas City, Missouri, wrote to *Radio Digest* in order to chide its readers for their parochialism. Ryan wrote:

I have read with interest the readers' controversy that has been going on in your magazine during the past several months. Brickbats have been flying thick and fast as one-half of the country shouts "low brow," while the other retaliates by saying "snob." Why all the argument? It's because the farmers and the city people have their own ideas on what constitutes an interesting program. Though some of the Mid Western stations render a very valuable service to the farmers, how are we going to get along without the chain stations to relay the messages of the President of the United States or John McCormick [*sic*] or Marion Tailey [*sic*], or a detailed ringside description of a world's heavyweight bout? It is alright to broadcast "hog calling" contests, the price of garden seeds, old time fiddlers, etc., for people who want to hear it, but the chain stations reach a much greater audience and it means more to hear national events broadcast than it does to hear some crossroads gossip about the neighbors.[30]

The July 27 issue of *Radio Broadcast* included the inverse sentiments of a correspondent in Nebraska, whose letter was identified by the editor as exemplifying a larger flow of "rabid" correspondence that routinely crossed his desk. The writer, identified as Mr. O'Hara, charged,

You want to see 500 stations eliminated and these 500 are to be the ones you New Yorkers and the chain don't own. . . . And by the way just what do you mean by high class programmes? Some cigarette smoking female dago or Russian warbling in upper C till they drive all the dogs in the neighborhood crazy? If that is your idea of a high class programme—and judging from the programmes we hear over WEAF it is—just keep them in the cultured and protected east, will you?[31]

If O'Hara comes across as an excitable type, the vehemence with which he expressed his preferences was pretty much the rule of the day. Early radio listeners were a thin-skinned lot, prone, as the pioneering radio journalist Hans V. Kaltenborn observed in 1931, to take umbrage at a "voice which penetrated the privacy of their homes to contradict their beliefs."[32] Similar, perhaps touchier responses were triggered when the intruding contradiction was cultural rather than semantic. Rural listeners hated jazz but hated opera and classical programs even more. Middle-class urbanites wrote to government officials demanding the suppression of urban lowbrow stations' nightclub jazz and farmer stations' broadcasts of primitive fiddle tunes. The urban working class tuned past the high-class offerings of the corporate stations in favor of the commercial lowbrows. The situation was fundamentally democratic: everybody got something to listen to, as well as something to abhor.

\* \* \*

In the 1920s middle-class America was wont to talk about the exciting new medium as if it were a single, monolithic agency—*the* radio—and to imagine its social consequences in similarly monolithic terms, as leading inevitably toward a rapid standardization of thought, taste, and sensibility. From the perspective of an age more inclined to deplore than celebrate the homogenizing powers of electronic media, this prospect may seem less than appealing, but to a broad spectrum of contemporary middle-class opinion leaders—educators, elected officials, ministers, clubwomen, captains of industry, journalists—the envisioned unification of the American mind seemed nothing less than utopian. Between 1922 and 1929 articulations of this millennial vision were everywhere: in newspaper editorials, magazine articles, public speeches, sermons, and poems.[33]

A representative elaboration of the unity-through-broadcasting theme was advanced by the prominent science writer Waldemar Kaempffert in a 1924 essay entitled "The Social Destiny of Radio," published in *The Forum.* "The telegraph and the telephone," wrote Kaempffert, "did much to weave us into a political and economic fabric, but a coarse fabric with wide meshes. How fine is the texture of the web that radio is even now spinning! It is achieving the task of making us feel together, think together, live together." Kaempffert's optimism, like that of the average utopian radio booster, was built on the presupposition that the content of the new medium could only be genteel, educational, uplifting. "Who," he asked, "when contemplating the marvelous potential of radio, can help conjuring up a vision of a super radio university educating the world, of a super orchestra bringing out the beauty of Beethoven's Ninth Symphony to millions on both sides of the Atlantic, of a super newspaper reaching whole continents not by printed word but by the living voice?"[34]

Only a few forecasters paused to consider the distinction between the miraculous medium and its contingent content. One was William H. P. Faunce, president of Brown University, who aired ambivalent thoughts on broadcasting in his commencement address to the graduating class of 1924. Like Kaempffert, Faunce accepted the premise that broadcasting was effecting a rapid standardization of the American mind. Faunce further welcomed this opportunity "for a hundred millions to think together, feel together, and to act as a single corporate irresistible force" as *potentially* utopian—"something that surpasses all the dreams of science or education or religion." But, qualified Faunce, unless appropriate efforts were taken to insulate radio against "the almost universal tendency to 'leveling down,'" radio might just as readily become an agency of degradation. "A democracy," warned Faunce, "which leads to an intellectual melting pot, a drab mass in which individual taste and conviction have disappeared, is a pseudo-democracy and a tyranny. When we allow noble music to be crowded out by jazz and lofty poetry to be submerged in cubist experiment, and high aspiration to be reproached as 'pious,' we are not demonstrating our democracy, we are exhibiting cheapness of soul.[35]

Cassandras such as Faunce were all but drowned out amid the utopian hubbub. While it lasted, the millennial mood nourished expectations of the imminent perfection of intelligent and totally transparent politics, the overnight assimilation of immigrants, the revitalization of rural life, the extension of higher education to any and all, the reinforcement of right religion, and the universal dissemination of genteel cultural values. "The variegated strands of religion, politics, education, and culture," observes the historian Clayton R. Koppes, "wove in and out, making it difficult to separate one thread from the others. Each relied on the others to make the whole garment. But the final design was clear. Radio, alone, unaided, could solve the pressing problems of the day."[36]

It was axiomatic among middle-class radio boosters that the use of radio as a mere merchandising tool would be inappropriate, if not immoral. Early on, this notion gained the imprimatur of Secretary of Commerce Herbert Hoover, nominally the supreme administrator of the airwaves. In his keynote address to the First National Radio Conference in 1922, Hoover declared it "inconceivable that we should allow so great a possibility for service to be drowned in advertising chatter."[37] On the strength of this and similar statements made by Hoover between 1922 and 1924, many Americans would form the impression that broadcast advertising was forbidden by the federal government and that the Commerce Department held the power of censorship over offending stations.[38]

In reality, there was no such rule on the books—Hoover's "ban" on advertising was closer to a recommendation than a decree. But no matter: according to an influential bit of contemporary conventional wisdom, advertising by radio could not succeed even if it were tried since, given a choice between a station that advertised and one that did not, listeners would tune out the former in favor of the latter. Thus, as the sociologist Marshall Beuick triumphantly announced in late 1924, "broadcasting possesses its own anti-toxins against advertising; and, like the human body, it becomes more resistant after prolonged attacks."[39]

The belief that broadcast advertising was both unfeasible and just plain wrong was nowhere stronger than among advertising professionals. In 1923 J. C. McQuiston, publicity director for the Westinghouse Corporation, appeared before a meeting of the Association of National Advertisers to tell them that "if radio were used for advertising, it would give advertising a black eye from which it would take a long time to recover."[40] McQuiston was preaching to the choir: *Printers' Ink*, the primary organ of the advertising trade, had been hewing to an editorial line against broadcast advertising since April of the previous year and would continue to do so well into the 1930s.

If this sounds incongruous, bear in mind that the advertising industry of the 1920s was quite different from today's. Born at the turn of the century and growing up alongside the new phenomenon of national name-brand consumer products and a new class of monthly magazines appealing to the middle-class reading public, the industry had by the 1910s begun to see itself as practitioner of a beneficial new "science," one that combined the insights of psychology and sociology with the rationalizing values of scientific business management. When mobilized by the Wilson administration to assist the Committee on Public Information in manufacturing popular support for American involvement in World War I, the advertisers grew still taller in their own estimate and began to talk up their craft not just as a science but as a force for education and moral improvement. The historian Roland Marchand writes, "Capitalizing on their wartime elevation in status, advertising leaders in the early 1920s began to seize every opportunity to associate themselves with high culture and 'business statesmanship.'" The climax of this surge of self-esteem saw the advertisers earnestly striving to promote themselves to the rank of a bona fide profession, commensurate in prestige and authority to medicine and the bar.[41]

Intent on advancing their standing, the advertisers were loath to gamble their reputations by tampering with the marvel of the ages. Industry analysts at *Printers' Ink* thus developed a battery of arguments, technical as well as moral, for steering clear of the airwaves. Even if listeners could somehow be made to tolerate "the intrusion of advertising in musical and literary programmes," the circulation of those programs would be impossible to measure. Furthermore, any significant diversion of resources to the new medium was bound to disrupt the advertisers' existing relations with the print media. And unlike magazines and newspapers, which easily accommodated the sensibilities of the individual reader, radio lacked that ingratiating capacity now called random access. The adman Howard Angus wrote, "Everyone has turned over the pages of a magazine, glancing casually at some advertisements and not at others, focusing his attention only on those in the magazine that interested him. You can't do that when listening to a radio program. Your ear bumps right into the commercial announcements." Radio, Angus further noted, lacked the silent discretion necessary to the tasteful promotion of personal articles: "A printed advertisement addresses its reader in comparative privacy. . . . when [it] offends, it outrages only one person at a time. . . . When radio blares forth a three-minute essay on some subject that generally is confined to the boudoir or whispered to the ear of a physician, the discourse is likely to jolt a bridge party—and cause indignant neighbors to close their windows."[42]

Genuine idealism also played a role in conditioning the advertisers' rejection of radio. A well-bred cadre of Ivy League-educated WASPs, the advertisers were just as prone as any segment of the educated urban middle classes to invest hope in radio's utopian cultural promise.[43] "As an advertising man," professed a prominent executive in 1926, "I can see the immediate possibilities of radio advertising. As a family man and radio enthusiast, I can also see the grave danger to radio if advertising were ever permitted to touch radio even remotely. . . . Those who cast longing glances at the radio receiver and dream of its possibilities for the advertising of their products are not only misguided in their judgment but may be guilty of an attempt to ruin one of the most beneficial forces of our times."[44]

However, the advertising industry's rejection of the airwaves was never quite categorical. A certain limited form of advertising was deemed permissible right from the start: the spare insertion of a "simple, brief and direct announcement" such as "By courtesy of R. H. Macy" at the beginning of a program. The problem with discreet sponsorship of this kind was that it was not truly *advertising* according to the lights of the industry; it was just "name publicity." And because it impeded the advertisers from doing their jobs effectively, name publicity represented a threat, not just to the advertising industry, but also to the national economy— "a barnacle on the distribution system of this country." The entire proposition, concluded one contributor to *Printers' Ink*, was "as impracticable as it is speculative"; if radio had any place in an advertising campaign, its costs were to be "entered on the books under an account headed 'experiment,' 'charity,' or 'philanthropy.'"[45]

Note that in fussing about the shortcomings of "name publicity," the advertising experts were *not* agitating for a relaxation of existing standards of broadcast etiquette. Rather, they hoped to avoid the airwaves altogether, to shield themselves from the unsought responsibility of becoming "the philanthropist of broadcasting." Albert E. Haase, an analyst of radio affairs for *Printers' Ink*, wrote, "Down deep in its heart, the radio industry believes that the public should pay for radio broadcasting." And yet, Haase warned, "the radio industry still plans to lean heavily on 'advertising' as a financial prop." Obviously, he concluded, "some means must be taken to rid advertising of this load, for the good of the country as a whole, for the good of advertising, and for the good of the radio industry."[46]

In 1925, under the auspices of *Printers' Ink*, a committee of senior executives was convened to look for a way to get advertising off the hook. In its reports, the panel heaped praise on Britain's BBC, deeming it the optimum "example of a plan the radio industry in this country could follow." But should a listener-financed state monopoly prove unworkable, the panel was open to alternatives. Funds, they proposed, might be raised through voluntary donations, or taxes on receivers, or a levy on the profits of receiver manufacturers, and then used to pay for commercial-free programs. Such a fund "could be placed in the hands of one man who would be a virtual Czar," much as Will Hays was the current "Czar" of the movie industry. Or perhaps "men like Morgan and Rockefeller" could be induced to act "as trustees for the radio listener." Whatever the solution, the committee declared themselves more than happy to help "explain the plan" to the public—so long as advertisers were not saddled with the burden of paying for programs themselves.[47]

\* \* \*

In 1925 American radio seemingly stood a slim chance of becoming a commercial medium. Although there was no positive consensus as to how broadcasting should be financed, all of the big guns—federal administrators, the Big Four corporations, the national advertising industry, the press, and the middle-class electorate—were arrayed against the option of commercialism. And yet, by 1930 the American airwaves had more or less descended to the commercial condition that would become the enduring hallmark of the "American System of Broadcasting."

The discrepancy between what was initially sought and what was ultimately got from radio is a problem whose salience in the historical literature on American broadcasting has grown over time. As Robert McChesney observes, the foundations of the field were laid by historians "sponsored by or affiliated with the commercial broadcasting industry," whose work consistently flattered the commercial network system as representing "the sole logical system for a society dedicated to democracy and freedom."[48] (Frank Bannister's *Education* can be considered a late entry into the corpus of the "business histories" but stands apart to the extent that it engages—however incoherently—with the issue of commercialism and its cultural effects.)

Of late scholarship on early radio has shifted in an opposite direction. To about the same extent that the early business historians passed lightly over resistance to broadcast commercialism in the 1920s, late twentieth-century studies by McChesney, Hilmes, and Susan Smulyan put that resistance near or at the center of their analyses. These works are alike in treating the commercialization of the American airwaves as the consequence of a hostile takeover, engineered from above by corporate interests and consolidated in the face of opposition construed to have been more or less universal. Toward this end Smulyan invokes the Marxist scholar Antonio Gramsci and his influential concept of "hegemony"— invisible mechanisms of social control whereby elites impose conformity to elite values upon subordinate classes.[49] To similar ends, Hilmes appeals to the authority of Gramsci's postmodern successor Michel Foucault.[50] McChesney drops no theoretician's name but cleaves to an essentially Gramscian line of argument, equating resistance to commercialism with the general will of the people and the triumph of commercialism with the frustration of the same.

This book will argue that commercialism triumphed in the American airwaves because most Americans did *not* object to it. The case will be made that what has been taken for unanimous hostility to broadcast advertising was in reality a consensus of the better-off and better-educated, and that American exceptionalism in broadcasting is rooted not in a hegemonic concentration of corporate power particular to the United States but in the inability of the corporate interests and government regulators to keep "the people"—in the form of the entrepreneurial, populist, independent broadcasters—out of the airwaves.

The independents owed their existence to the U.S. Commerce Department's singular openhandedness with radio licenses. This policy of liberality long predated the broadcast boom: its original beneficiaries were recreational technophiles known as the wireless amateurs, the earliest adopters of home electronics. This scattered fraternity (it was predominantly a boys' club) began to take shape around 1906, as scientifically disposed youths independently began constructing radiotelegraph receivers and transmitters out of odds and ends of domestic hardware, in emulation of the world-famous boy technologist Guglielmo Marconi. As their numbers swelled, the hobbyists began encountering each other's signals in the ether and soon began communicating regularly among themselves in Morse code, gradually annexing the night sky as one enormous predigital chat room.[51]

Before long this rising babble began interfering with official and commercial use of the radiotelegraph, a problem that led Congress to pass the first law governing the airwaves, the Radio Act of 1912. Although interested parties such as the U.S. Navy and the commercial radiotelegraph industry had pushed for outright suppression of the amateurs, the drafters of the Radio Act instead mandated their removal to a reserve at the short-wave end of the spectrum, thought at the time to be without much value. The act also required amateurs to license their transmitters through the Commerce Department, but the licenses were inexpensive and the threshold of qualification was low. Fatefully, the framers of the Radio Act neglected to reserve to the federal government the discretionary power to deny a license to any qualified applicant.

So matters stood when the idea of using the instrument known as the radiotelephone (invented in 1906) for mass communication (as opposed to point-to-point communication) suddenly reached critical mass in late 1921. In response to this development, the Commerce Department quickly established a new category of license for broadcasting stations and ordered all amateurs with radiotelephones to desist from the dissemination of "weather reports, market reports, music, concerts, speeches, news, or similar information or entertainments."[52] But the rules for acquiring broadcast licenses were no different than those for amateur licenses, so a lot of amateurs who for years had been using radiotelephones for broadcasting-like purposes traded in their old licenses for the new kind. Other people who had never previously had anything to do with wireless joined the rush to stake their claim in the ether. By late 1922 the number of free-standing private broadcast stations in the United States was edging toward six hundred; during a period of complete regulatory breakdown in 1927 it surged to nearly eight hundred.

In no other country did such a proliferation of private stations take place. The standard path to the creation of a national broadcasting system was the one blazed by Britain. Apprised by the American example of the radiotelephone's potential for mass communication, the British government enlisted the "Big Six" of the British wireless industry—Marconi, Metropolitan-Vickers, the Radio Communication Company, Thompson-Houston, and the British subsidiaries of General Electric and Western Electric—to cooperate in the capitalization and erection of a unified network of stations, linked by telephone lines to a central complex of studios in London. Incorporated as the British Broadcasting Company in 1922 (and reorganized in 1927 as the nonprofit British Broadcasting Corporation), the new venture was granted monopoly privilege in broadcasting by His Majesty's government. The Big Six were to realize a return on their investments through the sale of receivers to the public; the network's programs were to be financed through the sale of mandatory listener licenses.[53]

The U.S. Commerce Department effectively foreclosed the possibility of such a rationalized, centralized approach to broadcasting in America by giving away licenses to all comers. Regulators never stood a chance of coaxing all the genies back into the bottle, even if, according to the law, radio spectrum was inalienable public property.

While the government was heedlessly giving away the public airwaves, the American corporate interests with the largest stakes in radio technology were losing control of radio on other important fronts. Since the early 1910s, American Marconi, Westinghouse, AT&T, and General Electric had all been anticipating windfall profits from the radiotelephone, though none of them knew exactly how the technology was to be applied. The prevailing assumption was that the radiophone would conform to the point-to-point model of communication set by the telegraph, the telephone, and the wireless telegraph. From this angle, the fact that anyone with a radio receiver could intercept and understand radiophone transmissions was a glaring flaw. Only a few isolated individuals recognized this property as a virtue: one was the eccentric radio inventor and litigator Lee De Forest, who seems to have grasped radio's potential for mass communication as early as 1907. But De Forest was a self-marginalizing figure whose opinions held no weight in corporate boardrooms. In practice, the wireless amateurs treated all radio signals, telegraphic or telephonic, as mass communications, but no one was paying much attention to them either. Prior to the broadcast boom the corporations were counting on the discovery of a way to shield radio signals against eavesdroppers that would make radiotelephone service a viable commercial prospect.

Believing that the radiophone held the key to the future of global telecommunications, and hoping that America would dominate world radiophone service the way the British Marconi Company dominated the wireless telegraph, in 1919 the U.S. government compelled Marconi to sell off its American subsidiary, the assets of which were transferred to a new corporate entity, the Radio Corporation of America. So as not to alienate existing corporate interests, federal officials brought in GE, AT&T, and, eventually, Westinghouse as shareholders in the new venture, and then negotiated an agreement for the orderly division of any future market for radio goods among them. But like the drafters of the Radio Act of 1912, the architects of the RCA trust grossly underestimated the future importance of the amateur market and explicitly excluded sales to amateurs from the agreement. Because both broadcasting and "listening in" began as variants of amateur wireless play, the exemption would prove fateful.

Had the Big Four foreseen that radio was destined to be a mass medium, they doubtless could and would have engineered a monopoly over the broadcasting privilege, just as their British counterparts would do just three years later. And had they anticipated the popular craze for "listening in," the Big Four would surely have done a better job of keeping control over the receiver market, from which much of the profit in broadcasting would come during the first ten years of the radio boom. Instead, they were caught flat-footed by the popular demand for tubes and receivers. By 1922 a mushroom crop of smaller manufacturers—Brandes, Magnavox, Freed-Eisemann, Day-Fan, Crosley, Stromberg-Carlson, Mu-Rad, Thorola, Philco, Fada, Zenith, Grebe, Grigsby-Grunow, Atwater-Kent, plus innumerable nameless cottage workshops—had sprung up to service the market, often in blatant disregard for the patent prerogatives of the Big Four.

Of the six-hundred-odd stations operating in the United States by 1924, some two dozen were controlled by the Big Four. Another one hundred or so belonged to educational institutions ranging from universities to regional colleges to high schools, fifty or sixty were licensed to churches or other religious institutions (the math here is necessarily fuzzy, owing to the high mortality of stations and steady throughput of licensees). The Chicago Federation of Labor staked out a license; so did the American Socialist Party of New York. The balance of stations were licensed to business enterprises great and small: newspapers, hotels, automobile dealerships, department stores, vaudeville concerns, insurance companies, music shops, electrical retailers, seed companies, grain exchanges, schools of chiropractic, an oil refinery, a photography studio, a commercial laundry, a steel foundry, and sundry unincorporated individuals who wanted to make themselves heard. Of these, the ones who did not surrender their licenses early in the game would eventually need to find means of financial support for their stations—although some were calculating to make broadcasting pay from the outset.

The conventional wisdom of the American middle classes in the 1920s held that radio advertising could not possibly prosper because no one would put up with it. A corollary assumption was that genteel culture would inevitably triumph over popular culture just because it was self-evidently *better*. Although these beliefs persisted well into the 1930s, they were falsified in practice by independent broadcasters at a much earlier stage in the game. While these small commercial broadcasters have received short shrift in the corporate-centered historiography of radio, it was they who presaged the commercial and cultural future of American broadcasting, and who pioneered program formats and business practices that persist to the present day. The following chapter tells story of one such forgotten pioneer station, WHN of New York.

# Chapter 2

# Serving the Masses, Not the Classes

> It is not enough to say that decent people can turn their dials. The harm is that many people won't.
>
> —*Offended radio listener to Commerce Department, December 1924*[1]

Late in 1921 George Schubel decided that his corner of Brooklyn—the neighborhood of Ridgewood (today part of Queens)—would benefit from a radio station. Publisher and editor of the weekly *Ridgewood Times,* Schubel was not a "radio bug," but he asked around the neighborhood for technical help and found it in the form of twenty-one-year-old William Boettcher, who operated a radiophone transmitter (call sign 2WU) from the attic of his parents' house. Engaged as Schubel's engineer, Boettcher requisitioned a fifteen-watt radiophone transmitter from the De Forest Radio Telephone and Telegraph company and erected a horizontal transmitting antenna—some copper wire strung between two flagpoles—on the roof of the three-story building shared by the *Ridgewood Times* and the Ridgewood Chamber of Commerce.[2]

After persuading the proprietor of a Ridgewood music store, Joseph Stroehlein, to sign on as announcer and program director and to contribute a grand piano, a player piano, two Victrolas, and a supply of 78-rpm records to the cause, Schubel applied to the Commerce Department for a broadcast license. After an agent of that department inspected and approved Boettcher's handiwork in late January 1922, Schubel was given a call sign and permission to broadcast on the 360-meter wavelength. One evening in February, WHN made its debut with an improvised program of records, player-piano rolls, and a live piano set by maestro Stroehlein. Before long, according to an unpublished autobiographical sketch written by Boettcher in 1980, telephones in the studio began ringing with calls from appreciative local listeners. "After only a short period as Chief WHN Operations Engineer, I prevailed upon Mr. Schubel and Mr. Strohlein that we had to increase our power," recalled Boettcher. Given the go-ahead, Boettcher rebuilt the De Forest apparatus, boosting its power to one hundred watts, at which strength WHN began to reap "listener telephone calls from the Greater New York area, and complimentary letters from upper New York state, New Jersey, Connecticut, other New England states [and] distant cities."[3]

On the air an average of fifty-seven hours a week, the station quickly evolved a program schedule synchronized to the rhythms of household life in Ridgewood. As recorded in WHN's daily studio logbook, a typical weekday's programming for 1922 began at 9:15 AM with the *Weather Report, Overnight News, and Music*, followed by *Bible Lesson, Fashiongram, Beauty Talk*, and *Health Talk*. A musical interlude at 10:00 was followed by a lecture on *Our Wild Bird Friends*, a reading of recipes and dinner menus, and then an hour and a half of radio silence. At 12:30 PM broadcasting would recommence with the thirty-minute *Lunch Hour Gossip* program, followed by another intermission. At 2:15 programming resumed with Genevieve Berhend's daily discourse on "Mental Science"—probably some variant on "The New Thought," a proto–New Age spiritual fad—followed by *Afternoon Tea Discussion*, a feminine forum for topics such as "What Constitutes the Ideal Man?," "What Do You Think of the Habitual Borrower?," "Should Marriage between Cousins Be Prohibited?," and "What Constitutes True Happiness?" At 4:15 came *School News*, followed by the *WHN School Child's Forum*, a talent showcase for students of nearby Public School 77. At 5:15 came the *Radio Gossip* show, which covered subjects such as "The Potentiometer," "Direct Coupled Receiving Circuits," and "Radiation Resistance." An hour later came *Real Estate and Financial News* for the benefit of repatriated commuter dads. A quarter past 7:00 brought *Bedtime Stories* for tired toddlers. Three nights a week—Tuesdays, Thursdays, and Saturdays—WHN went off the air at 7:30, to resume with live music from 9:30 to midnight. On Mondays, Wednesdays, and Fridays music played uninterrupted from 7:30 to midnight. The evening concerts were eclectic, running the gamut from the minstrel antics of the Original Swanee Entertainers of Woodhaven, Long Island, to a classical piano recital by Henry Spector, "a graduate of the Petrograd Conservatory of Music and well-known in Brooklyn and New York as a piano and vocal instructor." On Sundays, WHN broadcast "sacred and classical music" from 10:00 AM to 3:00 PM, followed by an 8:30 band concert sponsored by the *Brooklyn Eagle*, a tabloid newspaper.[4]

It is unclear to what extent Schubel was using his radio station for commercial purposes at this time, but a file of his business papers preserved at the offices of the *Ridgewood Times*'s successor publication, the *Times Newsweekly*, reveals that he envisioned radio as an advertising outlet from the start.[5] Among these documents is a business prospectus that, though undated, clearly predates the January 1922 assignment of the station's license and call sign. Entitled "Wireless Advertising," this pamphlet touted the station-to-be as "the latest and most pleasing way of coming in touch with New York's vast suburban trade" and included a mock-up schedule of imaginary infomercials. For example, Schubel proposed "The Shopping News" as an aerial bulletin of informational tidbits such as "Ligget's Safe Drug Stores are offering ten day tubes of Pepsodent free all week"; "John Wanamaker: first sale in New York of Saddle Oxfords, flapper fad of the hour, $4.65"; and "Bloomingdales sale today: new spring suits, $19.95." The prospectus was complemented by a rate card listing the station's projected advertising fees, which were pegged on a sliding scale from five cents a word for fifty words a week to one cent a word for five thousand words a week.[6]

The two documents indicate that in establishing WHN, Schubel had leaped before looking, discovering only after the fact that candid broadcast advertising of the kind he had had in mind was impractical. How and when he came to recognize the need for discretion is unclear. Perhaps he approached and was rebuffed by one of the high-end retailers named in his wishful prospectus; perhaps he took his cue from AT&T, then inaugurating its own New York radio station and loudly asserting its patent-based monopoly over what it termed "toll broadcasting"—the sale of airtime to third parties. Whatever put him wise, Schubel seems to have modified rather than abandoned his plans: Among his papers is a 1922 contract documenting weekly payments of twenty-five dollars from the Williamsburgh Savings Bank of Brooklyn made in exchange for "privileges" relating to the station, although these privileges were left undefined in this otherwise precise legal document. Evidently Schubel was operating WHN as a stealth advertiser, selling airtime but tempering the directness of the publicity he broadcast on his client's behalf.[7]

By the summer of 1923 Schubel, like many other small broadcasting start-ups, was getting tired of keeping the voracious microphone fed hour after hour, day after day. But instead of letting his transmitter go dark, as hundreds of other station owners were doing, Schubel went looking for a professional middleman to furnish WHN's programs.

It is unclear how Schubel entered into partnership with the Loew's vaudeville concern. The way the eighty-year-old William Boettcher remembered it, the merger was proposed by Nils Thor Granlund, chief publicist for Loew's, who approached Schubel out of the blue late in 1922. But according to Granlund's 1957 memoir, *Blondes, Brunettes, and Bullets*, contact was initiated by Schubel. Looking back across a span of thirty-five eventful years, Granlund was blurry on many details, remembering Schubel as "George Schubert" and mistakenly identifying him as a stage electrician at the DeKalb Theater, a Brooklyn outpost of the

Loew's circuit. In Granlund's account, "Schubert the electrician" brought a radio transmitter—"a queer-looking tangle of wires and black glass bulbs"—to the DeKalb one night sometime in 1922 and, after explaining its function, invited the publicist to address invisible listeners by speaking into an object resembling a metal cup. "Ladies and gentlemen," Granlund recalled speaking into the microphone, "I don't believe anyone can hear me, but if this thing really works, give me a ring. The telephone number here is. . . ." To Granlund's amazement, the telephone at the DeKalb began to ring, bringing "twenty or thirty calls from people as far away as Newark."[8]

"Flabbergasted," Granlund returned to the DeKalb the following evening, "determined to give this thing a real trial." This time Granlund told his invisible audience that he would "pay $10 to the listener who telephoned me from the longest distance." The prize went to a party in New Jersey residing nearly thirty miles away.[9]

Sensing that "George Shubert's radio machine" had potential as a publicity medium for Loew's vaudeville acts, Granlund next put together a test bill of ten performers, including "an accordion player, a singer, a piano player, a quartet, and three others whom I've forgotten." He mustered them before the microphone, announced the impromptu program as a talent contest, and invited listeners to register their preferences on a postcard and send them to the theater. "Three days later," wrote Granlund, "the floor and every available inch of space on George's tables were covered with stacks of post cards and letters."[10]

With these three experiments under his belt, Granlund took the news of his discovery back to the Manhattan office of his boss, Marcus Loew. Known as "the Henry Ford of show biz," Loew controlled a national circuit of ten-cent neighborhood theaters, "small-time" houses catering to working-class audiences. On the cultural continuum of vaudeville, the Loew's empire was distinctly downmarket, offering variety fare that was considerably coarser than that found on the "big-time" stages of the Keith-Albee chain, the circuit that had done more than any other to make vaudeville safe for middle-class family viewing.[11]

Granlund recalled that Loew's reaction to his proposal that they get involved in radio was, "What do you want to do, put us out of business? You'd be encouraging something that could ruin the theater." But eventually Granlund persuaded his boss "that one couldn't hold the sea back by waving at it," and Loew grudgingly assented to a deal with Schubel.[12]

Under the terms of the contract hammered out between Schubel and Loews Inc., Schubel remained the owner of the station while leasing out its use to Loew's for a five-year period at a fixed weekly rate of one hundred dollars, with the vaudeville concern assuming all responsibility for programming. In the summer of 1923 WHN's transmitter was moved to an office in the Loew's State Theatre at Broadway and Forty-fifth. Soon afterward, WHN's power was boosted up to a respectable (for 1923) five hundred watts (it was doubled to one thousand watts in 1924). On 9 August the station took to the air under its new management with a gala broadcast featuring showbiz greats Eddie Cantor, Irving Berlin, George M. Cohan, Earl Carroll, the film star Richard Barthelmess, and Marion Davies, songbird protegée of the tabloid publisher William Randolph Hearst.[13]

Day-to-day oversight of the station was left in Granlund's hands. "Having no previous experience in this thing," he later wrote, "I was a little doubtful of what it might mean to me. I decided at the beginning to conceal my real name. If I laid an egg, I wanted to lay it anonymously. I identified myself only by the initials N.T.G." But instead of laying an egg, NTG quickly found a loyal audience, winning first place in a 1924 popularity poll of announcers organized by the *Evening Journal*, a New York tabloid. According to the showbiz weekly *Variety* and its New York subsidiary, *Clipper*, the buzz surrounding NTG quickly established WHN's studio as "an attractive drop-in for the 'wise' bunch" of Broadway— showbiz professionals "not down on the current program, but present just to take in the general fun."[14]

Though widespread, Granlund's appeal as a radio performer was not universal. The radio announcer was a new figure under the sun, but proponents of broadcasting as a tool of uplift had already developed specific notions as to what kind of man (announcing was generally construed to be men's work) was fit to approach the altar of the microphone. As delineated in *Radio Broadcast, Popular Radio, Radio Dealer, The Wireless Age,* and the radio-themed supplements of the broadsheet newspapers, hypothetical portraits of the perfect announcer reliably converged toward a standard set of class-coded attributes: crisp diction; pronunciation and grammar "in accordance with the best authorities"; facility with foreign words and names; and attainment "in rhetoric and polite, scholarly expression" since on any given evening he might "be called upon to comment intelligently in connection with such widely separated things as Tchaikovsky's 'Symphonie Pathetique,' or a lecture on the migratory habits of birds." Always, the essence of proper announcing was identified as *dignity*—"natural dignity," "dignity and courtesy," even "*otium cum dignitate*" (ease with dignity). And NTG was routinely singled out as the antithesis of these ideals. "Reverting to horrible examples," wrote one of the above-quoted theorists of the announcer's art in early 1924, "consider WHN. Speaking plainly, the announcers at this station, especially a certain one, have a misconception of their duties. They seem to be of the belief that they are entertainers."[15]

For want of surviving recordings, the best record of NTG's announcing style is a parody published in the column of "Pioneer" (Raymond
Francis Yates), broadcast critic for the *New York Herald Tribune*. Yates,
who affected to interpret WHN's call sign as standing for "What Hectic
Noise" (parenthetically adding that "better use could also be made of
the 'H'") was pleased to publish a lampoon submitted by one of his
readers, C. A. Hughes of Jamaica, New York.[16] To highlight Granlund's
unsuitability as a radio announcer, Hughes imagined how NTG might
introduce the renowned Polish piano virtuoso Ignacy Paderewski:

Hello, folks! This is Station ——— 'nouncing! We're gonna give you a real genu-
wine treat t'night. You're about to hear the classy vir-too-osoo Mister Ignatz Pad-
dyhoofsky, who will entertain you by poundin' th' ol' music box for yer! B'lieve
me, he's some bird at peckin' at the ivories! No kiddin'. Th' talented gent's perfeckly wunnerful and charming an', I might add, a marv'lous manipulater of the
old pianoforty! Y'know what I mean! Incident'ly, ladies and gents, the prof is
gonna utilize in his performance this eve a han'some, bran' new, perfeckly lovely
an' charming an', I might add—er—marvelous Blatzenburger Baby Grand, on
sale at $5 down, $1 per week, with a perfeckly lovely and charming pianner scarf
and a marv'lous pianner bench thrown in! Yo-ho, Paddy! Wherejer go to? C'mon
up to the mike an' make your little bow-wow! . . . .Whaddya gonna spiel first,
Paddy ol' scout? "The Moonlight S'nata?" Attaboy. Go to it! You know how 'tis!
Shoot! Let 'er go![17]

Hughes's pastiche targeted Granlund's unseemly exuberance, bad
grammar, faulty diction, and willingness to shill, but NTG also drew frequent fire for making what a journal for the radio retail trade called
"wise cracks and comments of decidedly poor taste and of questionable
character."[18] Even *Clipper*, generally partial to WHN as "the most entertaining [station] in the metropolitan district" and scarcely puritanical
in outlook, sometimes wondered whether NTG's fondness for bawdy
repartee, racial and ethnic jokes, and low humor did not exceed the
bounds of broadcast propriety.[19] To boot, scientific proof of Granlund's
unsuitability was provided in 1925 by a team of researchers at New York
University, who recorded and analyzed the voices of New York's radio
announcers, assigning each one a precisely quantified place on a scale
of "acoustical importance." Highest ranked on this scale was Graham
McNamee of the AT&T station WEAF. Near the bottom, reported the
critic Yates approvingly, "pulling up to about seventh place," was
NTG.[20]

Even those who took a broader view of NTG's antics expressed themselves in terms that emphasized his distance from the genteel ideal.
"Purists," wrote Edgar H. Felix in his pioneering 1927 study of broadcast advertising, "may shake their heads at the mention of his style of
announcing, lacking as it is in dignity and grammar, but, if appealing to

the tastes of the masses is an art, Mr. Granlund is an artist."[21] With similar ambivalence, *Variety* noted in 1925 that WHN "is paradoxically the most entertaining to some and the greatest nuisance to others. The extreme of the alleged comedy hits the average layman right, but is so much drivel to those a little above the moron classification."[22]

Still others, however, embraced NTG's kidding as a welcome relief from the formality of the corporate stations. "Most announcers," wrote an editorialist for the tabloid *Jersey Journal* in March 1924,

have about them a dignity which is comparable only to that of a department store floor walker. Not so with the chief of WHN, whatever his name may be. This announcer refuses to take the radio seriously. There are no funereal notes in what he has to say. He does not believe that every day in the week is Sunday. About him there is no refinement of restraint or restraint of refinement. "Let 'er go, boys," he sings out in the cheeriest of tones after he has announced the next number, and the "boys," catching the spirit of the thing, "let 'er go" with all the vim that's in them. WHN is what might be called a friendly station. The announcer thinks that everybody ought to get better acquainted. He sees no reason why the eight members of the volunteer fire department in East Rutherford, N.J., shouldn't know the folks from "up state," so night after night he invites everybody on the air to join in some popular chorus. Frequently he interrupts to say the singing is not all that might be hoped for and he wants everybody to do better. The studio of WHN evidently is not the holy of holies, for all sorts of persons are dropping in there from time to time during the evening. The announcer makes them all come up to the microphone and say "howdy" to the customers. Some of the newcomers are made to tell a funny story, but generally there is more laughing in the studio as to what the announcer has to say about the funny story than about the funny story itself.[23]

For his own part, Granlund offered no apologies for his or WHN's lack of gravitas. "The policy of the station is not to educate the masses," he told *The Wireless Age* in early 1925. "Let someone else elevate them. What I want to do is to entertain people and to bring some frivolity into their homes."[24]

From the moment he took control of WHN, Granlund began looking for new ways to make the station pay. His first step in this direction was to institute payola there. Many people mistakenly regard payola—the use of bribes in the promotion of music—as a transient phenomenon unique to rock and roll broadcasting of the 1950s. In fact, pay-for-play arrangements have been a universal and constant part of the American popular music economy since the mid-1880s. The word "payola," according to one researcher, was already part of the specialized argot of Tin Pan Alley by the 1920s, although the more common term for musical bribery at the time was "song plugging."[25]

Before broadcasting, music publishers plugged their latest and most promising songs to the public by paying cash bribes or other emoluments—a new suit or dress, some luggage, a crate of liquor, a percentage of the song royalties, the services of a prostitute—to flesh-and-blood performers. In the event that the song went over with the public, the publishers made their money back plus profit through the sale of copyrighted sheet music.

By far the most important performers to pay off were itinerant vaudevillians, who could carry a publisher's song clear across the continent, exposing it one performance at a time from the stages of hundreds of theaters to a cumulative audience of millions. The bigger the star, of course, the more valuable were his or her services as a song plugger. Headliners working the big-time circuits stood to make as much or more from song plugging as they did from their theatrical salaries. But smaller performers were also in line to receive their share of the graft. This was true even of performers whose talents were not primarily musical. Dancers, jugglers, and conjurers, for example, worked to music, and music publishers found it worthwhile to assist them in selecting appropriate accompaniment for their acts.

On the local level, practically anyone involved in mediating between the music industry and the public stood to benefit from the largess of the publishers. Cabaret singers and dance bands were all on the take, naturally; so was the blind busker whose one talent was winding the crank of a wheezing curb-side barrel organ; ditto the person in charge of stocking the rolls in the coin-operated player pianos in saloons and penny arcades.

Following a bouncing ball across a line of lyrics on a movie screen is a convention established in the early 1900s by a forgotten caste of entertainers called "illustrated slide singers," paid by Tin Pan Alley to drill newly minted pop songs into the heads of audiences as they waited to see a silent movie. And when the movie eventually hit the screen, the house pianist would accompany the flickering images with a medley that incorporated current pop songs that he or she had been paid to plug.

An insider's perspective on payola at WHN can be found in *A Hell of a Life*, the 1966 memoir of Harry Richman. A major star of stage and screen in the late 1920s through the 1930s, in the early 1920s Richman was working as a piano accompanist in Mae West's cabaret act until West fired him for upstaging her with his grandstanding antics at the keyboard. So it happened that Richman was in need of work when he crossed paths with Granlund in late 1923. Granlund offered Richman an unsalaried position playing piano and coannouncing at WHN. A wised-up vaudevillian, Richman recognized the sense of the offer: only recently a music publisher had offered him good money to plug songs "on something called radio." Assured by Granlund that he would be free to select his own material, Richman accepted. "I was thinking," wrote Richman,

about the publisher's five dollars per song per day. I thought I would plug their songs incessantly and that was exactly what I did. NTG's show came from Loew's Theater and I was on the air seven days a week for at least six hours a day. What a show! We may not have been the most expert masters of ceremonies in the world, but I'll say this for us—we were diligent. First he would recite something, then I would do four or five songs, sometimes more, and always the songs that the publishers had given me five dollars a day for plugging on the air. Then NTG would come up to the microphone and recite a long poem such as "Boots" by Rudyard Kipling. After that he would read headlines from some newspaper and weather predictions. Also, because they were giving him the theater to broadcast from, "Coming Attractions for Loew's." Then I would go back on and render some more of the publisher's songs. Money was rolling in from those publishers. Between songs I would tell a joke or two or argue with NTG, which the listeners loved.[26]

The next phase in the economic flowering of WHN saw the formalization of its relationships with the music publishers, as the station began openly selling time to Tin Pan Alley stalwarts such as Leo Feist, Jack Mills, Jack Snyder, and Breau & Tobias. In turn, these companies supplied WHN's studio with an army of free talent to fill up the afternoon and evening schedules. The commercial nature of these performances was overt, with the names of the sponsoring publishers announced after each number.[27] *Clipper* summarized the resulting programs as "a song pluggers' marathon relieved by several Loew's acts playing nearby houses with a big feature around midnight."[28]

WHN was scarcely the only station involved in promoting popular songs, but broadcasters who cared about their reputations took pains to moderate or conceal the impact of payola on their programming. In late 1923 *Clipper* reported that certain New York stations were responding to listener complaints about the repetition of heavily plugged songs by forcing performers to vary their repertoires. Especially prestige-conscious broadcasters strove to disassociate themselves from payola entirely. Thus, when the Gimbel's department store chain opened its New York station WGBS in 1924, it announced a ban on "all song pluggers" in keeping with its status as "a public service institution with no commercial angles." In 1924 the New York corporate stations WEAF (AT&T) and WJZ (Westinghouse) closed their doors to the Radio Franks, a popular singing duo notorious for making the rounds of broadcasting studios and grinding out unvarying three-song sets from the catalog of Waterson, Berlin & Snyder. Later the same stations tried to suppress "palpable song plugging" by barring any performer whose entire repertoire was published by a single firm.[29]

Granlund placed no such saving restraints on song plugging at WHN. In late 1923 *Clipper* voiced misgivings that the station's relentless exposure of "Me No Speaks Good English" and "Mamma Loves Papa" for the Leo Feist Company might forever destroy the popular appeal of "the 'wop' dialect song."[30]

\* \* \*

Although it was quite legal, payola was widely seen as a symptom of the ethical bankruptcy of those in control of the music industry, "well known," as *Radio Digest* put it in 1924, "to contaminate anything [with which] they come in contact with bribes of various kinds."[31] But what the moralizing critics of payola failed (and still fail) to grasp is that the music industry has always felt itself a victim, and not the perpetrator, of the system. Tin Pan Alley *hated* payola, and with good reason: in the 1910s and 1920s the major music firms were obliged to gamble as much as twenty-thousand dollars on every hoped-for hit—investments with a highly uncertain rate of return.

Seeking to free themselves from what they called the "payment evil," Tin Pan Alley's major players worked hard to organize a lasting industrial peace, repeatedly forging multilateral agreements to withhold all promotional payments to all performers. But in every instance the logic of the market undermined these boycotts, either because a few participating firms proved incapable of resisting the now-amplified advantages of resuming payments on the sly or because the suspension of bribes left the honest firms suddenly vulnerable to "unfair" competition from smaller, nonparticipating firms.

This recurrent drama was repeated yet again in the early days of broadcasting: throughout 1923 and 1924 officials of the American Society of Composers, Authors and Publishers (ASCAP) worked hard at organizing a Tin Pan Alley–wide radio boycott, but again competitive self-interests motivated individual ASCAP members to break ranks. Late in 1923, for example, the minor firm of Breau & Tobias seceded from ASCAP, informing *Variety* that "they preferred to broadcast where and when they liked." A few months later the defecting firm was penitently begging for readmission, having found the airwaves to be an over-crowded "happy hunting grounds" for even smaller firms. By this time, however, even nominally honest subscribers to the ASCAP boycott were finding covert ways of circumventing the letter of the agreement. A standard method of cheating involved transferring ownership of a promising song to a "dummy" company not affiliated with ASCAP and then plugging the number hard via radio. The moment the song "went over," its real corporate parent would "buy" it from the subsidiary. Such chicanery inevitably led to the collapse of the boycott. In mid-1925 *Variety* acutely summed up the mood of the music industry: "The publishers' attitude today is that 'if we get off the radio it permits others to step in and make song hits in competition with us.'"[32]

The necessity of doing business with radio was especially galling to the publishers because they were certain that broadcasting was going to ruin their livelihood. This was an understandable mistake: the orchestration of a successful song-plugging campaign was a delicate and intuitive art, the goal of which was to pay for the exposure of a song just until the exact point when popular demand for it took over. Before radio, putting a song over had been a gradual process whose speed was set by the creeping progress of vaudeville troupes crossing the country by rail. Under these conditions, the plugging phase in the life cycle of a popular song extended over a period of several months. If the song went over, the publisher could count on it to remain profitable for a year or two. Radio abruptly took control over the schedule of a song's exposure away from the publishers, rapidly reducing the average life span of a hit to an interval of months—and, in subsequent decades, to weeks.[33]

Ultimately, radio's accelerative effect would be of great benefit to the popular music industry, yielding an exponential increase in the market for its goods. In the short term, however, the veteran strategists of old-style song-plugging campaigns, whose nerves and instincts were conditioned to slower and more organic modes of promotion and exploitation, experienced radio as a disaster. For several years they would continue to construe broadcasting as a destructive force liable to kill promising songs overnight, overexposing them before they could reach their profitable prime.

*       *       *

By the autumn of 1923 Granlund was expanding WHN's commercial functions to include promotional work for cabarets and nightclubs in the Broadway theater district, charging each establishment fifty dollars a week for the privilege of sending its singers and dance bands to broadcast from WHN's studio. In turn, NTG touted each establishment at length, including the names, location, and, as *Clipper* put it, "all other details, necessary and unnecessary, excepting possibly the date of the doorman's birth."[34]

Around the same time, WHN began sneaking into its broadcasts what may have been the earliest paid "spot" advertisements, thinly disguised as listener telegrams of the kind many stations solicited from their audiences. *Clipper* saw through the ruse whereby "some doctor or hardware man or some merchant always includes his business and address in his stereotyped message that 'WHN is coming in great,' etc."[35]

Granlund's next contribution to the economics of broadcasting was to initiate in late 1924 what would come to be known as "cabaret broadcasting." Instead of summoning nightclub dance bands to the studio, henceforth the station began broadcasting by remote hookups from the clubs using telegraph lines leased from Western Union. As ever, the shilling was unrestrained. "NTG flatters and puffs and praises various cafes and ballrooms, although it is a laugh the manner in which each cabaret or dance hall is lauded as the zenith and the ultra-ultra in the field," observed *Variety*, and "[a]ll for $75 a week."[36] The system must have been profitable for all concerned, because by early 1925 WHN had remote lines and supporting apparatus in over thirty clubs in the theater district, including the Parody Club, Club Moritz, Janssen's Hofbrau, the Silver Slipper, the Mirador, the Wig-Wam, the Strand Roof, the Everglades, the Club Alabam' and the Hotel Alamac, as well as clubs in Harlem, including Connie's Inn, Small's Paradise, and the Cotton Club.[37]

The metropolitan nightclub of the 1920s was a novel kind of social space: a place where middle-class men and women went to shuck off the constraints of nineteenth-century bourgeois behavioral codes and try on new, liberating modes of personal expression. In contrast to traditional Victorian formality, with its rigid segregation of the classes and sexes, nightclubs were places of "institutional spontaneity": heterogeneous, informal, structured to promote unfettered interaction among customers. Here even the invisible "fourth wall" separating audiences from performers was leveled by the institution of eye-level floor shows, which encouraged well-lubricated audiences to consider themselves part of the spectacle.[38]

This defection from Victorian formalism began in the 1910s among the "smart set," a youthful segment of the upper bourgeoisie who, bored by the constraints of respectability, gravitated toward the colorful company of actors, musicians, gamblers, artists, bohemians, boxers, overt homosexuals, jockeys, prostitutes, and career criminals. By the 1920s the revolutionary habit of "stepping out" was spreading to the urban middle classes, to the consternation of moral traditionalists, who were especially disquieted at the sight of otherwise respectable women visiting places of commercialized "cheap amusement" of a kind once reserved to the lower classes and middle-class males on a slumming spree. Alcohol being an indispensable ingredient of nightlife, stepping out took on new dimensions of disrepute and raffish allure when Prohibition took effect in 1920.

The musical accompaniment to this middle-class countercultural revolt was jazz—though not the brow-furrowing, theory-driven, philanthropically subsidized conservatory music that goes by that name today. The jazz of the Jazz Age was not art music and most definitely not "America's classical music." Rather, it was intended and apprehended as a loud and rowdy negation of all things genteel, refined, and respectable. Above all, it was dance music, performed alongside dance floors for sweaty, inebriated listeners caught up in the latest fad dance—the shimmy, the Charleston, the toddle, the lindy hop, the black bottom.

WHN's alignment with the nightclubs of Broadway and Harlem fast established it as New York's foremost broadcaster not just of jazz but of "hot jazz"—the real McCoy performed by black dance orchestras, as opposed to the softer "sweet jazz" favored by white bands. Indeed, a canvass of WHN's weekly schedules for the years 1923 through 1926 yields a canonical roll call of black jazz pioneers: Clarence Williams, Eva Taylor, Ethel Waters, Wilbur Sweatman, Eubie Blake and Noble Sissle, Florence Mills, LeRoy Smith, Charlie Johnson, Leona Williams, Duke Ellington, Fletcher Henderson, and Louis Armstrong.[39]

As Granlund admitted in his memoir, the nightclubs that WHN promoted were all speakeasies controlled by organized crime. "In those days," he wrote, "if you wanted to do business with the nightclubs you did your bargaining with gangsters; it was impossible to avoid them. Anyone who had anything to do with show business in these places had to know gangsters, had to deal with the mob."[40] By 1924 both Granlund and Richman were expanding their professional ties to the underworld. Richman borrowed mob money to set up his own Broadway speakeasy, Club Richman, which joined the roster of WHN's remote sites. Granlund went to work for the prominent bootlegger and racketeer Larry Fay, producing floor shows for Fay's lavish speakeasy, the El Fay Club, which was also a regular WHN remote site until it was padlocked by court order in 1925.[41]

Assuming that Granlund's boffo memoir is reliable on the point, WHN played a role in Fay's smuggling operations. Taking advantage of the fact that the station's signal carried three miles out to sea, Fay communicated with his rum-running boats by sending henchmen into the studio to instruct NTG to deliver one of his famously boisterous poetry readings. "It always puzzled me," Granlund wrote, "when these big tough guys asked me to read." In time, supposedly, word filtered back to Granlund that the requested poem—usually a work by Kipling, Service, Frost, or Poe—was a coded message that told the rumrunners whether or not the coast was clear.[42]

While it is true that bootleggers sometimes used radio equipment to coordinate ship-to-shore rendezvous, Granlund was likely stretching the truth with this anecdote. Suspiciously identical signaling schemes were attributed to cheap, jazzy, commercial independent stations from coast to coast throughout the 1920s. In 1925 *Variety* reported that the Commerce Department was poised to investigate "the illegitimate use of broadcasting stations, who, it has been charged, are sending messages in code, either by popular songs or lectures, as advance information on rum-running conditions." But there is no sign that such an inquiry was ever conducted, and in its unvarying replication from region to region, the radio-and-rum-ship scenario bears the stamp of an urban myth.[43] But urban myths are mythic in a nontrivial sense—they feed on common values and fears, otherwise they would not be able to propagate themselves from place to place as the plausible experience of the friend of a friend. Even if every account about a lowbrow commercial station sending coded messages to smugglers offshore of New York, Chicago, and Seattle is purely apocryphal, the stories still say something about how such stations were seen by the first generation of broadcast listeners.

A backlash against WHN was not slow in coming. Yates of the *Herald Tribune* reported receiving a constant flood of protest mail concerning the Loew's station, enough, he said, to justify the organization of an "Anti-WHN Association." And the *New York Times* almost certainly had WHN in mind when it intoned the following judgment on radio stations broadcasting jazz: "Surely they assume terrifying responsibility who debase this marvel and miracle of the ages to low uses."[44]

Individual citizens registered their disapproval of WHN with various authorities. In early 1925 an offended listener wrote to New York Police Commissioner Richard Enright citing the station's "programs of jazz and 'girl stuff'" as contributing to the epidemic of "reckless youth and shootings and disrespect for the law."[45] More frequently WHN's enemies addressed their concerns to Secretary of Commerce Hoover. A typical complaint urged Hoover to stifle the station on the grounds that its "programs consist mostly of jazz, the lower forms of music, sometimes approaching the indecent, and a large percentage of entirely uninteresting advertising."[46] A like-minded New Yorker asked Hoover to consider his protest as representative of

the thousands of others who feel that the New York Station WHN should be suppressed or at least toned down. It is utterly monopolizing the air with its bad English, cheap jazz, advertising of doubtful resorts and speakeasies to such an extent as to be a source of common disgust. This most thrilling achievement of modern science should not be prostituted to the disgusting uses which are now its habit. . . . P.S. This is a confidential letter and not for publication. I do not want to invite a fight with the sort of gunmen and toughs who seem to be running WHN.[47]

A more detailed account of WHN's depravity was filed with Hoover's office by Justice Joseph Callahan, a New York municipal court judge. Callahan wrote:

The other evening in announcing a program from a cabaret known as The Silver Slipper in this city, the dialogue between the announcer and the alleged manager involved the use of the word "fags" as describing some of the persons present. This word is commonly used to describe a class of degenerates well known to the police. Again the announcer and manager described over the radio the beauty of the chorus girls and the scantiness of their attire. Then something of this sort occurred: The manager says "Isn't this girl marvelous? Did you hear what she said? She wanted me to kiss her where I just slapped her," and then the voice of the announcer is heard saying, "And did you see where he slapped her?" This is just a sample of what is constantly coming from this station in plain advertising of many questionable places of resort here.[48]

Callahan's reference to "fags" indicates that nightclubs publicized by WHN were involved in the "pansy craze," a gender-bending trend in nightlife that titillated middle-class cabaret-goers with lesbian- and drag-themed entertainments and a chance to mingle with gays and lesbians in the crowd.[49]

Responding to the rising volume of complaints, the Department of Commerce ordered the regional radio supervisor Arthur Batchellor to evaluate the station's operations. After interviewing Schubel and monitoring WHN's programs at length, Batchellor delivered an ambivalent report that spoke directly to the contemporary fragmentation of middle-class cultural tastes and standards. "The type of program given out over station WHN," he wrote,

differs somewhat from the programs usually given out over other stations. This station broadcasts from some of the leading New York cabarets and these cabarets are attended by many of New York's finest people. Frequently, vaudeville artists appear at this station and sing songs and talk on subjects which they are accustomed to present to the public from the vaudeville stage. No doubt some of these songs and talks might be construed by certain types of people to border on suggestiveness provided of course these people were inclined to think in that direction. . . . Generally speaking I do not feel that this station is intentionally violating any of the rules of decency, as the manager of this station can produce thousands of letters commending them upon the excellent service from this station, and they realize fully if their station is to continue to be a paying proposition, that they must furnish programs which are of general interest to the public[50]

Batchellor's finding was undoubtedly the pragmatic one, given the flimsy legal basis of federal authority over broadcasting at this time. But in early 1924 WHN came up against a better-armed and more determined opponent: AT&T. The telephone giant harbored two legal objections to the Loew's station's operations, the first of which concerned its transmitter. The corporate patent-pooling agreement that attended the formation of RCA in 1919 had given AT&T monopoly rights over the sale of radiophone transmitters and parts to non-Big Four purchasers. It was AT&T's position that any broadcaster using a transmitter not made by its manufacturing subsidiary, Western Electric, was guilty of patent infringement. In 1923 AT&T had put noncompliant broadcasters on notice that they must either pay for a patent license or face litigation.

AT&T's other grievance related to WHN's advertising. Here too the phone company asserted monopoly rights, a position based on a clause in the 1919 agreement that reserved "commercial applications" of the radiotelephone to AT&T. At the time this clause was drafted, AT&T was anticipating the advent of some kind of wireless telephone service. Hoping to perpetuate its control over private telephone subscriptions into a prematurely imagined wireless age, AT&T surrendered to RCA and GE the right to market receivers to the public in exchange for exclusive rights in the provision of radio messaging, in whatever form it might eventually take.

When it became apparent that radio was to be a mass medium rather than a point-to-point one, what had seemed to be a sharp bit of industrial bargaining on AT&T's part was revealed as a big mistake. By ceding the right to sell receivers to the public, the telephone company had cut itself off from the original source of corporate profit in broadcasting. By 1921 Westinghouse, RCA, and GE were all taking up broadcasting in order to stimulate sales of their receivers. Shut out of this market, AT&T was nonetheless determined to establish its own foothold in broadcasting. Groping for an alternative profit principle, it fell back on its exclusive rights to the commercial exploitation of radio, proposing the establishment of an experimental "toll station" in New York. The notion "that a broadcast, like a telephone call, should be paid for by the one originating it," wrote the company historian William Peck Banning, was one that came naturally to "the telephone mind."[51]

The toll broadcasting concept was immediately controversial. AT&T had no sooner announced its plan than the *New York Times* fired an editorial warning shot across its bow, preemptively condemning any sale of airtime "to soaps, home builders, razor blades, cocoa, hair tonics, and politicians, at so much an hour."[52] Sensitized by this and other rebukes, and meeting a high degree of what Banning called "business resistance" to the scheme, the station trod lightly in its advertising practices, restricting itself, as AT&T publicists defensively declared over and over again, to the cultivation of "goodwill publicity" for its sponsors.[53] Commercial interruptions of programs were not allowed; products and prices were not to be named. WEAF's favored way of promoting a client while minimizing offense to listeners was to name a program after a sponsor—for example, "The Silvertown Orchestra," underwritten by the Silvertown Tire Company.

To compensate for public resistance to the toll concept, WEAF took pains to establish itself as a cultural front-runner among New York stations, scoring a long succession of prestigious firsts in broadcasting, including early concert series by the Metropolitan Opera Company and the New York Philharmonic Orchestra. By late 1923 WEAF had forged a relationship with the New York Philharmonic conductor Walter Damrosch, whose lectures and recitals would adorn the station's schedule for years to come. And in an event heralded as the high-water mark of broadcast culture to date, on New Year's Day of 1925 WEAF broadcast a program centered around the operatic prima donna Lucrezia Bori and the world-renowned Irish tenor John McCormack. On this special occasion a relay network of eight "high class" northeastern stations was wired together, a temporary configuration that presaged the creation of the NBC network the following year.[54]

WEAF also had its lighter side: high-end vaudeville of the wholesome Keith-Albee kind, suitable for family listening, and a modicum of sweetened white jazz in the later evening hours. But presentation of pop culture did not come naturally to a station whose studio personnel had been selected on the basis of their knowledge of higher things. In September 1924 *Variety* complained about WEAF's supercilious treatment of pop music, declaring that the way that its announcers "continue and insist on assuming that condescending attitude toward 'the lighter music,' as they do, and evince it through studied and aloof pronunciation of the simple euphonious titles, is something to wonder at. In attempting to pronounce 'Ji-Ji-Bo,' part of the B. Fischer-Astor Coffee House orchestra's programs, an advertising regular weekly feature from WEAF, the announcer took particular pains to ad-lib 'whatever that means' and 'I wonder if I pronounced it correctly.' "[55]

Bridging the vertical gap between prestigious specials such as the McCormack-Bori concert and awkward attempts at presenting pop music was WEAF's first major hit program, *Roxy's Gang*, inaugurated in January 1923. Named after its master of ceremonies, the theatrical impresario Samuel L. "Roxy" Rothafel, *Roxy's Gang* has been imprecisely identified by some historians as a vaudeville revue. The label is correct insofar as the program originated from a commercial theater, but it overlooks the idiosyncratic place that Rothafel and the Capitol Theater held in the field of showbiz. Before coming to radio Roxy had already attracted favorable notice from cultural uplifters for having elevated the Capitol Theater's orchestra to respectable symphonic standards. The noted critic and composer Deems Taylor, in his contribution to *Civilization in the United States*, an influential but otherwise relentlessly pessimistic 1922 report on the state of American culture, went so far as to declare that even Theodore Thomas, the legendary nineteenth century patriarch of American conductors, had "rendered no more valuable service to music in America" than had Roxy. Although some critics condemned Rothafel's gushy, sentimental style of announcing, *Roxy's Gang* was more frequently praised as an accessible blend of entertainment and uplift that would help raise the brow level of the general public by teaching them to love the classics.[56]

In sum, after an initially rocky reception, WEAF successfully disarmed critics of the toll concept with culturally prestigious content. The AT&T station, declared *Radio Broadcast* in late 1926, "not only formulated and established the present method by which the public pays for broadcasting but it created such high standards for commercial programs that it robbed the method of its undesirability."[57]

While striving to legitimate the toll concept with virtuous programming, AT&T kept a close watch on independent broadcasters infringing on its monopoly. Although the company harbored no objection to a station such as WGBS providing publicity for its corporate owner, Gimbel's department store, it took exception to small stations selling time to third parties.[58] Early in March 1924 the telephone company initiated proceedings against WHN in Federal District Court.

AT&T claimed that in selecting WHN as a test litigant it was guided only by the convenience of a shared New York jurisdiction, but it is likely that the phone company was banking on a public relations dividend as well. In effect, the suit pitted the most prestigious radio station in the city against the most vulgar. "Perhaps," conjectured an editorialist for the *Jersey Journal*, "WEAF has thought WHN too undignified." But if that was the strategy, continued the commentator, then AT&T had made a mistake "from the standpoint of air psychology," WHN being "a selection calculated to cause more perturbation among the fans hereabouts than any other station which might have been selected." Thinking to single out a vulnerable pariah, AT&T had wreathed its opponent in the mantle of the underdog—"just a neighborhood pet until WEAF gave it national significance."[59]

AT&T also had no way of knowing that George Schubel had been mentally girding himself for battle against the "Radio Trust" since 1922. Schubel's longstanding conviction that the corporate powers were conspiring to push independent stations like his out of the airwaves apparently grew out of his correspondence with two other small station owners, F. H. Keefe of Newburgh, New York, and T. B. Hatfield of Indianapolis, who wrote to him in 1922 to report threatening visits from representatives of Western Electric. According to Keefe, a Western Electric salesman named Rainey had dropped by his station and quizzed him at length as to the make and design of his transmitter. Assuming that Rainey's interest stemmed from a desire to provide his station with maintenance service, Keefe was forthcoming as to the jerry-built nature of his gear, whereupon Rainey put heavy pressure on him to replace it with licensed Western Electric equipment. "On being told that we were getting out fine with our present apparatus and only interested in securing a supply for our equipment," wrote Keefe, "Mr. Rainey stated that the Western Electric Company could not supply any of the material which consisted of tubes, microphones, etc., for any 'unlicensed equipment.' . . . He further said that the attorneys of the Western Electric Company were at that time working on just what they (meaning, I suppose, the Trust) would ultimately do with the number of infringements of the many patents which were contained in ours and similar equipment being used by independent broadcasting stations."[60]

Hatfield, a retailer of receivers and parts, complained of a similar squeeze and added that RCA had cut off his store's supply of tubes. "We, of course, are in the dark as to what the situation really is," concluded Hatfield, "but it looks very much as though the Western Electric Company and the Radio Corporation of America, with, of course, the General Electric Company and the Westinghouse Companies, are endeavoring, in some way, to restrict the broadcasting end of it. If this is the case, we certainly want to fight with all our force against such a procedure."[61]

A fighter by nature, Schubel had taken Hatfield's challenge to heart. His plan, as revealed in a memorandum to his lawyer, Charles Pope Caldwell, was to argue his case in the court of public opinion while stalling the official proceedings with petty obstructions. He wrote:

The main element in the case is time. I think that we should use every tactic possible to have the matter dragged along. In the first place, I notice that the complaint is made out against Loew's Incorporated, etc., instead of against Loew's Booking Agency. Could the papers be returned with the request that they be made out correctly? Could a complaint be started through the Federal Trade Commission or the U.S. Department of Justice on the monopoly question upon which our own case could be made to hinge, so that there would be a delay in the case for which we would have to wait upon the government?[62]

One of Schubel's first countermoves against AT&T was to enlarge WHN's profile by forming a league of independent broadcasters, the Radio Broadcasters' Society of America. In reality, the RBSA seems to have consisted of little more than a letterhead, a ringingly patriotic constitution printed up as a trifold tract, and a mailing list containing the addresses of a dozen other small broadcasters. In the pages of the tabloid press, however, the RBSA became a "big radio society" representing twenty united independent stations. As executive secretary of the society, Schubel initiated what WEAF's chief executive William E. Harkness later characterized as a "particularly rabid" propaganda campaign, issuing a steady stream of press releases depicting the telephone company as a sinister monopoly intent on "controlling the religious, educational, entertainment, and political destinies of the nation" through a stranglehold on the airwaves. Implausibly, Schubel and Caldwell claimed to have heard representatives of AT&T baldly declare "that it was their plan to wipe out all independent broadcasters, to obtain a monopoly of the air, to charge speakers for broadcasting, and to charge each individual listener for listening." After eliminating the independents, asserted Schubel, "this radio octopus could go to the Government and apply for the valuable licenses and franchises which these independent stations would lose through non-operation, and capitalize what belongs to the American people at the rate of $400 or more an hour." Schubel further warned that if the "Radio Trust" had its way, "eventually no person will be permitted to have a radio set in his home not rented from the AT&T, precisely as virtually all telephone subscribers of the country now must get their telephone service from AT&T and its subsidiary companies."[63]

With consummate cheek, Schubel also went after WEAF's commercial practices. "Instead of worrying about how to make listeners pay," he piously declared, the telephone company

ought to worry about the time when listeners may demand to be paid for listening in. A broadcaster could not extol the merits of a certain brand of chewing gum, or candy, or urge its listeners to go to stores and ask for a certain brand of coffee if no one listens to such advertising. To sell advertising over the radiophone it is necessary to have a listening audience. Anyone can walk along Broadway and get an eyefull of illuminated advertising without spending a nickel! Why pay for getting an earful of advertising over the radiophone?

While hammering away at WEAF's commercialism, Schubel was careful to prop a back door open for himself, airily speculating in one of his public communiqués that "advertising of a highly desirable form, properly presented, might be one of the sources of revenue which can be applied to the maintenance of public broadcasting." But in that case, reasoned Schubel, broadcasting-for-hire was properly the business of "the newspapers of the United States," not of AT&T, which had "no more business to solicit and broadcast advertising than a newspaper would have to go into the telephone business."[64]

The tabloids of New York City and neighboring parts of New Jersey obligingly reported the story exactly as spun by Schubel. The *Brooklyn Eagle*, for example, publicly put the question to W. E. Harkness, manager of WEAF, whether "in the interests of fair play, he would permit the presentation of the opposite side of the argument" over his station's powerful four-thousand-watt transmitter, and then pounced on his refusal as proof of AT&T's "unfair and un-American influence."[65]

Spokesmen for AT&T sputtered in their attempts to defuse such accusations. "We have no desire for a monopoly of the air," protested AT&T president Harry B. Thayer. "The question presented is a plain, narrow one. We have brought it because we believe the defendants are violating our rights. Some of our broadcasting patents have been infringed—many times carelessly and sometimes wantonly. We have offered to license infringers at reasonable rates." Although AT&T's version of issues and events went nowhere in the tabloids, it received more even treatment from the *New York Times* and the *Herald Tribune.* The latter cut to the heart of the matter when it noted that the "sore points with independent broadcasters rest in restrictions which these stations must agree to when they purchase sending sets" that barred them "from receiving reimbursement for . . . broadcasting publicity."[66]

While cleaning up in the tabloids, Schubel opened up a second front on the airwaves—although according to the pro-WHN *Brooklyn Eagle* it was WEAF that "first used its transmitter to gain friends for its cause among radio fans" by interrupting its scheduled programs to set forth a defense of AT&T. In the first of a long series of scripts he wrote for attorney Caldwell to deliver on the air, Schubel wrote: "It was not, and is not now, the intention of WHN to carry its case into the upper regions of the air. The proper place to try a legal case is in the courts." However, added Schubel, AT&T's use of WEAF as a propaganda weapon left WHN no choice but to respond in kind with twice-nightly rebuttals "every evening hereafter, until the various points raised in the Telephone Company's statement have been covered." The ensuing lecture series were essentially reiterations of Schubel's press releases draped in an extra layer of patriotic bunting—comparisons of AT&T to George III and Schubel to Paul Revere, and so forth.[67]

NTG contributed to the propaganda campaign by poking fun at WEAF's highbrow programs on the air; informing listeners that WHN's agenda was "to be a service station, and not force our programs on you, like the others do"; and changing the WHN's self-conferred title from "Birthplace of the Hits" to "The Station of Human Interest, Serving the Masses, Not the Classes."[68] Granlund also went to the tabloids with the claim that AT&T was stooping to dirty tricks. "Since the fight with the telephone company has developed," he told the *New York American,* "the telephone service to WHN has suffered a decided change for the worse." The tabloid elaborated, "As a rule it is as much as two operatrices can do to handle the incoming calls" at the station, but now hours were going by without a single ring. The *American* also lent credence to the charge, attributed to unidentified radio experts, that "some mysterious agency is on the air drowning out WHN when the independent version of the controversy is being broadcast."[69]

Schubel's guerrilla media tactics were a great success, instigating neighborhood meetings of hundreds of WHN fans and independent radio dealers and eliciting, according to the *American*, "more than 10,000 letters of support" as well as petitions "signed by entire fire companies, community organizations and radio clubs." Almost a quarter of the correspondence reportedly brought support in the form of checks and currency "with instructions that they are to be used in the legal fight."[70]

The attacks on AT&T were also felt at the upper end of the social scale, among board members of the Radio Music Fund Committee. This committee was a charitable endeavor organized by some of New York's leading cultural philanthropists—among them Clarence McKay, Felix M. Warburg, and Frederic A. Juilliard—aimed at raising funds for the noncommercial support of radio concerts "of the highest class" to be broadcast from WEAF.[71] Describing the initiative as "laudable but misguided," Schubel charged that "most of the money collected from music lovers and others will be spent in high charges made for broadcasting instead of [going] to the artists and performers."[72] Rattled by accusations that they were "giving aid and comfort to the monopoly," the trustees of the fund suspended their activities for the duration of the controversy, never to resume in the aftermath.[73]

While publicly signaling his determination to "fight the octopus to a standstill," Schubel was privately preparing for the possibility that he might lose in court. But he already had a contingency plan up his sleeve. "If we should finally be restricted in any way in the matter of commercializing the station," he wrote to Caldwell, "then the way to overcome the matter would be to place the station on a . . . philanthropic basis as previously suggested by me, to be called the Marcus Loew Broadcasting Foundation, myself to donate the apparatus and Marcus Loew to finance the current expenditures. . . . This would make the entire broadcasting enterprise a philanthropic enterprise, one against which patent rights, as I understand, do not apply." Disguised as a vaudevillian philanthropy, reasoned Schubel, the station could continue advertising "if greater care, tact and judgment is exercised in putting over announcements."[74]

Schubel and Loew were spared the necessity of becoming cultural philanthropists by the entry of Grover Whalen into the fray. As commissioner of plants and structures for the city of New York, Whalen had been trying for some time to establish a municipal broadcasting station, WNYC. On 5 March he went to the newspapers with an account of how Western Electric had been frustrating his efforts. According to Whalen, the AT&T subsidiary had refused to sell him the four-thousand-watt transmitter he wanted, advising him to shelve the project and use WEAF's toll service instead. When Whalen rejected that option, the company tried to steer him toward a five-hundred-watt apparatus, simultaneously jacking up the price of the one he wanted. Asked by the *Morning World* to define the issues at stake, Whalen jumped onto Schubel's rolling bandwagon and declared that New Yorkers ought not "have to take our religion, our politics and our education from the Radio Trust." The commissioner also echoed Schubel's attack on the Radio Music Fund. "The public at large," he said, "is being asked to contribute generously in order to enable the telephone company to get high-priced artists and create a predominant position and demand for their advertising services." Whalen further signaled his intention to involve the federal government in the fracas. In open letters to Congress and the Federal Trade Commission, he accused AT&T of trying to "appoint itself virtual dictator of the air" by assuming "the prerogatives of the Federal Government in the control and regulation of radio broadcasting."[75]

Faced with the threat of a federal antitrust probe and morally depleted by weeks of Schubel's tabloid-amplified calumnies, AT&T began to back away from its lawsuit. As rumors spread that the phone company was seeking an out-of-court settlement, the about-face was satirically glossed by a tabloid editorialist, who wrote:

WHN and WEAF appear to be getting real friendly, sending invitations to each other now. WEAF says: "Dear WHN: Please meet us where we can have a little chat to see if we can't settle this nasty little question about who owns the ether. It seems to us that the ether is so small and unimportant that this question can be settled between friends without any hard feeling resulting. We'll bring the cigars. Yours, for better broadcasting, WEAF." WHN answers: "My Dear WEAF: Thanks for your kindly invitation. Sure will be glad to meet you, and see no reason why we can't fix this thing up. Grove Whalen just blew in while we were reading your letter, so we asked him along. You know Grove, so we guess this will be OK. Grove's a little sore because he has been trying to buy a couple of pounds of ether and has had to do a little shopping around without success, but believe this can be smoothed over. Marcus looks forward to the party and asks us to send his best. . . . Yours for stronger patents, WHN."[76]

In the ensuing settlement, the commissioner got a fair price on a one-thousand-watt Westinghouse transmitter and WHN paid AT&T fifteen hundred dollars for a patent license.[77]

Surrounding the resolution of the dispute was a certain amount of confusion regarding the issue of broadcast advertising. *Radio Broadcast*, usually well informed, mistakenly reported that in signing a license agreement with AT&T, WHN had admitted that it had no right to advertise. "We think," declared the glossy radio monthly, "the interests of the radio public are being conserved when such stations are prohibited from broadcasting for direct monetary profit. Direct advertising by radio is highly questionable even when tried by so excellent a station as WEAF."[78] In fact, however, the telephone company had quietly abandoned its asserted monopoly over commercial time sales. As correctly noted by *Clipper*, WHN now had "all rights and privileges to do as it [saw] fit with its own station."[79] So, by implication, did every other radio station in America.

AT&T's sudden surrender on this point is something of an enigma and an overlooked watershed in broadcasting history. Writing in 1946, by which time commercial sponsorship was entrenched as the economic basis of "the American System of broadcasting" and procommercial viewpoints could be aired without controversy, the AT&T historian Banning framed the capitulation as part of a deliberate program of "radically new steps" taken "in order to provide a better basis for broadcasting's development. These steps were impelled by a belief—directly opposed to the opinion just quoted [from *Radio Broadcast*, reproduced above]—that the interests of the radio public would be 'best conserved' by *not* prohibiting 'broadcasting for direct monetary profit.'" Banning continued, "Few outside the telephone organization realized the full import of this radical action, and the economic basis for broadcasting's support long continued to be the moot question in the broadcasting world."[80]

An interesting question is whether AT&T executives clearly anticipated the ramifications of lifting the ban, or whether they simply tired of defending themselves against the monopoly charge. Judging from an equivocal statement made by AT&T president Herbert Thayer, the company no longer had a fixed position on the issue of advertising. "I am inclined to think," said Thayer, "that we will at least stop broadcasting for hire ourselves. We may license a number of stations for hire, or we may throw it open for everybody. . . . Whether or not we continue to broadcast for hire, we believe that it is in our own interest as well as the interest of the public that others should broadcast and some should broadcast for hire. So, while we intend to maintain our title to our patent rights, we also intend to make it easy for others to use them."[81] As it turned out, AT&T never again challenged another broadcaster for infringing on its monopoly over toll broadcasting. Henceforth, the only impediment to the commercialization of the airwaves would be the public's objection to it.

Now given carte blanche in commercial matters, WHN pulled out all remaining stops and began doing a high volume of spot advertisements for a wide variety of small New York businesses—tailor and dress shops, a storage battery concern, furniture stores, a chain of barbershops, jewelers, small department stores, taxicab companies, drugstores, and restaurants. Bringing to bear his experience in print advertising, Schubel resumed an active role in the business affairs of the station, managing advertising accounts and sending out solicitors to attract new clients.

Long a critic of WHN's bad habits, Yates of the *Herald Tribune* gave the new WHN a backhanded salute for sheer industry. The station, he wrote, "has a talent that comes very close to being downright genius for finding new means of making 'broadcasting' spell 'advertising.' No matter how much we bewail the crudity of their methods . . . we are forced to give them credit for their unflagging zeal in squeezing revenue from the microphone."[82]

To his credit, Schubel did not lack the courage of his convictions. As a member of the committee on advertising at the Fourth Annual Radio Conference convened by Secretary of Commerce Hoover in November 1925, he was alone in proposing that overt commercial sponsorship was the proper financial basis for American broadcasting. His words fell on deaf ears, however, and the final resolution of the committee was the standard condemnation of "direct advertising."[83]

Schubel may have been the only broadcaster in America in 1925 willing to speak out publicly in favor of broadcast advertising, but his advanced views received unsolicited statistical support from the Radio Artists' Association (RAA), a musicians' equity group fighting to establish the right of performers to receive payment for broadcast performances. In a June report intended to undermine broadcasters' claims that they lacked an income stream from which to pay performers, the RAA stated that WHN was enjoying an annual income of three hundred thousand dollars with overhead of not more than fifty thousand dollars.[84] Another New York station cited in the report, WFBH, was said to be pulling in ninety thousand dollars annually with expenditures of thirty-five thousand dollars. The latter station was a recently established "cabaret broadcaster" similar to WHN but, according to *Variety*, "even less discriminating about its clients."[85]

By 1925 WFBH was just one of several independent New York stations emulating WHN's bad habits. Early that year a fledgling corporation called Associated Broadcasters Incorporated circulated a prospectus, much like the one Schubel had put together back in 1921, urging potential investors to "imagine the tremendous sums of money that will be spent by financial, industrial and merchandising concerns in radio advertising."[86] Situated in a Broadway hotel, the company's station, WMCA, took to the air on 22 February with a format much like WHN's, combining Tin Pan Alley song pluggers, vaudeville comedy, nightclub jazz, and a high volume of direct advertising that was described by Yates as an interminable "travelogue through realms of egg noodles, macaroni, progressive cheeses, metal polish and five minute frosting."[87]

Working the same profitable vein after December 1925 was WBNY, "The Voice of New York," a station that, again according to Yates, "unloaded more repulsive advertising than WEAF, WJZ, WOR and WGBS combined could in twice the time." Other stations in the New York area known for combining lowbrow entertainment and direct advertising were WPAP, located at the Palisades Amusement Park in New Jersey and operated by Marcus Loew's business partners, Nick and Joe Schenck; WBBC and WGCP, both of Brooklyn; WKBQ, "The Voice of the Bronx"; WEBJ, operated by the Third Avenue Railway Company of New York; and WPCH of Harlem.[88]

Parallel developments were taking place in the airwaves of Chicago. One station there was practically WHN's twin: WBCN, operated by the *Southwood Economist*, a neighborhood advertising circular in the *Ridgewood Times* mold. As described in numerous letters of complaint to Commerce Department officials, its programming consisted largely of song pluggers, cabaret shows, and advertising for small local businesses that was purchased, according to a survey of broadcast advertising practices published in *Variety*, at a rate of two hundred dollars per hour.[89] (It may have been a critic of commercial broadcasting who in July 1924 smashed the windows of the building that housed WBCN's studios and who planted a bomb that destroyed the same windows a second time a few weeks later.)[90]

The Chicago region had its answer to NTG in the person of Charles Erbstein, who seems to have modeled his announcer's shtick directly on Granlund's, right down to the boisterous recitations of Service, Frost, and Kipling.[91] A millionaire criminal attorney, Erbstein established his station, WTAS, in 1923. Situated on his estate in Elgin, Illinois, forty miles west of Chicago, the station had "an ornate studio fashioned like the radio control room of an American ship complete with navigation lights and illumined portholes."[92] Nearby sat Erbstein's roadhouse-cabaret, the Purple Grackle Inn, whose house band, the Purple Grackle Boys, was a jazzy mainstay of WTAS's musical programs. Between 1924 and Erbstein's death in 1927, the station was engaged in the defining economic functions of the urban lowbrow station: song plugging, publicizing Chicago cabarets and vaudeville houses, and relaying what *Variety* called "a vast amount of advertising propaganda" for small businesses.[93]

Two other Chicago stations conforming to the lowbrow business model were WBBM and WHT, condemned respectively by *Radio Broadcast* as "one of the foremost of the lowbrow stations" and "super-lowbrow." The former, established in 1923 by Ralph and Leslie Atlass, the jazz-loving sons of a wealthy produce wholesaler, would later attain greater respectability by becoming an affiliate of the Columbia Broadcasting System in 1928. The latter, an ephemeral five-thousand-watt giant with studios and transmitter in the upper floors of the Wrigley Building, took its call sign from the monogram of one of its owners, Chicago mayor William Hale Thompson, a celebrated super-lowbrow in his own right.[94]

Apparently not every Chicago lowbrow was involved in the cabaret trade. Identified by *Variety* in 1925 as "the cheapest advertising station operating in or about Chicago," WTAY of Oak Park promoted local restaurants, stores, and tradesmen for one hundred dollars a week, but the station seems to have steered clear of speakeasies. The same seems to have been true of its north-side contemporary, WKBI.[95]

With or without ties to cabarets, stations akin to WHN were popping up in virtually every urban broadcasting market after 1925. In that year, the stations WHAT and WAMD were competitively blasting Minneapolis-St. Paul with what one offended listener called "the jazziest of jazz," financed by ads for chiropodists, mail-order firms, and local retailers. Local feeling ran particularly high against WHAT for the way its poorly tuned signal interfered with the "fine classical music" and Sunday sermons broadcast by WCCO, the local upholder of genteel standards in broadcasting.[96] In Rochester, New York, station WOKT was charging local merchants one hundred dollars an hour for the privilege of sponsoring programs consisting, according to one detractor, of "senseless chatter, musty jokes and moth-eaten stories . . . mixed with worthless jazz."[97] In Detroit, front-runners in broadcast commercialism were WGHP, owned and operated by a local advertising firm, the George Harrison Phelps Corporation; and WMBC, where the former traveling salesman Frank Bannister would cut his teeth on broadcasting.[98] The Schubelian aspirations of the owner of KWKC, a one-hundred-watt station in Kansas City, Missouri, are reflected in a circular he sent out to local businesses inviting them to "tell the people about Yourself and Your products or the Business that You Are In" and promising them an audience of "ONE HUNDRED THOUSAND (100,000) HOMES!"[99] Pittsburgh was supplied by WJAS with direct advertising and what one listener called "trash music which neither elevates the morals nor improves the musical knowledge of the listener."[100] In Miami, Florida, WQAM, WMBF, and WGBU competitively plied a similar vein.[101] Listeners in Cincinnati wrote to the Commerce Department complaining about the cabaret broadcasting and other "smutty" commercial entertainments from station WMH.[102] A self-appointed spokeswoman of the "serious-minded, thinking people" of Saint Louis, Missouri, wrote the same office to protest the "jazzy, non-intellectual and commercial programs" of station WIL.[103] In Seattle, Washington, a leading offender against broadcast propriety was KXA; in Portland, KXL; in Jersey City, WAAT; in Akron, WADC; in Buffalo, WMAK; in Hackensack, WBMS; in Wilkes-Barre, WBRE, and so forth (my sense is that there are a lot more where these come from, but I leave their recovery to future researchers.)[104]

In certain respects, WHN was sui generis, distinguished from the average lowbrow station by its proximity to the hot black core of the metropolitan jazz scene and perhaps by a more daring attitude in general with regard to standards of cultural propriety. But in other ways, WHN typified the populist and commercial "station of local interest" referred to in the previous chapter, the kind that the Princeton researchers Meyrowitz and Fiske had in mind when they observed that "the little fellow likes the little station." By all evidence, stations like these represented the best that the airwaves had to offer to a large segment of the early broadcast audience. They also represented, in a way that the genteel corporate stations of the day did not, the future of American broadcasting.

Figure 1. George Schubel, publisher of a neighborhood newspaper in Brooklyn and founder of station WHN, felt he had every right to use the airwaves for advertising. When AT&T's legal department tried to stop him in 1924, Schubel thrashed the telephone company into submission with a canny guerrilla campaign of populist propaganda.

Figure 2. A business prospectus and advertising rate cards drafted by Schubel ca. late 1921.

Figure 3. Nils Thor Granlund, WHN's chief announcer, did not care if his bawdy, freewheeling style offended advocates of radio's higher cultural destiny. "The policy of the station is not to educate the masses," he told an interviewer in 1925. "Let someone else elevate them. What I want to do is entertain people and bring some frivolity into their homes."

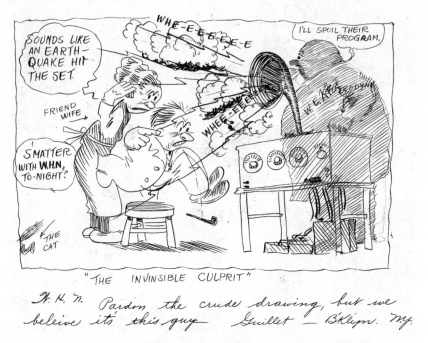

Figure 4. Sketched by a listener at the height of WHN's 1924 legal battle with AT&T, this cartoon refers to allegations that the telephone company was using its own radio station, WEAF, to jam the independent station's signal.

Figure 5. A former antiradical investigator for the U.S. Department of Justice, Franklin Ford was the primary announcer at WHAP, a well-financed New York station dedicated to classical music, ultra-right-wing politics, and heretical Christian Science metaphysics.

Figure 6. Forefather of the modern shock jock, William K. Henderson of Shreveport, Louisiana, held a national audience spellbound with his rustic insult comedy and foul-mouthed ramblings about chain stores, federal officials, and the "Radio Trust."

Figure 7. The Reverend Wilbur G. Voliva, supreme ruler of the fundamentalist utopia of Zion, Illinois, and proprietor of station WCBD. His hellfire sermons and lectures on "flat-earth" geophysics were heard and appreciated from Haiti to Alaska until federal authorities moved him to a less favorable wavelength in late 1928.

Zion Radio Station.

Interior of Radiophone Broadcasting Station, W. C. B. D.

Figures 8–9. Souvenir postcards of station WCBD, Zion, Illinois.

# Chapter 3

# Brows High and Fevered

The purpose of radio programs should be to convey ideas to the greatest public possible in a pleasing manner, but, as with any other means of entertainment, the elevation of the taste of the public, influence toward the cultural or moral and spiritual, should be the greatest point of consideration.

—*John Warren Erb, musical director of WHAP, 1927*[1]

By and large it was the large corporate stations that occupied the cultural and ethical high ground in the 1920s, while commercial independents espoused more commercial and populist cultural agendas. An exception to this rule was WHAP, an exceptionally well-heeled independent that joined the increasingly crowded ether above New York City in late 1925. Easily the most militant defender of genteel cultural values to hold a stake in the early airwaves, WHAP was anomalous in other ways as well. In its peculiarity, the story of WHAP throws the key themes of this study—the volatile utopianism that surrounded the birth of broadcasting, and the bitterness of the warfare over broadcasting's proper cultural content—into particularly vivid relief.

WHAP came into the world defining itself as the antithesis of stations like WHN. A publicity item for WHAP planted in the pages of *The Country Editor*, a suburban New Jersey revue, positioned New York's new "Station for Public Service" as an overdue antidote to broadcasters who polluted the airwaves "with the stormy clamor of jazz" and "thinly cloaked indecencies hurled upon the air from the lips of soaked or half-soaked announcers, to find lodgment in the sanctuaries of the just as in the malodorous dens of the vicious."[2] The *Herald Tribune* elaborated on WHAP's corrective mission on the day before the station's grand opening. "Believing that those who favor jazz and vaudeville songs are already receiving an ample volume of this material from other stations," the paper announced," WHAP will not broadcast any music of this type at any time."[3] Instead, reported the *New York Times* two days later, WHAP intended to "confine itself to classical and semi-classical music and to educational talks by noted university lecturers and well known authorities."[4]

WHAP additionally presented itself as the fulfillment of the frequently expressed hope that elite cultural philanthropy might rescue radio from the burden of self-support. Prior to WHAP, only one serious attempt had been made to implement such a solution for broadcasting's financial woes: the Radio Music Fund, which, as was related in Chapter 2, was cut down before its prime in the crossfire between WHN and WEAF.

Supposedly stepping in where the previous initiative had failed was William H. Taylor, identified in WHAP's press materials as a "well-known millionaire philanthropist, traveler, connoisseur [and] patron of the arts." Socially and financially speaking, Taylor was an insignificant figure compared to the Warburgs and the Juilliards, erstwhile patrons of the Radio Music Fund. Still, as owner of a railcar factory, a clutch of Pennsylvania coal companies, and controlling shares in a New York bank, Taylor was a bona fide millionaire. What's more, he was observed to be sparing no expense in endowing WHAP with first-rate technical facilities.[5]

Pricking up his ears at this hopeful new development, the radio critic Raymond Francis Yates of the *Herald Tribune* wrote in early December 1925 that "with the advent of WHAP, the subway-ridden island of Manhattan now presents the most complete and compact exhibition of broadcasting in all its phases that is to be found anywhere." Yates proceeded to categorize New York's radio stations according to their economic functions. "Direct financial return from persons and business desirous of public goodwill," he wrote, "is WEAF's reason for existence. The stimulation of receiving set-sales is the why behind WJZ and WJY [Westinghouse-RCA]. . . . Direct financial return from persons and business desirous of ethereal advertising keeps WMCA, WHN, and WFBH on the air. . . . And now WHAP blossoms forth as a purely philanthropic station." Each motive, noted Yates, produced "its own type of program-presentation." In his estimation, it was the "goodwill seekers among the broadcasters" who were most successful in producing good programs, as opposed to "those stations in search of quick returns, either for themselves or their sponsors." But the goodwill impulse seemed troublingly vulnerable to the critic, predicated as it was on a "paradoxical platform; namely, the exploitation of altruism" for commercial gain. "Take away the altruism," he warned, "and you have objectionable program matter." Now, concluded Yates, it was up to WHAP "to prove that altruism free from the spurs of commerce can produce uniform excellence in broadcasting."[6]

For a time it seemed that WHAP would live up to Yates's expectations.

The station's grand opening on the eve of 30 November 1925 was built around a two-part recital by the renowned Australian composer and pianist Percy Grainger, featuring selections from Chopin, Grieg, and Brahms as well as Grainger's own works. The recital was followed by chamber music from the WHAP String Quartet, a lecture on the topic of "Radio as Educator" by Professor Thomas J. Wertenbaker of the Princeton University history department, a speech from Assistant Secretary of the U.S. Treasury Byron P. Newton on "Radio as Molder of Public Opinion," and vocal selections by various staff artists.[7]

For a few months WHAP's programming continued in the same genteel vein. Every broadcasting day opened with a recital of classical works by the WHAP Orchestra. Ensuing programs of conservatory or sacred music were provided by WHAP's women's chorus, male quartet, woodwind quintet, and string quartet—ensembles that drew on the finest musical talent in New York, including members of the New York Philharmonic Orchestra.[8] Professor Wertenbaker of Princeton returned to give a series of thirteen weekly lectures on American history, and another Princeton scholar, the English professor John Duncan Spaeth, gave a concurrent series of fourteen lectures on American literature.[9] Ernest Thompson Seton, a renowned author of nature-themed children's books, gave weekly talks about the Woodcraft League, a youth organization he had founded. Yates followed these programs with enthusiasm, noting the excellent diction of the speakers, calling its musical offerings "graceful" and "beautifully played," and praising WHAP's signal for its "perfect" reproduction of piano tones.[10]

Behind the scenes, however, there were indications that WHAP was not quite what it seemed. Three weeks after the grand opening, the station's announcer and studio director, Leslie Joy, who had been lured away from an announcing job at WEAF, abruptly resigned, complaining that the purposes of the station had been misrepresented to him.[11] Joy's departure presaged other changes. As winter gave way to spring, the character of WHAP's nonmusical programs underwent a gradual transformation. A new crop of speakers began to be heard, their names gradually supplanting those of Ivy League academics in WHAP's daily program listings. The new lecturers were all militant conservatives propounding extreme views on race relations, immigration policy, the menace of political radicalism, and national military preparedness. Among the new orators were Joseph T. Cashman and William Bosler of the hypermilitaristic National Security League, Harry F. Atwood of the antiradical Better America Federation, Hugh White Adams of the antiimmigrant American Protective League, and William H. Anderson of the American Protestant Alliance. Also coming to new prominence at WHAP was Franklin Ford, who had earlier replaced the departed Leslie Joy as the station's primary announcer. Ford now began supplementing his role as the host of WHAP's musical programs with thrice-weekly "News Digest" programs, in the course of which he excoriated Roman Catholics and Jews as parasitical enemies of the United States.

Yates tracked WHAP's transformation with puzzlement, then disillusion. Perhaps in the hope of eliciting reform, he continued for several weeks to compliment WHAP's musical offerings even as he reproached the station's speakers for their "sustained ferocity," "irate emotionalism," and "strange mingling of historical and religious argument" and for the "curious and inexplicable psychology" behind their "sectarian and political arguments of militant aspect." But by late spring he had formally washed his hands of "The Station for Public Service."[12]

Four months after the station's grand opening, WHAP's studios made a significant pilgrimage from their original home in Brooklyn to a stately brownstone building at the corner of 96th Street and Central Park West. One door down from New York's First Church of Christ, Scientist, this was the residence of the person who had been the station's unofficial but true proprietor all along, Mrs. Augusta Stetson.[13]

By 1926 Augusta Stetson had been a well-known figure in New York for nearly four decades, owing to her role in the growth of Christian Science there. Born Augusta Simmons in Maine around 1842, she was ostensibly destined for a life of conventional Victorian domesticity when, in 1864, she married Frederick Stetson, executive of a Maine shipbuilding firm.[14] But after her husband's health was broken by privations suffered in a Confederate prison during his Civil War service, Augusta was obliged to find a way to support her household. She was trying to establish herself as an elocutionist on the Boston lyceum circuit in 1884 when she met Mary Baker Eddy, the founder of Christian Science. Then in the ninth year of the prophetic mission she had begun in 1875 with the publication of *Science and Health with Key to Scriptures*, Eddy recognized in Stetson a personality as forceful as her own and cultivated her as a disciple.

Dispatched by Eddy to New York City in 1886 to oversee the expansion of Christian Science there, Stetson demonstrated gifts as healer, evangelist, organizer, and administrator to rival those of Eddy. By 1903 Stetson had assembled the largest and wealthiest congregation in the entire Christian Science organization and housed it within a splendid granite temple on Park Avenue erected at a reported expense of $1.25 million.

As watchful as a Mafia don of her subordinates, Eddy had a long history of turning against her favorites, and by the 1890s Stetson's successes in building up the church in New York had awakened her jealousy. That Stetson was twenty years younger than Eddy and widely seen as her probable successor probably contributed to the breakdown of relations between the two—especially since, according to the magical logic of Christian Science, all thoughts touching on Eddy's mortality represented an assault on her well-being. In 1909 Stetson was excommunicated at Eddy's behest, following a headline-making heresy trial. Among the charges against Stetson were that she and her followers had perverted Christian Science techniques of mental healing by afflicting others with invisible bombardments of "malicious animal magnetism."

Stetson withdrew from public life for the year following her expulsion but continued to minister privately to a few dozen disciples who had followed her out of orthodoxy, including William H. Taylor, the future patron of WHAP. But after Eddy's death in January 1910 Stetson arrived at a new understanding of her banishment, reinterpreting it as Eddy's way of sending her forth to advance Christian Science through the establishment of a new, "purely spiritual" church destined to supercede the lapsed authority of "the material organization," as Stetson and her followers styled the Boston-based Christian Science orthodoxy. Stetson also began preaching that Eddy would shortly be resurrected to join her in ushering in the new millennium predicted in the Book of Revelation.[15]

Drawing on Taylor's fortune, in 1919 Stetson inaugurated a lavish and long-running national publicity campaign, filling entire pages of major newspapers from coast to coast with announcements promoting herself as Eddy's successor. WHAP had been conceived as a high-tech supplement to this campaign. In mid-January 1926 Stetson began making twice-weekly broadcasts from WHAP, on Sunday afternoons and Wednesday evenings.[16] In its larger details Stetson's radio message was congruent with orthodox Christian Science doctrine. Like Eddy, Stetson preached that physical reality—especially the human body—was a harmful mirage, but that the illusion would in time be dispelled once a critical mass of minds came to Christian Science. Stetson went beyond orthodoxy, however, in rejecting the reality not just of sickness but of death and by proclaiming her own immortality and that of her followers. Moreover, Stetson categorically proscribed sexual intercourse, a position that Eddy had once looked into but ultimately rejected on pragmatic grounds.

Stetsonite Christian Science was also anomalously politicized. A predominantly upper-middle-class movement, orthodox Christian Science was (prior to the 1960s) conservative in its social tendencies but, in keeping with its studied otherworldliness, politically inert. The Stetsonites' idiosyncratic sympathy with far-right political causes was closely connected to their leader's obsession with "Anglo-Israelism," a pseudohistorical doctrine that identified the Anglo-Saxon people as one of the biblical ten lost tribes of Israel. Originating among the English middle classes in the 1870s, Anglo-Israelism (also called British Israel) soon spread to the eastern seaboard of the United States, where it ignited some interest among the bourgeoisie, including Mary Baker Eddy, who absorbed the theory from an English follower sometime in the 1890s.

While Eddy had only flirted with Anglo-Israelism, Stetson embraced it as doctrine. The hybridization of Anglo-Israelism and Christian Science in her mind triggered an onslaught of xenophobic prophecies whereby white Protestant America equaled the lost tribe of Manessah and Protestant Britain the tribe of Ephraim. Together these brother nations were the only true Israel, other Jews having lost God's favor by rejecting Christ. On Eddy's resurrection, Manessah and Ephraim would rally to her and Stetson's standard, vanquish all foreign elements, and destroy the biblical "red dragon"—a figure which to Stetson represented the Roman Catholic Church. In the wake of this convulsive cleansing, Stetson declared, "America will finally be revealed to our spiritual senses as heaven."[17]

While she had no definite timetable for these events, in 1920 Stetson began to feel that the time was nigh, an intimation she based on the fresh triumph of the American women's suffrage movement (which she approved of) and the recent military cataclysm in Europe.[18] To hasten the millennium, Stetson and her acolytes drafted a detailed political program calling for the disfranchisement of Catholics and unassimilated immigrants in America; the suppression of the foreign language press, the repatriation of African Americans to Africa; the "recognition of the tendency toward moral disintegration resulting from the activities in this Christian country of the anti-Christian Jews, in our theaters, our motion pictures, and in American business circles; the discontinuance of these anti-Christian activities; and the exclusion of Jews of this character from America."[19]

It is unclear whether Stetson's willingness to put WHAP at the disposal of various right-wing fringe groups was motivated entirely by political sympathy or if there was a financial quid pro quo involved. As for the initial concealment and gradual revelation of WHAP's true colors, the Stetsonites seem to have been angling first to capture a broad, cultured, middle-class audience and then to convert it to Stetsonism by degrees. It was the second time the sect had experimented with a Trojan-horse media tactic of this kind; the first attempt had been a magazine called *The American Standard,* whose covert purpose was to recruit the resurgent Ku Klux Klan into Stetson's camp. The keystone of this remarkable plan was a copy of the Klan's closely guarded national membership list, which the Stetsonites obtained through bribery from high-ranking Klan officials in 1923.[20] Armed with the mailing addresses of millions of Protestant nativist households, the Stetsonites hired a prominent Klan leader named C. Lewis Fowler to serve as the magazine's editorial figurehead and began sending out *The American Standard* twice monthly beginning in February 1924. Though the periodical's content was penned by her followers from the start, Stetson waited until its eighth issue before tipping her hand and addressing its readers directly.[21]

It is hard to imagine what the rank and file of the lumpen Klan would have made of the strange, unsolicited magazine, which combined inspirational quotations from Ralph Waldo Emerson, William Gladstone, and William Ellery Channing with advice on how to "tune out" the nefarious influence of the Jesuit and Jewish "hypnotists" whose "mental broadcasting" was corrupting American culture and politics.[22] Demand for subscriptions was apparently tepid, however, because the *American Standard* ceased publication in November 1925.

Although WHAP's declared status as a disinterested philanthropy was a lie, the Stetsonites were wholly sincere about promoting musical high culture. More than just bait for a better class of listener, WHAP's polished musical offerings were an integral element of Stetson's spiritual battle plan. A former church organist schooled in musical classicism since childhood, she had long emphasized the spiritual importance of music in her teachings. Her flock included many gifted musicians, and as an evangelist Stetson had long courted New York's concert-going public. In 1917 she established a choral society through which to disseminate her musical ideals and inaugurated a long-running annual concert series of "spiritual music," held (on a for-hire basis) at Carnegie Hall and the Metropolitan Opera House.[23]

"Spiritual music" as defined by Stetson was a narrow category more or less limited to the conservatory classics, with particular preference to her favorite composers: Mozart, Haydn, Handel, Bach, Beethoven, and Mendelssohn. Everything else, she taught, was "counterfeit music, introduced and maintained in America by aliens and enemies of Christ."[24] Quizzed about her philosophy by the classical-music journal *Musical America* in 1917, Stetson proffered opera as a prime example of musical counterfeit, citing the "mental pictures of human cruelty, jealousy, envy, hatred, murder, licentiousness and death" prevalent in operatic libretti as the likely cause of the war then raging in Europe.[25]

Popular music, it went without saying, was beyond the pale. And as WHAP's musical director John Warren Erb explained to the journal *The Musician* in 1927, the Stetsonites were especially opposed to popular music in the airwaves. "The radio," declared Erb, "is dealing with the realm of the invisible. Broadcasting is a mental inoculation without the physical presence of the artist. It is a most powerful influence for either the upbuilding or deterioration of public taste. Therefore, there should be no place for jazz or the cheap type of music hall songs in programs broadcast from reputable stations."[26]An esteemed vocal coach and choirmaster, Erb was just the sort of disciple Stetson was inclined to dote on. Another was Miss Kitty Cheatham, an acclaimed soprano singer who discoursed regularly from WHAP on the excellences of her Nordic racial heritage and served as the hostess of the station's weekday afternoon children's program of songs and stories.

Another Stetson favorite frequently heard from WHAP was Vida Milholland. Born in 1888, Milholland was the progressive era's equivalent of an upper-class red-diaper baby. Her father, John E. Milholland, made a fortune building pneumatic-tube messaging systems beneath the streets of New York and was a founding member of the NAACP. Her older sister, Inez Milholland Boissevain, with whom Vida cofounded the National Woman's Party, was hailed as a martyr to the cause of female suffrage after dying of acute anemia in the midst of a 1916 speaking tour. Shortly after her sister's death, Vida fell into Stetson's charismatic orbit. As a speaker at WHAP, she attacked sex, alcohol, and tobacco and espoused American political isolationism and military preparedness. Trading on her sister's legacy, Milholland was prone to putting a feminist spin on her leader's mission, exalting Stetson as a "fighter for the true emancipation of woman, which emancipation frees her from the age-old bondage of sex."[27]

But the predominant voice at WHAP was that of Franklin Ford, who had taken over as the station's chief announcer following the departure of Leslie Joy. A Princeton graduate (class of 1913) and son of a Princeton professor of politics, Ford had briefly served as an operative of the U.S. Justice Department's Bureau of Investigation (precursor to the FBI) during the Red Scare of 1919.[28] In that same year Ford's parents converted from Episcopalianism to Roman Catholicism, an anomalous transition that might have conditioned Ford's transformation into a professional anti-Catholic. It is not clear how or when he entered Stetson's service, but by 1920 Ford had left the Bureau of Investigation to become her live-in personal secretary.

In addition to presenting WHAP's musical programs, Ford gave inflammatory "News Digest" talks on Monday, Wednesday, and Thursday evenings and capped the week with a special Saturday "Lecture on Political Romanism," the texts of which were also published as a column in *The Fellowship Forum*, a Ku Klux Klan weekly out of Washington, D.C. While most of Ford's radio talks differed little from the garden variety anti-Catholic demonology of the day, at times he was led down lonelier polemical paths by Stetsonite metaphysics. In a 1927 lecture entitled *Tammany Hall's Roman Catholic Greeting to Colonel Lindbergh*, for example, Ford interpreted the participation of Catholic officials in the ceremonial welcome extended by New York to the aviator-hero as the reenactment of the Calvary of Christ. To Ford, Lindbergh represented the "Nordic

stock which gave us Leif Ericson [*sic*] . . . , a true man possessing the
mind of Christ sufficiently to command the winds and the waves to obey
him." That Lindbergh had suffered exposure to a boxing match and a
"Ziegfield girl-show [*sic*]" by Catholic ward heelers proved that the avia-
tor had been made "the victim of Romish psychological mental manipu-
lation." Similar blasphemies had been perpetrated against the pilot's
mother, Evangeline Lindbergh, who, "like Mary, the Mother of Jesus
Christ, gave to the world her son." Especially revolting to Ford was the
fact that the Catholic governor Al Smith, "a heavy smoker of strong
cigars and an advocate of strong drink, [had] planted his pendulous lips
against her pure face." Thus, shuddered Ford, "the same mouth that
kissed the papal ring of Cardinal Bonanza has now made a public connection with the face of Mrs. Lindbergh."[29]

Adding to the notoriety that these strange and offensive harangues
brought him, Ford courted notice as a litigator, bringing three well-
publicized lawsuits against the city of New York between 1927 and 1930,
all relating to the overlap between Roman Catholicism and city government. In the most prolonged of these unsuccessful suits, Ford applied
for injunctions to restrain the municipal station WNYC from broadcasting Catholic fraternity functions, citing the programs as violations of the
First Amendment. Between his broadcasts and lawsuits, Ford momen-
tarily established himself as one of the most hated men in New York and
was publicly denounced by religious leaders, Broadways stars, and public
officials, including New York's playboy mayor Jimmy Walker. Reveling in
the attention, Ford sent out press releases enumerating the death
threats he received.[30]

Odd as they were, there seems to have been an audience for WHAP's
programs: Stuart Hawkins, who replaced Raymond Francis Yates as the
*Herald Tribune*'s radio columnist, "Pioneer," in 1926, reported receiving
blizzards of hostile mail from touchy "WHAP addicts" every time he criticized the station. But if WHAP had its friends, it did not want for enemies. Chief among the latter was the Christian Science orthodoxy, which
placed letters and notices repudiating WHAP in scores of northeastern
magazines and newspapers. Also active in attacking the station were the
American Jewish Committee and the Knights of Columbus. Two members of the U.S. Congress, Samuel Dickstein and Solomon Bloom, both
Jewish Democrats from New York (the latter a sometime Tin Pan Alley
songsmith), lobbied for the suppression of WHAP. After polling its readership, *Radio Broadcast* ranked WHAP alongside two notoriously mercenary midwestern commercial stations as the most "widely disliked
stations" in America.[31]

As they had in the case of WHN, Commerce Department officials met
demands for the suppression of WHAP with boiler-plate disavowals of

the government's power to censor the airwaves. But providence twice intervened on behalf of WHAP's enemies in early 1927; first when the coffers of the station's patron, William H. Taylor, were exhausted; and second when Taylor himself expired weeks later at the age of sixty-eight.[32]

The loss of Taylor's support came just as the Stetsonites had committed themselves to replacing WHAP's original transmitter, located atop the Printerion Building in Brooklyn, with a new twenty-five-thousand-dollar transmitting tower to be situated across the Hudson River in Carlstadt, New Jersey. The station's finances suddenly strained to the breaking point, Stetson was obliged to downsize WHAP's operations. Until this time WHAP had held the distinction of being the only independent station in America paying wages to a permanent, full-time staff of musicians. In late May 1927, however, Mrs. Stetson was obliged to issue a general layoff notice. "The present transition," Stetson optimistically explained to her staff, "means that the station is changing still more toward the status of a wholly spiritual church, supported by the voluntary efforts of its congregation." In other words, it was Stetson's hope that WHAP's roster of topflight classical musicians would continue to serve the station pro bono.[33] Her expectations proved to be misplaced, and only the hard core of her following—Franklin Ford, Kitty Cheatham, John Warren Erb, and Vida Milholland—stayed on.

WHAP now began appealing directly to its listeners for financial support. Response to these requests, claimed Franklin Ford, was highly encouraging, bringing in as much as fifteen thousand dollars per month.[34] The fortunes of the station reportedly received a boost when the Democratic Party selected a Catholic, Al Smith, as its candidate in the presidential race of 1928. With its new transmitter in the Jersey meadowlands up and running, WHAP launched a year-long propaganda attack against Smith, coloring its fund-raising appeals with warnings of an imminent papal coup should Smith attain the White House.[35]

But close on the bankruptcy and death of William H. Taylor came another, more wrenching blow to WHAP: Stetson, who was nearly ninety, was ailing to the point that she was obliged to retire from broadcasting. Characteristically, she glossed this setback in the material realm as a promotion in the dimension of spirit. "I have decided," she confided to her listeners in August 1928, "to withdraw from the microphone and rise still higher into the wholly spiritual work of mental reflection. To my air audience I say, 'Listen for my voice in the wholly spiritual chambers of thought.'"[36] On October 12 she passed away under the care of a regular physician. According to the Stetsonites' contemporary chronicler Alton K. Swihart, Stetson's inner circle anticipated a swift resurrection and kept her remains lying in state for several days before bowing to the necessity of a funeral. Absent from this protracted wake was Franklin Ford, to whom Stetson had left control of WHAP.

Within a month of Stetson's death, the thirty-eight-year-old Ford manifested a definitive break with her teachings by wedding a lady pianist in the employ of the National Broadcasting Company. Henceforth, he defined himself religiously as an Episcopalian. Under his direction WHAP made no further references to Christian Science and had no further truck with Cheatham, Milholland, and Erb.

While no longer a Stetsonite, Ford stayed true to WHAP's established agenda of anti-Catholicism, antisemitism, antiradicalism, and "good music"—although the musical side of WHAP's programs depended increasingly on phonograph records.[37] Now operating on the cheap, he improvised a new format much like modern talk radio, including call-in segments during which he broadcast his live telephone conversations with listeners on such topics as the secret orgies conducted by monks and nuns behind convent walls, and the ritual sacrifice of infants clandestinely practiced by priests and rabbis.[38]

It is hard to tell what sort of profit Ford was able to reap from WHAP in its post-Stetsonite phase, but in 1930 he had enough money to revive *The American Standard*—this time as an organ of nativist opinion with no connection to Christian Science. That same year he acquired control of a second independent broadcasting station, WOAX of Trenton, New Jersey, which functioned for a time as a relay station for WHAP's programming. In the pages of the *Standard*, Ford touted WHAP and WOAX as the first links of a projected nationwide network of listener-supported stations dedicated to the promotion of "100 per cent Americanism."[39]

By late 1931, however, his dreams of a national media empire were in peril. "Certain forces," disclosed Ford in the *American Standard*, "known for their hatred of free speech have been campaigning in Washington against station WHAP. News to this effect has appeared in the press. The response of the friends and supporters of WHAP has been emphatic and unanimous. A lot of letters are pouring into this office. The writers profess their hearty approval of the station, declaring its continued maintenance to be a public necessity. We cannot get too many of these letters. They will aid us materially in any possible struggle in the future."[40]

The enemies of free speech to which Ford referred were a league of Italian American fascists whose feelings had been repeatedly hurt by statements made by one of Ford's new colleagues, Dr. Carlo Fama. An Italian-born Protestant evangelist, Fama had been broadcasting from WHAP since December 1928, voicing harsh criticisms of the Roman Church, Mussolini, and New York's Italian-language press. According to the *New York Telegram*, the fascists had obtained the ear of someone at the

State Department, who in turn had persuaded the newly created Federal Radio Commission (FRC), precursor to the FCC, to investigate WHAP.[41]

Then in its fourth year of existence, the FRC was conducting a systematic crackdown on troublemakers in the airwaves. This cleanup operation had begun in earnest in the summer of 1930, when for the first time federal authorities denied a broadcaster's application for license renewal on the grounds of broadcast content. On the receiving end of this unprecedented sanction was John Romulus Brinkley, owner of station KFKB of Milford, Kansas, which functioned as a publicity organ for a profitable but disreputable alternative-medicine clinic that Brinkley ran there.

The revocation of Brinkley's license was a legal wake-up call to all broadcasters operating from the margins of the airwaves and to the American Civil Liberties Union (ACLU), which began casting about for a client to defend against the government's newly asserted power to kill stations on the basis of content. Contacted by ACLU spokesman Hatcher Hughes, Ford expressed a provisional willingness to stand in the docket.

In November 1931 Hughes wrote the FRC asserting that WHAP's broadcast attacks on Mussolini, the Italian government, and Roman Catholicism were protected under the First Amendment.[42] FRC secretary James W. Baldwin's responded with a bland reiteration of the commission's position that the denial of a license renewal somehow was not censorship. Baldwin patiently explained to Hughes,

The Federal Radio Commission is specifically prohibited by the Radio Act of 1927 from the exercise of censorship over programs broadcast by radio stations; however, the Commission may, when programs have been broadcast, consider them in connection with applications for renewal of license, in order to determine whether they are operating in the public interest, convenience, or necessity. If it appears that a station's operation is not in public interest, the station license may be set for hearing and the licensee has opportunity to present evidence that the station should be renewed.[43]

Baldwin's reply seems to have been enough to discourage Ford from gambling his license at a legal hearing. Instead, he broke off contact with the ACLU and made a last-ditch effort to recast WHAP in a less controversial mold. Signaling his change of heart to federal authorities, he wrote to the Radio Division in March 1932 requesting a new call sign, WFAB. "The reason for this request," Ford meekly explained, "is that we wish to change the policy with respect to our programs. . . . In the future we desire to place our programs on the same basis as any other station, and, in order to assist in accomplishing this purpose, we deem it essential that our call sign be changed."[44]

In response to this white flag, the FRC granted Ford's request and terminated its inquiry into WHAP's affairs. Starting afresh under his new call sign on 12 March 1932, Ford began selling airtime to all comers and found that most of his business came from the minority groups he despised: Polish, Jewish, and German interests, who filled WFAB's schedule with commercially sponsored foreign-language programs. Presumably this state of affairs helped Ford decide to sell his station and its license, which he did in September 1932.

Subsequent to the sale of WFAB, Ford took one last shot at sustaining his radio career by canning his anti-Catholic and antisemitic diatribes on transcription discs (electrical recordings custom-made for airplay) and paying to have them broadcast from various northeastern commercial stations. Back in WHAP's well-financed glory days Ford had insisted that commercialism in broadcasting led to a "commercial dictatorship" that rendered freedom of speech impossible. The censorious reaction of the commercial stations whose time he was purchasing for his transcription talks now confirmed this judgment. "If we are to continue with this series," wrote the manager of Cincinnati station WSAI to Ford in early 1933, "it will be necessary for you to refrain from any attacks either directly or indirectly on other religions. If this is not in keeping with your plans, I am very sorry to say that we will have to terminate this series."[45]

Ford's ambitions for a radio career appear to have died with the transcription scheme. Subsequently he moved to Florida and launched a successful career in real estate. In later life, according to family members, he never spoke about his involvement with the Stetsonite cult. But in January 1952 he enjoyed a brief reprise in broadcasting as a contestant on *Songs for Sale*, a CBS television show hosted by Steve Allen, in which amateur songwriters submitted their work to be evaluated by a jury of music business professionals.[46]

As Lawrence Levine has shown in his influential work *Highbrow/Lowbrow: The Emergence of Cultural Hierarchy in America*, cultural hierarchy, though never reducible to a purely disciplinary power, is inextricably rooted in the hegemonic ambitions of the cultured classes. In their musical beliefs, the Stetsonites represent an especially radical expression of high culture's disciplinary side. It was an article of faith among the upper bourgeoisie in the early twentieth century that the spread of "good music" equaled the spread of moral and political goodness—that initiatives of cultural uplift could counteract vice and criminality, promote temperance and chastity, pacify class antagonism, neutralize labor unionism, and hasten the integration of unassimilated immigrant groups into the Anglo-Protestant mainstream. (Today belief in the salutary power of classical music is greatly diminished, but weak echoes of the old faith persist: in the pseudoscientific notion, for example, of "the

Mozart effect," which associates exposure to the classics in early infancy—or even in utero—with improved math scores later in life.)

Stranded on their strange plane of metaphysical abstraction and vitalized by hatred, the Stetsonites took the disciplinary conception of broadcasting's musical mission to its furthest possible extreme, redefining transmissions of chamber and conservatory music as a sort of Anglo-Protestant death ray aimed at the "dangerous classes" of American society. Although it may seem inappropriate to associate the term "genteel" with such a fevered worldview, Stetson and her followers definitely belonged to—represented, in a sense, a dying scream of—the Anglo-American genteel tradition.

*Chapter 4*
# "Exit the Jonas Hayseed of 1880"

Those who listen to KMA and KFNF help feed the world. Some of those stiff necks who haven't the energy to feed themselves, let them have their highbrow stations after the backbone of our country has gone to bed.

*—Arkansas radio listener, 1927*[1]

In early 1925 Omaha grain merchant Charles Vincent acquired a broadcast license and a two-hundred-watt transmitter and, under the call sign of WAAW, began providing daily program service to his region of the midwestern grain belt. As Vincent explained to the Radio Division of the U.S. Department of Commerce, his motives for doing so were largely prudential, stemming from a desire to ingratiate his firm, the Vincent Grain Company, in the hearts and households of local farmers. "The post-war period, with its attendant deflation of values," Vincent wrote,

was especially embarrassing to the grain trade. Always since Joseph managed the conservation of grain for Pharoah and the rationing of the reserves, grain dealers have been considered fair game for a certain class of critics. . . . Our exchange came in for its full share of misrepresentation, and among the sins charged against us was the "suppression of market reports" and "withholding of market news" until the shapeless monster, called the "Board of Trade" or "Grain Exchange" had "appropriated" all the benefits supposed to go with a knowledge of market changes. Of course, there was no truth in the charges, but in the inflamed condition of the minds of the farming public, we were in the position of a ship sailing the strait between Scylla and Charybdis. If we kept silence, it was construed as a confession that the charges were true. If we replied, it would add fuel to the flame. Just at that time, radio was being introduced to the west. Two of us, Mr. Frank J. Taylor and the writer, conceived the idea of broadcasting the market reports, placing the latest market news up-to-the-minute in the instant possession of every person, whether trader, farmer or stockman, who would provide himself with a receiver. We have broadcast band concerts, religious services, musical programs, Agricultural Department bulletins as a means of cementing the friendship of interested peoples and building up a spirit of goodwill between city and country to replace the old antagonisms that formerly existed and which are not yet fully eradicated.[2]

The antagonisms Vincent referred to were real enough. In the 1920s the urban economy was flourishing as never before: gross industrial production, stock values, and wages were all soaring to new heights. But the agricultural sector was suffering a slump commensurate to the success enjoyed by industry and finance. Coming down off a period of exceptional wartime prosperity, American farmers were beset by plummeting crop prices and collapsing land values.

Adding insult to injury, the 1920 U.S. census reported that, for the first time, the urban populace of the union had surpassed the rural. On one level, this well-publicized fact was only a statistical artifact, the function of a recent change in the criteria of enumeration. At the same time, a genuine shift of national demography was definitely taking place, one that rural dwellers were experiencing in direct and personal ways: by watching their neighbors, relatives, sons, and daughters migrate to the cities in unprecedented numbers in search of opportunities that farm life could not match.

Moreover, there hung in the air a generalized sense that rural life had somehow been comprehensively superseded, left in the dust by progress. Metropolitan civilization was distinctly ungracious in ringing in the changes. The ruling motif of contemporary literature was, as the historian Richard Hofstader observed, that of "a revolt against the village" and "an attack on the country mind."[3] In the realm of popular culture, comic strip artists, Tin Pan Alley songsmiths, and vaudeville performers spun infinite comedic variations on themes of rural imbecility. The extent to which these insults reverberated in the countryside is difficult to judge—vaudeville circuits did not reach there, and it is safe to assume that few farmers subscribed to *The American Mercury,* the monthly bible of metropolitan self-regard. But whether or not they heard all of the distant laughter enjoyed at their expense, country people understood that their way of life was fast being redefined as a backwardness: something trivial and obscure taking place *out there,* beyond the pale of electric light, indoor plumbing, prosperity, sophistication, modern convenience, and modern pleasure.

Schooled by generations of political flatterers from Thomas Jefferson to William Jennings Bryan to consider themselves the backbone of the republic and the source of all its virtue, rural Americans took the news of their irrelevance hard and kicked back angrily against the rising power of the cities. The backlash dominated the domestic politics of the day. Prohibition, though also supported by the swing votes of Anglo-Protestant "progressives," was largely a punitive expression of rural nativist hostility toward the immigrant-infested cities, and the battle to enforce the Eighteenth Amendment would continue to pit the nominally dry countryside against the defiantly wet cities for thirteen tumultuous years. The fundamentalist controversy, kindling for decades and ignited by the Scopes Monkey Trial of 1925, would blast the major Protestant denominations into two separate camps, liberal and fundamentalist, a schism that closely coincided with the urban-rural division. Ku Kluxism, the strain of militantly nativist Protestant fraternalism that attracted as many as four million adherents by middecade, cut across the urban-rural boundary and extended into many smaller American cities, but its values and the balance of its numerical strength derived from small towns and the countryside.[4]

Little wonder, then, that the same class of prophets who dreamed aloud about broadcasting's capacity to "Americanize" immigrant groups made comparably rosy predictions about how radio would pacify and cosmopolitanize the countryside. The favorite theme of this subgenre of the utopian discourse inspired by radio was the one emphasized by the grain buyer Charles Vincent in his letter to Commerce officials: the notion that broadcasting fresh market news to farmers would restore rural prosperity, or at least assuage rural suspicions that the market was a crooked game rigged in favor of the cities.

Faith in the power of rapidly distributed market reports to appease rural anger was seconded by utopian projections of radio's mollifying cultural effects on the countryside. At their least astute, urban radio boosters wrote as if the typical country dweller were simply a cultivated bourgeois who happened to live at an inconvenient remove from the nearest concert hall or lyceum. "The high-class entertainments and educational lectures which were previously available chiefly to city dwellers are now within reach of every farmer," trumpeted *The Literary Digest* in 1922. "He need no longer make a special trip to the city to hear an opera or lecture by some noted explorer."[5]

Other observers showed a clearer appreciation of the cultural chasm separating the city from the countryside but made predictions that were still only slightly less sanguine. In a 1924 essay entitled "Exit the Jonas Hayseed of 1880," for example, the journalist Christine Frederick introduced the readership of *The Wireless Age* to a radio-equipped Illinois farmer of her acquaintance. "He is far from a 'bearded hayseed,' I'll tell the world," vouched Frederick. "He lives in a very modern home indeed—two bathrooms, electric toasters at breakfast (and using electricity generated on his very own farm, too!) and he has an *office!* . . . a roll-top desk, a typewriter, and a filing cabinet." Frederick did not claim that this paragon of rural enlightenment, so reassuringly like an urban white-collar worker in his accoutrements, was at all representative of his class, but merely that he was "an augury of more cosmopolitan farmers to come." Of course, she qualified, "there are farmers and farmers." Another she had met flatly refused to spend money on a radio, but this poor specimen belonged "to the degenerating days of native stock, thinned out by the live farm boys going to town, leaving all the poorer types behind." Regardless, Frederick expressed confidence that there was nothing wrong with country folk that radio could not soon fix. "The stolid, set look upon peasant faces," she opined, was primarily a consequence of "isolation, the demon of the rural spaces." She reassured her readers, "I have sat in a farmhouse in Utah far up in the beautiful mountain section there, miles and miles from the city, and heard the splendid broadcasting available and seen the farmers' faces shine with a real human interest and sociability."[6]

Judging from such titles as "Coal, a Factor in Industry and Health," "Glass, One of Man's Blessings," and "Heat and Cold: What They Seem to Us"—all features presented by Westinghouse's Pittsburgh station KDKA in 1924 as fare tailored to rural needs and interests—the premise that rural radio listeners were craving uplift from the cities exerted considerable influence among early corporate programmers.[7] Only occasionally did an urban observer question the reality of this rural hunger for formal instruction. In 1926, for example, John Wallace, critic for *Radio Broadcast*, glossed a report recently issued by the National Farm Radio Council and based on a survey of 44,550 radio-equipped rural households. "The average urban listener doubtless has the impression, as had we," wrote Wallace, "that the farmer is most interested in having himself uplifted and educated—for the reason, no doubt, that every program we hear announced as a 'special feature for farmers' is of such uplifting or educating nature. But lo and behold! it seems the tired farmer, just as the tired business man, is more eager to be entertained by his radio than taught." As a further surprise, noted Wallace, the Farm Council's report revealed that farmers insisted on being entertained on their own cultural terms. Jazz and soprano singers, according to the survey, were especially displeasing to the rural audience. Desired in their place was more "old time music."[8]

"Old-time" was a catch-all category for music pleasing and familiar to rural ears. At its core was fiddle-based folk music meant for dancing: ancient and authorless melodies such as "Turkey in the Straw," "Arkansas Traveler," and "Pop Goes the Weasel." Old-time was not a purely folkloric category, however. The term was just as applicable to Tin Pan Alley songs as long as they had been around for a good while. Sentimental "heart songs" and parlor ballads from the pre-ragtime era—"Silver Threads among the Gold" and "When You and I Were Young, Maggie"—were every bit as old-time as "Barbara Allen," a song dating back to the English Civil War.

In subsequent decades—and thanks in no small part to radio—the rural demand for old-time music would support the rise of a new idiom of commercial popular music known at different points in its history as "hillbilly," "hillbilly and western," "country and western," and "country." Over time this music would absorb any number of distinctly nontraditional elements and influences, including Tin Pan Alley song structures, jazz rhythms, exotic instruments like the steel guitar (of Hawaiian origin), and electric amplification. The persisting, legitimating element of this invented musical tradition was a stance of antiurbanity, a mood that would survive even after the genre became as urban as any other form of popular music in terms of its audience demographics and its modes of production.[9]

The same defining mood of antiurbanity informed the rural response to radio in the 1920s. Early rural radio listeners were in no mood to accept cultural dictation from the cities, and a few urban stations in farm-belt regions recognized this fact early in the game. For example, WLS of Chicago, operated by the Sears-Roebuck corporation, began catering to rural tastes in 1924 with a folk music revue called *The Old Fiddler's Hour*, later renamed *The National Barn Dance*. Station WSM of Nashville, Tennessee, property of the National Life Insurance Company, scored a similar success four years later with *The Grand Ole Opry*. In both instances, however, the corporate owners of these stations initially regarded these programs as embarrassments to their public image; only massive popular response prevented their replacement with more genteel alternatives.[10]

Beyond the city lights, however, there existed a class of broadcaster, known as the "farmer stations," who did not need to be led by the nose to an understanding of the old-time aesthetic but practiced it right from the start, by instinct bred in the bone. In many respects the farmer stations were analogous to urban lowbrow stations like WHN. They were founded by entrepreneurial types whose minds worked a lot like George Schubel's—visionaries who, on hearing of the ease with which a broadcast license could be acquired, recognized commercial opportunity and seized it. Like their lowbrow city cousins, the rural independents were brashly commercial, culturally populist, and given to defining themselves in opposition to corporate stations and the potted-palm aesthetic.

In other respects, however, farmer stations were different from the urban independents. The latter shared a basic uniformity of function and format owing to their involvement with a common set of sponsors and content providers: cabarets, neighborhood vaudeville, local business advertisers, and the song-plugging economy. But in the places where farmer stations sprang up, there were no cabarets or vaudeville houses and fewer small businesses to enlist as sponsors. Neither was there an old-time payola system for rural broadcasters to tap into—at least not yet. In the absence of these financial and cultural inputs, the rural independents developed their own modes of commercialism. The typical farmer station adopted what was called the "direct sales" model, selling consumer goods by mail order to listeners. The rural independents also differed from urban lowbrows in that they tended to be more sharply stamped by the personalities of their owners, who were also their primary announcers—"Ego Stations" is how two early radio historians referred to them.[11]

The idiosyncrasy of the farmer stations makes it difficult to generalize about the rural broadcasting scene, but at a broad level of analysis it can be stated that their fans loved hearing folk music such as fiddle reels and jigs; felt the same way about low church Protestant hymns and gospel songs from the late nineteenth century; disliked classical music as "high hat" and European; disliked opera for related reasons but even more intensely; disliked jazz with comparable passion but for different reasons, perceiving it as natively American but sinful, toxically modern, and "wet"; accepted the products of Tin Pan Alley so long as they were familiar and long out of date; disliked contemporary Tin Pan Alley products, all of which they subsumed indiscriminately under the rubric of "jazz" or "ragtime"; made an isolated exception to the previous rule in favor of "Hawaiian music," a national pop craze at the time;[12] enjoyed fundamentalist preaching and lay expressions of Protestant piety; tolerated or enjoyed broadcast commercialism as practiced by the farmer stations; bridled at the genteel corporate style of announcing as pompous and snobbish; and disliked the urban lowbrow style of announcing for opposite reasons, perceiving it as profane and jocose.

Again, the foregoing derive from the broadest level of generalization. In the following profiles of popular farmer stations, complicating exceptions abound. Stations KWKH and WCBD, for example, deviated from old-time musical aesthetics, each in its own way. KWKH of Shreveport, Louisiana, violated the pattern by salting its old-time musical menu with hot jazz and blues; WCBD of Zion, Illinois, deviated in the opposite direction by incorporating classical music into its programs.

The rural independents also varied in their emotional tone. Women's magazines of the present day have been observed to fall into one of two basic categories, "smiling" and "nonsmiling"; much the same can be said of the farmer stations. It is plain that a lot of rural listeners enjoyed the sound of a rurally-inflected voice raised in anger against the cities and the conditions of contemporary life, and most of the stations profiled in the following chapters were happy to oblige. Two conspicuous exceptions on this count were KFNF and KMA, both of Shenandoah, Iowa. Both stations were dominated by the personalities of their owners, who presented themselves on the air as men of peace and good cheer rather than as populist firebrands. Despite their generally irenic character, however, they were widely decried by proponents of radio's genteel mission as two of the most offensive broadcasters of the day.

There is no obvious reason why Shenandoah, Iowa (population five thousand), should have become an epicenter of early American broadcasting. Nestled in the southwest corner of the state, a hundred miles or so east of the Nebraska border, Shenandoah was a prairie hamlet much like any other. Perhaps it was the sheer ordinariness of the place and its people that enabled its two broadcasting stations, KFNF and KMA, to capture the loyalty of the huge rural audience they shared.

Tracing the origins of Shenandoah's brief apotheosis as a media capital leads us 120 miles westward to Omaha, Nebraska, where a fraternal organization called the Woodmen of the World established the area's first radio station, WOAW, in 1922. In the spirit of regional fellowship, the Woodmen routinely made their microphones available to parties of volunteer talent from outlying towns and villages. In 1923 Shenandoah businessman Henry Field, proprietor of the Field Seed Company, started taking advantage of this standing invitation, arranging for the transportation of speakers, singers, fiddlers, and pickers from the Shenandoah area to WOAW's studios. The homespun cultural offerings of these delegations were satisfactory to the Woodmen, but lodge officials had difficulty convincing Field that the airwaves were not an appropriate place to promote his seed business. "We gave him the privilege of our station four or five times," wrote WOAW station manager Orson Stiles to federal officials in 1924, "insisting, however, on his last three appearances that he personally stay away from the microphone, as he was inclined to exceed our right as a first-class station in his direct publicity talks." Frustrated by these constraints, Stiles further recounted, Field eventually fell out with the Woodmen, "declaring that our statements to the effect that direct or undisguised indirect publicity was prohibited were all 'bunk.'"[13]

Soon after Field broke with the lodge, his competitor in the seed business, Earl May, owner of the May Seed and Nursery Company, began sponsoring his own programs of rural talent at WOAW. A dues-paying Woodman in good standing (awarded the special rank of consul commander in charge of radio affairs), May enjoyed an inside track with the fraternity. By the summer of 1924 he had acquired a private studio at his place of business in Shenandoah, which, linked to the Nebraska station by telephone line, relieved him of the necessity of traveling to Omaha in order to conduct his weekly programs.

Determined not to cede the airwaves to his competitor, Field applied to the Commerce Department for a broadcast license of his own, then recruited some local wireless amateurs to build him a transmitter from scratch. The resulting apparatus was reportedly unlovely to look on— Field later called it "the darnedest rig you ever saw"—but it functioned more than adequately. "On a good clear night," reminisced Field in 1952, "we would pour on the kilowatts and really tear a hole across the midwest."[14] In late February 1924 Field took to the air under the call sign of KFNF, which he variously deciphered as "Known for Neighborly Folks" and "Keep Friendly, Never Frowning."

Born on a cattle farm near Shenandoah in 1871, Field was a born entrepreneur who began selling flower seeds to his neighbors at the age of six. When the U.S. postal system extended rural free delivery to his corner of Iowa in the 1890s, he saw an opportunity to get out of farming by setting himself up in the expanding field of mail-order seed sales. As his enterprise grew, Field carefully monitored the tone of its correspondence, taking pains to preserve the common touch. "Make your letters conform to the spirit and policy of our business," he directed his staff in a 1918 memorandum that presaged his broadcasting style. "As I see it, it means cheerfulness, liberality, honesty and a spirit of what you might call human nature—the small town or common-folks idea. . . . Don't put on any airs. Don't be upstage, or, as we say, 'biggity.' . . . Cut out the book English and talk what I call Missouri English. I mean a forcible, direct, possibly somewhat provincial style."[15]

Like George Schubel of Brooklyn, Field saw radio as a sales medium from the start. A key difference between KFNF and WHN, however, lay in the nature of Field's business. By integrating the station into the operations of his mail-order house, Field moved beyond mere "direct advertising" for third parties to create the first of what would soon come to be recognized as a separate and specifically rural category of commercial broadcaster, the "direct sales station." Initially, Field applied the "direct sales" principle to his existing line of seed and nursery products, whose sales showed a gratifying gain of 33 percent within a year. In 1925 he experimentally broadened his stock in trade to include radio receivers, house paint, automobile tires, dried fruit, and coffee. When these products proved more profitable than his seed business, Field moved wholeheartedly into general retailing, and soon built up an inventory to rival that of Sears-Roebuck, including, according to a 1930 profile published in *The Nation's Business*, "alfalfa, auto awnings, baling wire, bug dust, can sealers, chains, cocoa, coats for men and women, coffee, curtains, fencing, fire extinguishers, fruit (canned), gladioli, hose for men and women, jewelry, jugs, luggage carriers, mattresses, overalls and jackets, paint, peonies, pressure cookers, radio supplies, roofing, rubbers for men and women, rye, shirts, shoes for men and women, silverware, spices, stoves, suits for men, sweaters, tea, ties, tires, towels, and underwear for men and women."[16] The new lines of merchandise also performed well for the Field Company, whose gross income reportedly increased from seven hundred thousand to three million dollars per annum between 1924 and 1927.[17]

The simplicity of KFNF's economic plan was complemented by an equally straightforward musical policy rooted in barn dance music and gospel hymns. These musical forms being native and ubiquitous, Field did not have to search far for talent: he simply turned his clerical and menial staff into radio stars. Unlike city stations, which strove to distance themselves from the taint of amateurism, KFNF proudly advertised the fact that its most popular female vocalist, LuEtta Minnick Armstrong, was the office assistant to company treasurer Fred Tunnicliff, who was familiar to listeners as the announcer of KFNF's Sunday night devotional services. KFNF's star harmonica player, Cecil "Pete" Yarger, doubled as station engineer. A singing quartet called the Seed House Girls were all company telephone operators and secretaries, and singing banjo player Ira Randall worked in the paint and oil department. Mrs. Leanna Field Driftmier, hostess of the daily *Kitchen Klatter* program for farm wives, was Field's sister. The male vocal trio known as the Cornfield Canaries worked as company bookkeepers and shipping clerks when they were not moonlighting as the KFNF Hawaiian Trio, a ukulele-guitar-mandolin ensemble. In fact, with the exception of a blind teenaged piano prodigy named Minor Clites, all of the forty-seven regular performing personnel at the station were full-time employees of the seed company—"never professional singers," as a KFNF souvenir program schedule boasted, "but just our own folks."[18]

Program presentation at KFNF was commensurately free of pretension. "Everything seems more or less impromptu," explained *Radio Digest* in 1930. "Listeners may hear an occasional snatch of conversation which is not on the program. The rendering of a humorous ballad may be interrupted by the laughter of performers and announcer. It is somewhat as though a bunch of boys and girls had just dropped in and were being called upon to 'sing that cowboy song of yours, Bill,' or 'Eli, play the *Virginia Reel* for us.' The entire program is presented with a spontaneity which never suggests rigid professionalism or exacting program etiquette."[19]

To a broad cross-section of rural listeners, the plain style of broadcasting conceived by Field was deeply satisfying, especially compared to the programs emanating from the cities. "Just had Radio three weeks and wouldn't do without it," wrote Jacob Rasmussen of Schaller, Iowa, to Field in late 1925. "But we wish all them Jazzie Chicago stations would go broke and let decent people have a chance to broadcast. We sure like those good old Familiar songs, harmonicas, Fiddles & Accordion . . . that's old country style & sure is fine."[20]

Meanwhile, Shenandoah's other seed sales baron, Earl May, impeded from competing directly with Field by the Woodmen's strictures against direct advertising, applied for his own broadcast license and went into debt to purchase a brand-new five-hundred-watt transmitter from Western Electric.[21] In January 1925 Shenandoah's second direct-sales station, KMA, went on the air. Essentially a carbon copy of KFNF, KMA differed in minor details. Like Field, May recruited performers from among his existing staff, but he seems not to have applied the principle as broadly and consistently as Field did, drafting a larger percentage of his talent from the surrounding community—a mandolin orchestra made up of local businessmen, for example, and the Southland Jubilee Singers, a local "colored" quartet of spiritual singers. Of the two stations, KMA was perhaps slightly more cosmopolitan in its cultural policies. Henry Field, as one of his employees later recalled, was immovably "prejudiced against grand opera or anything that he called 'high and flighty' music, and wouldn't tolerate it."[22] May, on the other hand, was able to find a niche in KMA's schedule for the likes of the Farnham Trio, a classical string ensemble consisting of a local music teacher and her daughters, all graduates of the Northwestern University Conservatory of Music.[23]

By and large, however, the two stations were two peas in a pod, and any rivalry between was amicable. At several junctures in their linked histories, KFNF and KMA cooperated in sharing time on a common wavelength, an arrangement that relieved listeners of having to choose between them. It is not surprising, therefore, that listener correspondence to the stations should indicate that fans of one were all fans of the other. Often, in fact, the two Shenandoah stations were lumped together as if they were a single entity. A 1927 letter from a farm wife to *Radio Broadcast* is typical in this regard: "Too much is said against the Henry Field and Earl May stations, KFNF and KMA. Both are clean and satisfy our Iowa farm homes. They are a temperance people and we need more like them."[24] Some listeners even presumed that Field and May had to be kinfolk, until Field pressured May into broadcasting a statement quashing the rumor that he was Field's son-in-law.

Neither station seems to have held a clear lead in popularity over the other. In 1925 Field took second place in *Radio Digest*'s poll of the "Most Popular Announcers"; the following year May placed first. When the *Omaha World Herald* conducted a popularity poll of regional stations in 1927, it found KFNF and KMA to be "neck and neck" at the head of the pack, garnering 42,840 and 41,104 votes respectively. "The contest," elaborated the paper, "served to establish one fact definitely and that was that the farmer radio fans are 'strong' for their stations."[25]

The popularity of the two stations turned Shenandoah into a tourist draw. In June of 1927 the annual Jubilee Flower Show cooperatively sponsored by both stations drew twenty-five-thousand weekend visitors to Shenandoah (without, as the *Shenandoah Sentinel* proudly noted, "a single instance of drunkenness or disorder"). According to *The Nation's Business*, more people visited the KFNF studios each year than attended the Iowa State Fair. In summertime, visitors came from as far away as Texas, New Jersey, and Canada to stay at the KFNF tourist camp and enjoy the "refreshment booths, home museums, dinners-for-35-cents, popcorn wagons, trinket counters for the children, and tire repair places which surround KFNF headquarters."[26]

Beloved as they were in the countryside, the Shenandoah stations were proportionately reviled by urban upholders of the genteel ideal. In 1927 *Radio Broadcast* awarded KFNF and KMA first and second place on its list of "most hated stations" and opened its pages to Francis St. Austell, president of the Iowa Radio Listener's League, a Des Moines-based citizen's group formed to combat the direct-sales plague in the Midwest. St. Austell took the opportunity to portray Henry Field as a dangerous spellbinder whose "magnetic personality" was capable of arousing "a feeling among his followers that is akin to worship." Field, he warned, was on the cusp of becoming "a national figure, a creation of radio, a leader of hundreds of thousands, almost a prophet, a Moses of the common people."[27]

In fairness to St. Austell, Field was not entirely above the temptations of demagoguery. In 1927, C. E. Crow, publisher of the *Massena* (Iowa) *Echo*, reported to the Commerce Department that Field had "gone crazy as Hamlet on the idea [that] he must broadcast over the country that merchants of all kinds are exacting usurious profits and that he is the only benefactor the farmer has." Field, continued Crow, "day by day poisons the minds of the farmers that the 'High Brows' are trying to put it over on the farmers by jumping on their best friend, KFNF."[28] Apart from self-interested agitations of this kind, however, Field was no provocateur. To the contrary, the essential components of his radio persona were optimism, good cheer, and piety. As KFNF employee Pate Simmons recalled in 1957, Field "often told the audience of his concern with world conditions and that he usually felt that common sense and friendliness would set things aright."[29] The forum for these soothing discourses was Field's twice-daily half-hour program, *The Letter Basket*, during which he answered listener queries about agricultural problems with plugs for appropriate products from the Field Company's inventory. These pitches came couched in an unhurried flow of Field's folksy geniality. "Quite often," reported *The Nation's Business*,

> he spends some time laughing over a letter he has received, or expressing sympathy for some bereaved family in a home several states away, or boosting for good roads, or trying to find a good dog for a sick boy in Montana. Along with mention of our $30 stove and extra good shoes (if you don't know your number, just put your foot on a piece of paper and mark around it, holding the pencil straight up) there is much about the weather, crops in general, an old fiddler's illness (send him a post card, folks) and the new baby in the family of Tom Jones, down at seed house No. 4.[30]

Conscious of the mounting urban backlash against his station, in 1925 Field initiated an interesting correspondence with Commerce Secretary Hoover wherein he defended direct-sales and broadcast advertising as practices conforming to the cultural standards and values particular to the farm belt. According to Field, KFNF's commercialism simply reflected the rural preference for straight talk and plain dealing. "I was really surprised myself," wrote Field,

> to find how universally the farm people and especially the farm women really want to hear prices named. They consider it really the important part of the talk sometimes. I thought I knew farm people pretty well already, but this gave me a new insight which I had vaguely suspected, but had never realized before. The astonishing thing of it is that the farm people are really very, very much in favor of so-called direct advertising, and show a latent hostility to the so-called courtesy programs. In other words, they seem to like frank speaking and direct methods better than any polite evasions.[31]

In hearings before the Federal Radio Commission in 1927, Earl May offered a similar defense of KMA's hard-sell practices, claiming that he had "been just pushed into that" by "all kinds of letters saying, 'The music is fine, but tell us what this costs.'" Both broadcasters claimed to have made attempts at curtailing their quotation of prices on the air— widely considered a cardinal sin of broadcast commercialism—and both claimed that the change of policy had provoked resistance ("the darnedest cussing," in May's words) on the part of listeners.[32]

Plainly this is testimony to be taken with a grain of salt—Field's account of how he was dragged into direct advertising by his listeners, for example, is belied by the Woodmen's experiences with him back in 1922. Still, there is much evidence to support the claim that farmers liked direct advertising and demanded prices. Archived federal files on KFNF brim with correspondence from rural listeners to this effect. Identical sentiments were routinely expressed in the letters column of *Radio Digest*. "KMA and KFNF provide our best all around programs," wrote *Digest* reader Anna E. Shannon of Liberty, Nebraska, in 1927: "Suppose they do tell the farmers the prices of things for sale—that is what farmers want. All stations advertise, so why not do it direct? I don't suppose you will ever read this, but it is written anyhow."[33] "I am a reader of your paper," wrote Elmer Redke of Amboy, Minnesota, "and I would like to say a word or two. We want direct advertising. If they can afford to sell at a low price, everybody else can too. We don't want to hear the chain stations. If anybody wants to hear WEAF, they can tune in direct. We don't want WEAF all over the dial. If every station has its own program, maybe we could pick up a good one more often than we do. We want old-time music. We understand it and like it."[34] Advertising, concurred Edgar H. Cox of Acester, South Dakota, "is interesting and helps lower the prices on what we need. The Shenandoah stations and KTNT are the stations we like best. . . . Why not let the farmers have a few stations that will give the programs of old-time singing and talks about things we need. They are surely easier to tune out than a couple dozen powerful stations all broadcasting the same grand opera line of bunk."[35] "Why," demanded Luther Bruere from his homestead outside of Bussey, Iowa, "hasn't the farmer a right to have the prices of things he wants?"[36]

Assisted by listeners' letters of support (over a million of them, according to the journalist John M. Henry), by 1928 Field and May managed to extract grudging acknowledgment from the Federal Radio Commission that the agrarian Midwest was distinct in its attitudes toward broadcast advertising.[37] "The commission realizes," wrote the commissioners in their second annual report,

> that in some communities, particularly in the state of Iowa, there seems to exist a strong sentiment in favor of such advertising on the part of the listening public. At least there are some broadcasters in that community who have succeeded in making an impressive demonstration before the commission on each occasion when the matter has come up for discussion. The commission is not fully convinced that it has heard both sides of the matter, but is willing to concede that in some localities the quoting of direct merchandise prices may serve as a sort of local market, and in that community may thus be rendered.[38]

Had they been more determined to explore "both sides of the matter," the commission would have done well to consult Francis St. Austell's screed against the farmer stations in *Radio Broadcast*, in which the reformer expressed definite opinions as to where the battle lines were drawn. The recipient of correspondence "from all over the country, from Rhode Island to California, from Maine to Mexico," St. Austell reported that "most letters from opponents of the principles of direct selling are on excellent paper and represent a highly educated class, while those from the supporters of the direct seller are not noted for cleanliness." It was an insight that St. Austell credited to his clerical help: "The young lady who sorts my mail," he explained, "was discovered once making two piles of letters before opening them. One was a clean, neat pile, the other was quite different. When asked the reason for such a procedure, she remarked, 'The clean ones object to direct selling, the dirty letters support it.'"[39]

Hundreds of letters expressing listener support for KFNF bundled together in the archived files of the Commerce Department's Radio Division sustain the judgment of St. Austell's secretary. Few would qualify for prizes in penmanship, spelling, or grammar; many are written on scrap paper, and some are marked with the grime of toiling hands. An even more impressive feature of this correspondence, however, is the sense of connection between listener and broadcaster it gives. "You ask for real heart to heart information about Programs from your station," wrote D. J. Cowden of Adair, Iowa, in December 1925,

[but] I cant see where you can improve on it much. I think your station fills a needed place in the Radio World that we cant do without. You give information on all farm questions. You tell the markets and weather. You give a whole Sundays religious program and quit at reasonable hours at all times. Everything broadcasted is of an uplift nature. . . . Let the dance halls and leg shows hold open all night if they want to and play their Jazz and sing their smutty songs, and have their TRAINED????? singers tremulo nonsense like a Coyote ad-lib-itum, but you just stay where you are. You are doing the country more good than all the Jazz houses in the world.[40]

Just as WHN's "lowbrow" commercial format replicated itself across the urban landscape after 1924, KFNF and KMA inspired a crop of rural imitators. Some of these were simply small-scale versions of the original models. KSO of Clarinda, Iowa, licensed to the A. A. Berry Seed Company, fell into this category, as did WNAX of Yankton, South Dakota; KMMJ of Clay Center, Nebraska; WAAW of Omaha, Nebraska; and KTFI of Twin Falls, Idaho.

Similar in certain respects to the KFNF-KMA school of farm broadcasting, but distinct in others, were another linked pair of midwestern rural broadcasters—KFKB of Milford, Kansas, and KTNT of Muscatine, Iowa. Licensed by the Commerce Department in September 1923, KFKB was owned and operated by John Romulus Brinkley. Born in a log cabin in the mountainous backwoods of North Carolina in 1885, Brinkley served a brief apprenticeship as a station agent and telegrapher for the Southern Railroad at Sylva, North Carolina, but by the age of seventeen he had raised his sights to a career in medicine. For want of access to formal training, Brinkley began his practice as an itinerant "Quaker Doctor," a stock type of the traveling medicine show business, who, dressed up in colonial garb and using no direct pronouns but "thee" and "thou," promoted bottled patent medicine throughout the countryside.[41] Determined to improve his professional standing, in 1908 Brinkley invested twenty-five dollars in a medical license from the Bennett Medical College of Chicago, a diploma mill associated with the eclectic school of botanical medicine. It was the first of many such fast-track diplomas he would acquire.

The year 1917 found Brinkley briefly employed as a plant surgeon at a Swift and Company abattoir in Kansas City. It was here that he claimed to have hit on the surgical operation that would bring him fame and fortune. Observing the vitality of the goats headed for slaughter at the Swift plant, Brinkley hypothesized that a transplantation of plugs of testicular tissue harvested from live goats into the testes of human males would have a restorative effect on the latter's sexual powers. Relocating to the tiny hamlet of Milford, Kansas, Brinkley opened a clinic and began testing his treatment on volunteer patients. The operations, he later wrote, were successful from the start, barring one undesirable side effect: a strong goatish smell emanating from the revitalized subjects. After further experimentation with different breeds, Brinkley found that Toggenburg goats provided optimum rejuvenation with no unpleasant odor.

Despite the forbidding nature of the "Brinkley Compound Operation" and its steep price tag of seven hundred and fifty dollars, the Milford clinic was initially a commercial success. By 1923, however, business was slumping and Brinkley was casting about for new promotional strategies. Newspaper advertisements were vulnerable to legal attack from the AMA, whose policies forbade medical advertising. Broadcasting was different, though: in establishing KFKB, Brinkley acquired the means to generate publicity entirely on his own terms.

Possessed of a well-oiled line of patter perfected in his medicine show days, Brinkley was a folksy, unpretentious, and pious broadcaster. Moreover, as two Kansas sociologists observed, his twice-daily broadcasts included something for almost everyone in the rural listening audience: "Old men who retained undying hope for the return of youthful vigor; the morbidly curious and the repressed who relished his ultra-frank discussions of the sex glands; devout Church people who accepted him as a defender of the old-time religion; all watched the clock for the hour when Brinkley went on the air."[42]

Culturally, the self-styled "Sunshine Station at the Heart of the Nation" conformed to the old-time template of the Shenandoah stations. Among KFKB's regular performers were "Uncle" Bob Larkan, "an old time fiddler from Arkansas, one of the best in the South"; Roy Faulkner, a.k.a. "the Singing Cowboy"; a guitar-and-banjo trio called "The Old Timers"; "Dutch, the Boy Blues Singer"; and local church choirs.[43] Like

Field of KFNF, Brinkley devoted much of his airtime to reading and answering letters from his listeners. In the latter 1920s Brinkley spun this practice into a new money-making scheme that would quickly equal the goat-gland side of his practice in profitability. The market for the "compound operation" was limited to older adult males, but now Brinkley expanded his therapeutic repertoire to include an extensive line of bottled botanical nostrums suited to the treatment of ailments of the young and the old, male and female alike. These remedies were exclusively available from crossroads apothecaries belonging to the "Dr. Brinkley National Pharmaceutical Association," a new professional group that attracted over five hundred members practically overnight in 1929. Renaming his program *The Medical Question Box*, Brinkley now began dispensing individualized medical advice to correspondents over the airwaves. In 1930, for example, a female listener who signed herself "Somewhere in Missouri" wrote to Brinkley complaining that operations on her appendix and ovaries had left her nervous and subject to dizzy spells. Diagnosing her surgery to have been a botch, Brinkley counseled "Somewhere" to adopt a salt-free vegetarian diet and dose herself daily with his "Special Prescription No. 50" plus remedies 64 and 61, available at $3.50 per bottle from participating merchants.

It was shrewd of Brinkley to involve five-hundred-odd regional retailers in his new prescription scheme. A direct sales approach as practiced by KFNF and KMA would have garnered Brinkley 100 percent of the profits from sales of his patent medicines instead of the one-dollar kickback he received from every sale, but the Shenandoah stations and their imitators were under continual fire from competing merchants who resented what they saw as unfair advantages enjoyed by radio merchandisers. Where Field and May had incurred organized regional antagonism against their stations, Brinkley's Pharmaceutical Association scheme created an instant and influential network of political support for KFKB throughout the so-called "Brinkley belt," which extended through Oklahoma, Missouri, Kansas, Iowa, and parts of Arkansas. Merchants participating in the scheme reported that it netted them between seventy-five and one hundred dollars per day. According to KFKB's assistant studio manager D. D. Denver, the station's income from the racket was around five thousand dollars a week, while the goat-gland clinic was taking in between five thousand and seven thousand dollars a week.[44]

Another prominent rural broadcaster, who stood midway between Field and Brinkley in his business practices, was Norman Baker, the proprietor of station KTNT of Muscatine, Iowa. Born in Muscatine in 1882, Baker trained and worked as a machinist in a local button factory in his teens. At the age of eighteen he left Muscatine to pursue a career in vaudeville. According to Clement Wood, author of vanity-published biographies of both Baker and Brinkley, Baker discovered at an early age that he had psychic gifts that enabled him to send and receive "wordless wireless messages," predict the future, and cure disease. Capitalizing on these abilities and his matinee-idol good looks, Baker worked the lower-tier midwestern vaudeville circuits as "Charles Welch," a top-hatted hypnotist who performed mental marvels with the help of an attractive female assistant called "Madame Tangley." By 1914 Baker had tired of the footlights and returned to his home town accompanied by a new bride, the second Madame Tangley.

Back in Muscatine, Baker invented an automated musical instrument he called the "calliaphone"—essentially a circus calliope driven by compressed air instead of steam.

In taking up broadcasting, Baker was at first seeking a means of publicizing his invention to its potential customers: "skating rinks, circuses, road theatrical companies, amusement parks," and so forth.[45] Realizing that public demand for calliaphone concerts was limited, he soon adopted a roster of old-timey programs similar to those of KFNF, KMA, and KFKB. Simultaneously, Baker adopted the direct sales model of radio merchandising. Taking a page from Brinkley's book, Baker offered local producers and merchandisers a piece of the action, proposing to market their goods to the radio public on consignment. In soliciting these partnerships, Baker thoughtfully offered to shield his suppliers from any possible reputational damage that might result from their association with KTNT. "We will sell your goods under our own label," he vouched in a 1927 prospectus, "or under your own label. It is immaterial to us. We will protect you against complaint. Perhaps you will want us to use our own label and you simply be our manufacturer of the 'TANGLEY BRAND'—your name not mentioned over radio."[46]

As was the case with the Shenandoah stations, Baker successfully promoted his station as a tourist attraction. Toward this end, he took pains to endow KTNT with a physical plant worth traveling to see. The resulting architectural sport was described by Clement Wood as incorporating "a bit of American, a dash of Moorish, a gob of Spanish, an ort of Egyptian, and so with all the rest."[47] To accommodate tourist traffic, Baker established a service compound that included a garage; a concession area serving ice cream, "near beer," and souvenir knickknacks; and a two-hundred-seat family restaurant called the KTNT Cafe.

Although Baker would not take up a Brinkley-style medical practice until late in his broadcasting career, he had early established himself as an authority on public health and consumer safety. Among his early pet causes as a broadcaster was a crusade against aluminum, a material relatively new to the countryside and subject to much suspicion. According to Baker, the use of aluminum cookware and baking powder containing powdered aluminum (an anticlogging agent) were leading causes of cancer. Baker was also active in organizing local campaigns of resistance against the compulsory vaccination of cattle and schoolchildren, medical practices that he claimed caused more death and disease than they prevented.

At some point in 1929 Baker crossed paths with Harry Hoxey, an Illinois-born naturopath and self-proclaimed inventor of a sure-fire cure for cancer. In partnership with Hoxey, Baker set up his own cancer clinic in Muscatine, the Baker Institute, which was soon treating as many as three hundred inpatients at a time. The partnership between Baker and Hoxey was short-lived, but Baker kept the clinic running after Hoxey's departure in 1930.

As a broadcaster Baker had none of the droll folksiness that worked so well for Field and Brinkley. Rigid and splenetic by nature, Baker's stock-in-trade at the microphone was rage, and most of his airtime was consecrated to attacks on his perceived enemies, local and distant, great and small. Disrespectful regional newspapers, political enemies in Muscatine, the Federal Radio Commission, and the American Medical Association—each received a due lacquering from Baker, whose favorite interpretation of his call sign was "Know the Naked Truth." According to an unlucky representative of the FRC assigned to interview him in the summer of 1930, the sincerity of Baker's opinions was above question. "However," continued the shaken agent in his report,

there are many evidences indicating insanity. He, apparently, has hallucinations of grandeur, thinks of himself as Baker the Great Emancipator of the People in the war against the financial octopi of the country and with these hallucinations he is troubled with a great physical fear, having in his office a sub-machine gun, together with a box of ammunition in his desk, with two automatics at hand, while four armed guards patrol the grounds of the Institute and at night searchlights are played over the grounds continually. The same equipment of machine guns, automatics, etc., is in evidence at the radio station.[48]

Despite or because of his seething anger and paranoia, Baker commanded a loyal radio following, albeit perhaps not so large as those of Field, Brinkley, and May. Unlike the former, Baker only placed, but never won, in the various journalistic popularity contests among farmer stations.

In operating on the wrong side not only of good taste and commercial decency but also of the American Medical Association, Baker and Brinkley had prioritized themselves as the stations subject to earliest removal from the airwaves during the clean-up campaign launched by the Federal Radio Commission in 1929. Brinkley was the first to go. At the behest of the AMA, in June 1930 the FRC moved to deny the renewal of

KFKB's license on the grounds that it was operating in no one's interest and necessity but those of its owner. The commission also cited Brinkley for "obscenity," referring to the candid treatment he gave to sexual matters in his daily "health talks."

The first independent broadcaster to have his license pulled on the grounds of program content, Brinkley mounted a vigorous campaign of defense that would provide irrefutable proof of the loyalty of his public. The terminal date for KFKB's license had been set by the FRC for 20 June 1930. On 23 June, however, the courts granted Brinkley's petition for a stay order that would enable KFKB to stay on the air until 31 October, pending an appeal of the decision.[49] Making the most of this continuance, Brinkley threw his hat into the political ring, entering the Kansas gubernatorial race as an independent just five weeks before the election.

Running on a platform that promised free health care for the poor, old-age pensions, workmen's compensation, free textbooks for schoolchildren, the creation of an artificial lake in every county ("to increase rainfall, and promote healthful recreation"), the abolition of convict labor, and lower taxes, Brinkley undertook an energetic tour of every county in the state, traveling in his private airplane, *The Romancer.* Accompanying him on this barnstorming tour were old-time entertainers and preachers familiar to the Kansas electorate from KFKB's programs. Because he entered the race too late to get his name on the ballot, Brinkley was running as a write-in candidate, a handicap that led his Democratic and Republican rivals to underestimate him at first. In short order, however, the enormous crowds that Brinkley was attracting—numbering into the tens of thousands, according to some accounts—became a matter of real concern to his opponents.

Just two days prior to election day Brinkley's opponents obtained from the attorney general of Kansas a helpful ruling stating that only ballots marked "'J. R. Brinkley,' with a capital 'J,' a period between the 'J' and the 'R,' and a capital 'R,'" would be counted; that all ballots written Brinkley, Doctor Brinkley, Mr. Brinkley, J. R. Brinkley, M.D., and so on, would be thrown out."[50] It was generally conceded by informed observers that this timely decree cost Brinkley the election. Under its terms 56,000 Brinkley ballots were disallowed, cutting Brinkley's polling numbers down from 239,000 to 183,000. The election went to Democrat Harry Woodring, who garnered 216,000 votes.[51]

Two years later Brinkley ran again, this time with his name on the ballot and a well-organized statewide network of "Brinkley Clubs" supporting his candidacy. Not having a radio station at his disposal this time, he compensated with a spectacular touring road show, traveling about the countryside in a circuslike motorcade complete with a sound truck and a stage on wheels, led by a shining sixteen-cylinder Cadillac. This time

Brinkley came in third with 243,938 votes; victory went to Republican Alf Landon, with 275,100. Although he threatened to run again in 1934, this was Brinkley's last run at the governor's mansion.

In the interim between his two political campaigns, Brinkley sold off KFKB and his Milford clinic and shifted his medical and media operations to the southern banks of the Rio Grande, establishing a new hospital and radio station in the Mexican border town of Villa Acuna. Situated on Mexican soil, Brinkley's new station was immune to FRC's regulatory control. In establishing his pirate station, XER (later renamed XERA), Brinkley was taking advantage of bad diplomatic blood between Mexico and the United States. Feeling shortchanged by the United States in the international allocation of clear channel wavelengths, Mexican authorities were happy to let Brinkley occupy a prime American wavelength and bombard the continent with his new seventy-five-thousand-watt super-transmitter, whose signal was twenty-five-thousand watts more powerful than any then allowed by the FRC. By 1935 Brinkley further boosted his signal strength to five-hundred-thousand watts, making XER the most powerful radio station in the world.

Norman Baker, meanwhile, had lost his own battle with the FRC, which denied him a license renewal in June 1931. In 1932 the imitative Baker made a run for the governorship of Iowa as a Farmer-Labor candidate but was hampered from touring the state by an outstanding warrant for his arrest on charges of medical malfeasance. Obliged to campaign from an undisclosed location out of state, he won a paltry five thousand votes. In 1933 Baker followed Brinkley down to the Mexican border, establishing a new cancer clinic and a high-power pirate station, XENT, in the Mexican town of Nueva Laredo.

Culturally speaking, the new "border blasters" continued in the grand tradition of the farmer stations—"homey rather than highbrow," as a 1932 publicity notice for the grand opening of XENT put it—but seasoned with a regional accent of Mexican folk music. For another decade Brinkley and Baker would continue to serve large rural listening audiences with a mixture of mail-order advertising, dubious medical counsel, hillbilly and gospel music, fundamentalist religion, and populist political commentary. But in 1941 the United States and Mexico arrived at an understanding on the clear channel issue, and Mexican authorities shut down Brinkley's superstation. Days after the demolition of XERA, Brinkley suffered a heart attack, after which his health speedily declined. In the spring of 1932 he was back in the United States awaiting trial on charges of mail fraud when he died of a second heart attack at the age of fifty-six.

In 1940 Baker was extradited to the United States, also to face mail fraud charges. Convicted, he was sentenced to a four-year term in Leavenworth prison. Upon his release he retired to Florida, where he lived out the rest of his days in luxury on a yacht previously owned by the financier Jay Gould. He died of liver cancer in 1956 at the age of seventy-six.

Having kept clear of rural medical rackets, the Shenandoah stations were spared extinction at the hands of the FRC. And by the 1930s the corporate broadcasting interests were all reneging on their vows never to plague their listeners with direct advertising, a development that undercut criticism of the direct-sales model. The Depression hit both stations hard, however, such that Field was obliged to cede ownership of KFNF to a group of creditors, who reorganized the station under the corporate aegis of KFNF Inc. Although Field continued to deliver his daily *Letter Box* program until 1938, the station rapidly lost its idiosyncratic local character under its new management, henceforth deriving most of its musical programs from transcription services in the business of providing smaller stations with "canned" programs distributed through the mails on giant phonograph discs. The new KFNF also took a portion of its programming from the Mutual Broadcasting System, one of several minor commercial networks active by the mid-1930s. By 1950 KFNF had become a full-time affiliate of the Mutual network. Earl May continued broadcasting until his death in 1946, but by the mid-1930s KMA too was rapidly losing its distinctive rural character, becoming increasingly reliant on transcription programs and network hookups for its programs.

The absorption of farmer stations such as KFNF and KMA into the mainstream of broadcasting reflected a concurrent mainstreaming of rural listening tastes. It was commonly observed in the 1920s and 1930s that rural youth were less averse to jazz and contemporary Tin Pan Alley pop than their parents were; over time generational succession would erode the rural resistance to urban pop culture. Even highbrow offerings from the metropolitan concert halls won a degree of rural acceptance over time. The opening of the rural mind on this score was presaged by the sentiments of Duke Bettelton, a resident of Rural Route #1 outside of Dayton, Ohio, who wrote to *Radio Digest* in 1929 to say that he had initially hated "opera, classical music, soprano singing, etc., over the Radio," but that he had since "lost a little ground" and could occasionally "enjoy some of the above mentioned music."[52]

The stations profiled in this chapter exemplified the mainstream of rural broadcasting in the 1920s and early 1930s. The following two chapters concern stations which, although usually lumped in with the farmer stations, pursued distinct programming paths.

# Chapter 5

# That Doggone Radio Man

Hello, doggone, here's a telegram from Gulfport: "We in Gulfport get a kick out of your unique program." When I listen to those dignified announcers on the chain stations of the north, I don't wonder.

—*William K. Henderson, 1928*[1]

As a radio personality, Henry Field of KFNF was often observed to be especially popular among farm women. No one ever said the same of Field's notorious contemporary, William K. Henderson—a.k.a. "Doggone" Henderson, "Ol' Man" Henderson, and "Hello World" Henderson—owner and operator of station KWKH in Shreveport, Louisiana. Where Field played the upright and temperate Christian gentleman to perfection, Henderson personified an opposite rural social type, the crossroads hell-raiser: bawdy, profane, and according to many hostile listeners, often "beautifully soused."[2] The good-ol'-boyishness of the Henderson phenomenon is captured by the following exchange between the broadcaster and his fans. In February 1928 Henderson received a telegram of friendly greetings from "Henry and the boys" at the Cozy Cafe in Bremen, Texas, accompanied by a request that he play a hillbilly record entitled "I've Got Some Lovin' to Do." As the requested disk was being cued up, Henderson replied, "We know where Henry gets his lovin'. Right down on Matamora Street in San Antonio, Texas. Try and deny that, Henry."[3] What backslapping hilarity ensued down at the Cozy Cafe can only be imagined.

Owner and president of the Henderson Iron Works and Supply Company, a concern specializing in the manufacture of oil drilling and saw milling equipment, Henderson caught the radio bug from a Shreveport wireless enthusiast named William Patterson, who, with the intent of stimulating a local market for radio receivers of his own manufacture, had been broadcasting locally under the call sign WGAQ since 1922. In

1923 Patterson invited Henderson to help capitalize an upgrade of the station's low-watt, jerry-built transmitter. Initially dubious, Henderson came on board as a minority investor, but by 1924 he had become sufficiently enthusiastic about the project to purchase a controlling share in the station. A year later Henderson was obsessed with radio and had rebuilt his rambling country estate in Kennonwood, eighteen miles north of Shreveport, into a broadcasting compound complete with its own power plant, a new one-thousand-watt transmitter, studios on the first and second floors of his mansion, and dormitories and a commissary to accommodate technical personnel and visiting guests. A third studio, for remote broadcasts, was installed in Henderson's offices in Shreveport. All three studios were outfitted with special phonographs called panatropes, designed for the high-fidelity broadcast of phonograph records.[4]

A raging extrovert, Henderson approached broadcasting less as a business proposition than as a platform for self-expression, an agenda reflected in his 1925 request to the Commerce Department that his station's call letters be changed to WKH "in honor of William K. Henderson who so unselfishly has given his time and money to the development of his community and country."[5] Informed that call signs for all stations west of the Mississippi had to start with the letter *K*, Henderson settled for KWKH and parsed it as standing for "Kennonwood, William K. Henderson."[6]

The format Henderson developed was simple, economical, and prescient, anticipating the emergence of both the disk jockey of the 1940s and the present-day shock jock. On the air only at night, when atmospheric conditions allowed for the widest possible coverage, Henderson always began his broadcasts with some variation on this greeting, delivered in a peculiar croaking drawl that suggested a talking bullfrog: "HELLO, WORLD—This is KWKH at Shreveport, Lou-ees-i-ana. Shreve-port on the air, telling the world. Don't go 'way!"[7] The salutation was followed by unstructured hours of Henderson's impromptu remarks, punctuated by the playing of phonograph records requested by listeners, who communicated their preferences to him by letter, telephone, and telegram. This listener-request principle was set forth in the station's theme song, "The KWKH Blues," commissioned by Henderson from a regional black jazz band, Eddie and Sugar Lou's Hotel Tyler Orchestra: "I got the KWKH, KWKH blues / I got the KWKH, KWKH blues / So just tune in baby / I'll dedicate these blues to you."[8]

Although he was a college-educated millionaire living on inherited industrial capital, Henderson styled himself a "country boy" and spoke like one. The bulk of his discourse was aptly described by a Commerce Department field agent in 1928 (one of several assigned to monitor and transcribe Henderson's nightly tirades) as consisting of "vile epithets and accusations directed at the senders of telegrams of acknowledgement and request in general."[9] A large contingent of early radio listeners found this rustic insult comedy enormously entertaining. "Early in the days of the Radio," explained a correspondent for *Radio Digest* in 1929,

> Mr. Henderson found out how to get and keep an air audience. The way, he found, was to set off plenty of verbal pyrotechnics—bawl out somebody unmercifully—give them a good show. Whether or not they like what he is telling it, they listen and come back for more. They like to hear him get hot. And when he shows signs of cooling off they send him a batch of scathing, blistering telegrams to make him hotter, and he responds obligingly to this form of prodding. "People don't care about gentle modest talk," Mr. Henderson said a short time ago. "They want it strong. They want to hear you ride somebody. If not, why do they spend their good money for telegrams? They want to be entertained. They razz me and wait for me to bawl them out over the Radio. I never disappoint them if they sign their names." And that's why KWKH, even though its facilities for musical programs are limited largely to phonograph records, remains one of the most popular stations in the South and likewise one of the most popular in the country.[10]

Although it was not strictly necessary for KWKH listeners to goad Henderson in order to receive a personalized portion of his bile, a lot of his correspondents went out of their way to rattle his cage. "We have a telegram here from Helena, Montana, which I shall read," announced Henderson in late September 1927. "It says, 'We don't care for your station or the South!,' signed by I. M. Smart. He thinks he is smart. He no doubt is a cross between a hyena and a gila monster, gotten in a nigger graveyard and raised by an idiot. We will consider the source of this telegram and dedicate the next selection to him, which is 'Good Night.'" A similar challenge from a Des Moines, Iowa, listener read, "Get off the air—we want to hear something worthwhile." Provocations like these never found Henderson at a loss for a resonant retort, such as the following:

> What's the matter with you, you sawed-off, hammered-down, pusillanimous lollypop!
> Here you low down dirty pup, why didn't you sign your name? You're as yellow as this telegraph blank I have in my hand.
> Why in hell don't you turn the little knobs of your radio set? Every radio set has little knobs on it. You made an ass out of yourself by sending me this telegram.[11]

The tenor of Henderson's discourse changed little on the occasions when he spoke out on the larger issues of the day. His commentary on the presidential race of 1928, for example, consisted largely of slurs on the character of Republican candidate Herbert Hoover, whom he variously maligned as "a harebrained ninny-com-poop," "a yellow shit," "a Quaker skunk," "a son of a bitch," "a half-assed Englishman," and "a cross between a jackass and a bulldog bitch."[12]

Inevitably, Henderson's nightly harangues triggered an avalanche of complaints to Commerce Department officials and, after 1927, to the Federal Radio Commission. It is a curious comment on human nature that Henderson's critics seemed to have been almost as fascinated by him as his fans were. "One night several months ago," wrote a conflicted complainant in 1929,

> I listened for about three hours to a tirade of billingsgate, semi-profanity and vulgar abuse from the man who does most of the talking or announcing from this station. I had listened to this man's peculiar, characteristic utterances several times before but this night, as near as I could judge, he was drunk and repeated his abusive remarks over and over again. I listened in for the purpose of seeing how long he would keep up this disgusting sort of thing and to the best of my recollection it was almost three hours.[13]

"I am a frequent 'listener in' on Radio Station KWKH of Shreveport, Louisiana," wrote another hostile yet spellbound listener, "and believe that the disgusting language and profane remarks by W. K. Henderson over the air from said station are sufficient reason for the Federal Radio Commission to invoke its own Rules and Regulations and revoke the license of such station."[14]

By all indications, however, affronted yet regular listeners such as these stood at the margins of a much larger audience who simply adored Henderson. "There is no doubt," wrote the regional radio supervisor Theodore G. Deiler to his superiors at the Commerce Department in 1928, "that KWKH is rendering a distinctive service of its own, particularly to its followers who are very numerous." In a 1929 brief on the station, FRC chairman Eugene Sykes concurred: "That KWKH is a station of considerable popularity cannot be gainsaid." Sykes had witnessed an impressive material demonstration of this fact earlier in the same year when he summoned Henderson to appear at hearings relating to the continuance of his license. The broadcaster arrived bearing 163,000 notarized affidavits of support raised on short notice from his listeners across several southern and midwestern states. He later furnished the commission with a glossy studio portrait of the trophy he received from *Radio Digest* magazine in 1930 naming KWKH the "South's Most Popular Radio Station."[15]

Next to Henderson's foul mouth, KWKH's most valuable programming asset was its collection of some six thousand records, the contents of which were alphabetically listed in a catalog that Henderson made available by mail to listeners to facilitate their requests. An undated edition of the "Directory of the Musical Library of KWKH" surviving in the files of the Federal Radio Commission reveals KWKH's musical offerings to have covered a more eclectic range than did those of the midwestern farmer stations profiled in the previous chapter. In addition to a predictable preponderance of cowboy songs, gospel hymns, old-time fiddle tunes, sentimental Tin Pan Alley ballads, and banjo breakdowns, the KWKH library also included a substantial number of jazz records by the likes of Fletcher Henderson, Jelly Roll Morton, Clarence Williams, and Bennie Motten, as well as "hot mama" blues numbers such as Ethel Waters's "Shake That Thing" and Sadie McKinney's "Brownskin Flapper." How a farmer station got away with playing such music, typically abominated by rural listeners, is something of a mystery. It is imaginable that there existed alongside the pious, upright, and jazz-hating rural audience served by the Shenandoah school of broadcasting a significant number of rural listeners who enjoyed being exposed to the forbidden urban sounds of sin and syncopation. It seems reasonable that such a subset of the rural population would have been the same one disposed to appreciate Henderson's brand of humor. Then again, it is possible that Henderson was musically way out in front of his public but that the latter prized his wit so highly that they were willing to tolerate his predilection for jazz. According to the station's engineer, interviewed by the graduate student Lillian Jones Hall in 1959, the songs most frequently requested by KWKH fans in the 1920s—"My Horses Ain't Hungry," "Missouri Waltz," "Dead Cat on the Line," and "Them Golden Slippers"—were all solidly in the old-time tradition. In any case, it was widely conceded that the main draw of the station was not the music but the man. As one fan put it in 1930, "Practically every station on the air has [jazz], but only one station has ol' man Henderson: KWKH."[16]

KWKH also deviated from the general run of farmer stations in that it was not originally operated for profit. Between 1924 and 1928 Henderson financed the station entirely out of his own pocket and frequently boasted on the air that "this station don't sell or advertise." Periodically he even lashed out on the air against broadcast advertising, proposing that all stations operated for profit should be sequestered on a single wavelength in order to clear the air for altruistic stations like his own. By mid-1928, however, Henderson's anticommercial principles began to slip as he began making experimental forays into the direct merchandising game. The seeds of change lay in Henderson's habit of calling for coffee while at the microphone and then remarking that it was "doggone good coffee." A spate of listener inquiries as to where they could purchase some of the same brew inspired Henderson to package a souvenir brand of beans in tins bearing his own image and market it C.O.D.

over the airwaves. Despite a steep price tag of one dollar per pound, "Hello World Coffee" proved to be a great success, moving at a reported rate of a hundred pounds per day.[17]

Once having tasted the fruits of direct merchandising, Henderson quickly stepped up his retailing. By early 1929 KWKH was plugging a wide range of mail-order goods, including radio aerials, whisk brooms, a lockable gas tank cap for automobiles, patent medicines, insurance policies, truck tires, citrus fruits, and a privately published biography of Henderson, *The Life of a Man*. After 1930 Henderson was also promoting a variety of get-rich-quick investment schemes, including shares in an oil-drilling venture called the Depression Oil Company, a pecan farming operation called the Mayhem Pecan Orchards, and sundry pyramid sales schemes. At about the same time he began selling time to a real estate interest, the National Property Exchange, whose prerecorded transcription program, ancestor of today's late-night infomercials, rounded out the closing hours of the KWKH schedule between 1930 and 1932.[18]

Characteristically, Henderson was not at all embarrassed about this sudden reversal of policy. "I am not a charitable institution," he told the Federal Radio Commission in September 1932; "I expect to make some money with my station."[19] When pressed by FRC examiners to explain the appearance of bad faith on the issue of advertising, Henderson contended, like Field and May of Shenandoah, that he had consulted his listeners and that they had approved KWKH's new commercial agenda. "I had never done any advertising whatsoever on my station," he testified. "Then I went on the air and I asked my friends and listeners if there would be any objection to my advertising, and said if they said there was I wouldn't do it. There wasn't a dissenting vote; in fact they told me I was crazy for not doing it because all the rest were doing it.[20]

Henderson's conversion from philanthropic to commercial broadcasting coincided with an intensification of his interest in political matters. He had always enjoyed speaking out on current affairs, but prior to 1927 he had hewn to no particular cause beyond an intense antipathy to the growth of the national debt and twinned commitments to the superiority of the South over the North and the Democratic Party over the Republican.[21] Following the passage of the Radio Act of 1926, however, Henderson became increasingly voluble on the subject of broadcast regulation, and by 1927 he was nightly assailing the newly appointed members of the Federal Radio Commission by name as "crooks," "skunks," and "grafters" working on behalf of what he called "the electrical and financial monopoly." Were the commission allowed to continue unopposed, warned Henderson, it would deliver to this "infernal chain Combine" a complete monopoly over the American airwaves, which "from top to bottom" would carry "nothing but chain," to the exclusion of independent stations like his own. "The Teapot Dome Scandal," he roared, "would fade away in comparison with the stealing of the air away from the American people."[22]

In late 1929 Henderson became obsessed with a second political cause: the rural crusade against chain stores. Particularly strong in the South, this strain of antiurban populism had been gathering steam since the 1910s, as chains of variety, grocery, and shoe stores began penetrating the countryside and threatening the livelihoods of independent crossroads merchants. Organizing in their own defense, the mom-and-pop retailers of the countryside charged that the chains were diverting profits to the cities, evading their fair share of local taxes, and undermining regional cultural character with their standardized inventories. The message caught on among the rural electorate, and by 1927 several southern legislatures were attempting to levy special punitive taxes on chain stores and to place statutory limits on the number of chain outlets per county. The regular reversal of these popular measures in state supreme courts further fueled local perceptions that chain stores represented an omnipotent threat to regional autonomy.[23] Henderson was brought to the cause by a Shreveport banking official, Phillip Leiber, who had been making the rounds of local civic clubs for some time with a speech entitled "The Menace of the Chain Store." Already battling against the radio chains, Henderson invited Leiber to speak over KWKH in late 1929 and by his own account underwent an instantaneous conversion while listening to him. Henceforth, Henderson conflated the networks and chain stores into a single conspiracy, "the chain gang interests."

In early 1930 Henderson undertook the organization of a nationwide voluntary association for small merchants and their supporters. Dubbed "the Modern Minute Men," the club had attracted thirty-two thousand members by September of that year, despite steep annual membership dues of $12. Hard times notwithstanding, the Minute Men promotion quickly netted Henderson donations reportedly in excess of $373,500.[24]

The Commerce Department flagged Henderson as a troublemaker as early as 1926, on the grounds of his coarse language and reliance on phonograph records. A regulatory bias against "canned music" dated back to the earliest days of broadcasting, when phonographs and player pianos had been tiresomely ubiquitous staples of "wireless concerts" transmitted by amateur radiotelephone operators. Adopting the position that such programs provided inferior sound reproduction while duplicating services elsewhere available to the public, the Commerce Department began giving preferential treatment to stations foreswearing mechanically reproduced music in late 1922. Official opposition to the broadcast of records was not lessened by the dramatic improvements in recording technology after 1925, which dramatically narrowed the gap in fidelity between a well-engineered phonographic broadcast and a live performance. Because their superior capacity to furnish live entertainment put them in a class apart, the corporate stations and later the networks favored strictures against the use of phonographs, as did leaders of the record industry and major recording stars, who, prior to the 1940s, saw broadcast exposure of records as a threat to sales rather than a potential promotional boon.[25]

Lacking the resources to enforce an outright ban on records, in 1927 the Federal Radio Commission instituted a new policy whereby canned music was permissible so long as it was clearly identified as such, a directive designed to prevent "fraud upon the listening public." Small independent stations did sometimes connive at misrepresenting records as studio appearances by famous performers, but Henderson was above such chicanery and always forthrightly defended the legitimacy of canned music as broadcast content. "You have never heard anything better than these records," he told his listeners on one occasion. "We can give you Caruso if you want him. There are 12,345 artists here in the room waiting for me to stop talking." Another time he interrupted the opening bars of a record to bawl into the microphone, "Isn't that good? If it wasn't good, they wouldn't *can* it!"[26]

A third trait that made Henderson a thorn in the side of Commerce Department officials was his Napoleonic attitude toward signal coverage. Perpetually unsatisfied with his station's reach, Henderson was continually lobbying the government for higher power and a better wavelength. Following the Zenith Corporation's successful 1926 legal challenge of the Commerce Department's right to assign frequencies to broadcasters and limit their hours of operation, Henderson unilaterally moved KWKH's signal to a portion of the spectrum previously ceded by federal treaty to Canada and then boosted his signal power up to three thousand watts. Although the resumption of federal regulatory power in 1927 was supposed to bring a comeuppance to "wave-jumpers" and "pirates," the Shreveport station did very well in the ensuing reallocation of wavelengths, receiving a favorable wavelength at 394.5 meters and holding on to its self-authorized power boost. The best was yet to come for KWKH, however, after the passage of the Davis Amendment to the Radio Act in 1928. The fruit of a sectional backlash against the Northeast's domination of the airwaves, the amendment mandated an equal division of licenses and wavelengths among the five geographical zones created by the Radio Act. In the resulting second reallocation of wavelengths, KWKH was awarded the use of one of forty coveted clear channels, a privilege Henderson grudgingly time-shared with WWL, a New Orleans station operated by Loyola University.[27] With clear channel status came a power increase to five thousand watts, followed by another authorized increase to ten thousand watts in 1930.[28] Though it is hard to state with precision the range of KWKH at any given moment in its history, by 1927 Henderson was already a national presence on the airwaves, reliably reaching listeners as far away as Seattle, Washington, and Pennsylvania and, depending on meteorological conditions, enjoying intermittent coverage throughout North America.[29]

Even as he pushed for permission to boost his signal strength, Henderson seems to have regarded the power limits imposed by the FRC as little more than a baseline for what he could get away with on the sly. Internal memoranda of the Radio Division of the Commerce Department reflect awareness that KWKH was surreptitiously exceeding its assigned signal strength in 1926. By 1928 Henderson had abandoned any pretense of compliance and was overtly boosting and lowering his signal power from moment to moment according to his mood, barking on-air orders at his engineer to "give us some more power, doggone you, give me all the power you've got."[30] Irksome as all this was to federal officials, the Radio Division's field agents found themselves unable to catch Henderson red-handed, owing to the fact that the KWKH transmitter was situated at the center of Henderson's sprawling estate, such that it was "impossible to make a surprise inspection without sufficient time for the power to be reduced."[31]

KWKH's programs would have been a provocation to regulators even had Henderson not been given to broadcasting blistering ad hominem attacks on members of the FRC or calling the regional supervisor of radio, Theodore G. Deiler, at his home in New Orleans and baiting him on the air.[32] But this ongoing campaign of abuse personalized the tensions between broadcaster and regulators to such an extent that in 1929 FRC member Orestes Caldwell publicly charged Henderson with having precipitated the death of the commission's first chairman, Rear Admiral William Bullard, with his relentless slanders upon the latter's name. That Henderson was able not only to remain on the air but also to increase his privileges as a licensee in the face of such official enmity was primarily a function of his shrewd cultivation of friends in high places. Taking advantage of his strong signal coverage of the South and the Midwest, Henderson had at an early point in his broadcasting career adopted the habit of placing his station at the disposal of senators, congressmen, governors, and other elected officials from Louisiana, Iowa, Texas, Oklahoma, Montana, Missouri, Alabama, and Kansas. At times his political friends would join him in the studio to assist in reading listener letters and dedicating requested records; on other occasions they would call in by telephone to chat on the air.

By far the most valuable of Henderson's political patrons was Louisiana governor Huey Long. A friend and associate of Long's since the late 1910s, Henderson had been one of the Kingfish's early financial backers, contributing ten thousand dollars and the propagandizing powers of KWKH to Long's first, unsuccessful gubernatorial campaign in 1924. Henderson again supported Long in his second, triumphant campaign of 1928 and thereafter frequently brought him on the air as a guest star. Henderson was also generous in giving air time to Long cronies such as the Reverend Gerald L. K. Smith, whose jeremiads against the utility companies and other corporate interests were regularly broadcast over KWKH via remote pickup from Smith's Shreveport pulpit.

In return for these favors, Governor Long made KWKH's cause his own, treating any proposed regulatory action against the station as an intolerable infringement on the sovereignty of Louisiana. The evening of 5 March 1928, for example, found Long at Henderson's side at Kennonwood propounding the theory that the relative population densities of the Northeast and the South justified maximum signal power for KWKH. "Stations in the congested districts of the east," reasoned Long, "could reach thousands of listeners with only a few watts whereas the stations in this vicinity in order to reach the listeners desired would have to have much more power as we have to reach 2000 to 3000 miles." Long further warned the members of the FRC that any regulatory sanctions against KWKH would not be tolerated: "You're going to have to fight Louisiana and other states too, buddy, and you won't get away with it. We are going to expose you and not allow you to steal the air." Assured of Long's protection, in early 1931 Henderson went so far as to declare that the Louisiana state militia stood at his disposal in the event of any federal attempt to interfere with his station.[33]

That Long's protection was fundamental to Henderson's success in defying the government is suggested by the fact that federal radio officials, having tolerated Henderson's arrogance for years, moved against him with sudden assurance once relations soured between Henderson and Long in late 1931. Then again, Long's decision to break with Henderson at that time may have reflected an intuition on Long's part that Henderson's days on the air were numbered once the FRC's power to deny license renewal on the basis of previous performance had been tested and affirmed before a federal court. In any case, in the autumn of 1931 Long, now a U.S. senator, traded his affiliation with KWKH for a similar sweetheart relationship with WWL, the Jesuit university station with which Henderson had uneasily been sharing his clear channel wavelength since 1928.

Fresh from regulatory victories over comparably vexatious rural broadcasters such as Dr. Brinkley and Norman Baker, and armed with hundreds of hours of transcripts of Henderson's harangues and numberless listener complaints, in 1931 the FRC moved in for the kill with a final series of hearings on the renewal of KWKH's license. Primary among the charges under consideration was the accusation that Henderson routinely used "near-profanity" on the air. Dismissively likening the concept of "near-profanity" to "near-beer," Henderson's legal team initially denied that he was guilty of verbal impropriety, attributing any such perception to a cultural gap between northern and southern standards of polite usage. Moreover, asserted Henderson's lawyers, the defendant was "not ready to believe that the power of this great Government was meant to be applied to the standards attained by Oscar Wilde or even with the character, opinions, and doings of Madam DuBarry." As the review process wore on, however, the KWKH legal team began to give ground, allowing that the demands of Henderson's ongoing battles on behalf of the "common people" had perhaps caused him "to fight with weapons and language probably without a due regard to their propriety." Suddenly stricken by the thought that "any one of the innocent children of this Nation could hear anything over Station KWKH coming from my mouth that could, in the slightest, shock their tender sensibilities," in early 1931 Henderson pledged himself to reform his speech, enabling his lawyers to claim in December of that year that "from the first part of February, Mr. Henderson has at no time or any occasion used any language which might be considered objectionable to the most refined and technical moral person." In actual practice, the supposedly reformed Henderson displayed a technical bent of his own by delegating the pleasures of broadcast swearing to his listeners, who accommodated him with letters and telegrams peppered with "hells" and "damns." These Henderson would read on the air while legalistically covering himself with fig-leaf caveats such as "I didn't use those words; I merely read them out to you."[34]

Even as Henderson stretched himself to accommodate the conflicting demands of his semi-profanity-loving listeners and the censorious FRC, the latter body was pursuing other avenues of inquiry into the affairs of KWKH. Of particular interest to the commission was the fate of the monies Henderson had raised through his anti-chain-store league, the Modern Minute Men. After stonewalling the commission on this issue for several months, Henderson came forth with a less than reassuring account of the Minute Men's finances. According to Henderson, the gross sum of donations collected was actually $350,846, owing to bad checks received. Of this amount, $150,330 had been absorbed by the organization's pyramidal system of recruitment, which, like that of the contemporary Ku Klux Klan, paid incentives to members leading new joiners into the fold. Employing an arithmetic all his own, Henderson calculated that these deductions left to the Hello World Broadcasting

Corporation a sum of $250,516. Of this, he testified, another $89,119 had been defrayed by administrative expenses—"printing, stationery, postage, telegrams, telephones, salaries, etc.—" leaving the corporation with just $111,396. Without actually accounting for this sum, Henderson used the diminished figure to dispute the FRC's charge that he had diverted $151,800 of the Modern Minute Men's funds to paying off debts of the Henderson Iron Works and Supply Company. He stopped short, however, of actually denying that he had used Minute Men funds to bail out his ironworks, whose finances had been wobbly since the market crash of 1929.[35]

Despite the loss of Long's protection, Henderson kept up a bold front throughout the waning days of KWKH, swearing that "if monopolistic tyranny can only be resisted and met by offering myself as a burning sacrifice on the altar of liberty and an untrammeled medium of communication, then I say to all enemies of Constitutional Government and the Shylocks of the jingling guineas: 'Come and get me.'" Henderson apparently also held a contingency plan up his sleeve: according to an Oklahoma listener, Henderson boasted in early 1929 that if he lost his license he would relocate to Mexico to "set up a stronger plant which will cover all wavelengths in the U.S.A." When push came to shove, however, the bankrupt Henderson quietly folded his hand. Apprised by his lawyers that he stood no chance of retaining his broadcast license, in September 1932 Henderson sold KWKH to a group of Shreveport investors for fifty thousand dollars. Although Henderson's threatened Mexican pirate station never materialized, for the first year after the sale he and his audience enjoyed a period of mutual weaning, during which Henderson was permitted brief daily access to the airwaves to air his thoughts and opinions.[36]

After KWKH's studios and transmitter were repatriated from Kennonwood back to Shreveport in late 1933, the station's new management opened negotiations with the Columbia Broadcasting System, and in October 1934 the station became an affiliate of that network and thus a slave of "the chain gang" that Henderson reviled. Henderson slipped into obscurity, although in the summer of 1935 he took a stab at a comeback with an advertisement placed in the *Shreveport Times*. Entitled "I'm Still W. K. Henderson," the announcement read: "I have everything I used to have except money. I'm not in any business and I don't know what business I'd get in if I had any money. But you can bet I'm still Old Man Henderson to my friends throughout the land." Henderson optimistically signed off with the hint that "maybe you have some ideas to our mutual interest" and included his postal address for the benefit of interested parties.[37]

Speaking to a reporter from his deathbed in 1945, Henderson looked back on his broadcasting career and regretted nothing. "I was right, you know," he said. "I was right about the chain stores. I was right about the government control of radio. I guess I was fighting for free speech and free enterprise."[38]

# Chapter 6

# Wilbur Can Beat the Devil

From the uttermost part of the earth have we heard songs . . .
—*Isaiah 24:16*

In early 1923 the Reverend Wilbur Glenn Voliva, who liked to style himself as "the world's richest holy man," signed a contract with the Western Electric Company for the delivery of a five-hundred-watt radio transmitter.[1] In short order the apparatus was delivered to Zion, Illinois, a theocratic exurb of Chicago that Voliva had ruled with an iron fist since 1906. Licensed by the Commerce Department after a quick technical inspection, the new broadcaster took to the air in early summer under the call sign WCBD—parsed by local schoolchildren as "Wilbur Can Beat the Devil." For the next five years the Zion station would be one of the most widely heard in the world and, by all evidence, one of the best loved. Although often lumped in with the farmer stations, WCBD was pretty much sui generis. Culturally, it pulled off the impressive feat of hybridizing the old-time aesthetic with the highbrow while holding on to a large rural audience; commercially it hewed closer to corporate standards of reticence and discretion than any other independent with the exception of WHAP in its financial heyday.

This anomalous station grew from the soil of an anomalous community. As the historian Grant Wacker observes, the town of Zion "ranks among the largest and most grandly conceived utopian communities in modern American history."[2] Incorporated in 1902, the town was built on sixty-six hundred acres of shore land just south of the Wisconsin border. A cross between a company town and a spiritual commune, it was designed as a theocratic solution to the problems of the modern industrial order: class antagonism, labor unrest, crime, moral disintegration. The project was the brainchild of the world-famous evangelist and faith healer the Reverend John Alexander Dowie.

Born in Scotland in 1847, Dowie was trained as a doctor of divinity at the University of Edinburgh in the 1860s and served in Australia as a Congregationalist minister until 1878, when he withdrew from the Congregational order to pursue an independent ministry. Freed from orthodoxy, Dowie began to propound an idiosyncratic doctrine of "divine healing" and to condemn conventional medicine as a work of the devil. After serving a brief prison term in Adelaide, Australia, for disrupting the peace with his radical temperance agitations, Dowie immigrated to the United States in 1888 and established a new headquarters in Evanston, Illinois, in 1890. By the mid-1890s he had built a chain of "divine healing homes" in Chicago. In 1896 Dowie formalized his doctrine of divine healing under a new denominational rubric, the Christian Catholic Apostolic Church (hereafter, the CCC).

The ten thousand followers whom Dowie persuaded to invest and settle in Zion were to be employed in various collectively owned industries, including a lace factory, a confectionery, a printing shop, a lumber mill, and a bakery. To keep this hive of industry on the straight and narrow path, Dowie forbade his followers to purchase property outright. Instead, the citizens of Zion leased their homes for a generous term of eleven hundred years, their tenancy subject to termination should they attempt to exploit Zion property for any immoral enterprise. Expressly forbidden by the terms of the lease were saloons, tobacco shops, opium joints, theaters, opera houses, gambling dens, dance halls, circuses, brothels, and "any place for the manufacture or sale of drugs or medicines of any kind, or the office of a practicing physician."[3]

A better promoter than businessman, Dowie crippled an otherwise promising experiment in industrial socialism by mortgaging Zion's assets in order to leverage other, still more ambitious initiatives, including the "Zion Paradise Plantations," a million-acre agricultural commune he proposed to establish in Mexico. While running the infant economy of Zion into the ground with deficit spending, Dowie declared himself Elijah the Restorer, messenger of the second coming of Christ. Settling into his new identity, Dowie began swanning about in an Old Testament prophet costume of his own design, complete with elevated patriarchal headgear, jeweled breastplates, and an ornately carved shepherd's crook. Panicked by Dowie's increasing instability and by the fact that nearly half of Zion's original labor force had already abandoned the city, in 1906 the town's leading citizen-investors summoned Dowie's second in command, Voliva, back from missionary work in Australia. Born in Indiana in 1870, Voliva had begun his ministerial career a Methodist but switched to the CCC in 1899, attracted by the higher standards of discipline that Dowie demanded of his followers.[4] After taking one look at the books and another at Dowie in his prophet's drag, Voliva staged an ecclesiastical coup, usurping Dowie's position as "General

Overseer in Zion." The following year Dowie, now in an advanced state of dementia, died.

From the time of Dowie, the CCC had placed a high spiritual premium on musical literacy and performance skills. In keeping with these precepts, music education in Zion was socialistically funded and free to all community members. Unfortunately, the separatist character of Zion sharply limited opportunities for public displays of its musical talent. With the acquisition of WCBD, however, the meaning of the surplus was revealed. "It was God's plan," explained the church official Michael Mintern in 1928, "to withhold from us the real purpose in providing a corps of trained singers and players for the radio work."[5]

Blessed with what must have been the highest per capita supply of trained musicians in the nation, Zion enlisted more than ten percent of its citizenry to take an active part in the radio programs. In addition to the Zion Symphony Orchestra and the three-hundred-voice White Robed Choir, this army was subject to reconfiguration into a variety of more intimate permutations: a children's choir; vocal duos, trios, quartets, and quintets; a marching band; brass, woodwind, and string ensembles; a mandolin and guitar band; a marimba band; a melodic troupe of handbell ringers known as the Celestial Bells; and a host of solo artists. All this talent, as Apostle J. H. DePew, the station manager, proudly pointed out in 1925, was available to WCBD free of charge, thanks to the perfected way of life practiced in Zion: "Not a dollar has been paid to any artist for any service rendered. Even the staff and personnel, with an exception or two, have made the radio work their vocation, maintaining their former duties regularly."[6]

To make the most of these gifts, the citizens of Zion collectively plowed $120,000 into perfecting their broadcasting facilities, placing WCBD among the best-financed stations of the day. After a careful study of the relevant acoustic principles, the enormous Shiloh Tabernacle, epicenter of spiritual life in Zion, was expertly wired for sound. An array of eight microphones strategically distributed throughout the temple and controlled from a central mixing panel located in a soundproof control booth at the rear afforded separate pickups of the speaker's platform, the choir, the band, the organ, and the orchestra. In addition to this careful retrofitting of the tabernacle, Voliva commissioned the construction of a separate studio building adjacent to the church, a facility that boasted "every convenience," including an independent power plant, advanced acoustic surfacing from floor to ceiling, and indoor plumbing. Flanking the ultramodern brick studio building was a brace of steel towers 150 feet high, between which was suspended WCBD's 90-foot horizontal antenna.[7]

Zion's lavish investment in WCBD was money well spent given the station's extraordinary performance, which far surpassed the manufacturer's guarantees. When they purchased their transmitter the citizens of Zion were advised by Western Electric to anticipate a 150-mile radius for night transmission and a 100-mile radius for daylight transmission. Whether through God's favor or some quirk of geography, WCBD's signal reached much further than expected. "As a matter of fact," noted a church official with satisfaction, "the evening concerts of this station are heard quite regularly, not only up and down the Atlantic coast, even in midsummer, but last winter, under the most favorable conditions, they were heard clearly and distinctly in remote parts of Canada, in California, Alaska, Mexico, Cuba, Central America, and on ocean steamers far out on the Atlantic."[8]

Capitalizing on WCBD's atmospheric advantages, in mid-1924 Voliva moved to increase the station's signal power tenfold by contracting with Western Electric for delivery of a five-thousand-watt transmitter, one of only three such superpower transmitters then in operation. "In signing the contract for the new station," exulted a CCC spokesman, "the Western Electric Company has guaranteed a 250 percent distance increase over the present station, and if the distance actually reached is as much greater proportionately than that guaranteed for the present station, the results will be gratifying indeed. This will put Zion in the forefront of all radiocasting, such that the concerts and services will be heard regularly in all parts of the United States and Canada, except under the most unfavorable conditions."[9]

The new transmitter began operating in early February 1925 and more than matched these anticipations. For the next three and a half years WCBD enjoyed truly international stature, as demonstrated by the steady stream of correspondence from appreciative year-round listeners in Canada, Panama, Cuba, Haiti, Bermuda, every region of the continental United States, and the territory of Alaska.

Signal coverage of this kind was exactly what the Christian utopia needed to combat what it perceived as persistent misrepresentation in the national press. As Voliva explained to a reporter in 1928, WCBD "was conceived and born in prayer to counteract the evil that the newspapers and their atheistic writers have done us." J. H. DePew elaborated: "For 30 years certain newspapers in this country had lied about Zion with impunity. The radio station took care of this. It was God's rebuke to a crooked press. We go over their heads now, and reach the ears of the multitudes."[10]

The publicity problems to which Voliva and DePew alluded were real enough. When the town was founded, the considerable attention paid by the press to Zion wavered back and forth between skepticism about Reverend Dowie's integrity and/or sanity and guarded admiration for the communal ideals that Zion embodied. By the Prohibition era, however, Zion had become a national joke, lampooned by journalists from coast to coast as a microcosmic symbol of repressive Protestant moralism. On slow news days the national wire services turned a brisk trade in anecdotes concerning hapless motorists who, having taken a wrong turn into "the hair shirt town of the universe," were pulled out of their automobiles and carted off to jail for smoking cigarettes or forcibly escorted to the town limits for wearing lipstick and bobbed hair.[11]

External perceptions of Zion as an enclave of fanaticism were reinforced by newspaper coverage of Reverend Voliva's pulpit antics. Voliva liked to keep his name in the news by making calculatedly outrageous theological statements. Especially fruitful on this count was his insistence that the earth is a flat plane suspended midway between a physical heaven and a physical hell. Outflanking the leading anti-Darwinists of the day, Voliva asserted that his monopoly on this flat-earth doctrine made him "the only true fundamentalist in America," the competition being disqualified by their complacent acceptance of the erroneous "Pythagorean-Copernican-Newtonian system."[12]

There is no way of telling exactly how large WCBD's audience may have been, but the station reported receiving thousands of pieces of listener correspondence every year. Among the hundreds of these preserved in the pages of the CCC's weekly magazine, *Leaves of Healing*, a striking number include references to WCBD's popularity in their communities of origin. Equally impressive is the number of letters from fans whose occupations afforded them a privileged viewpoint from which to vouch for the station's wider popularity. In 1925, for instance, a traveling radio salesman based in Emlenton, Pennsylvania, wrote to say that WCBD's "programs are mentioned more often by the people I meet than those of any other station." Another commercial traveler wrote from Gary, Indiana, to share his conviction that WCBD was "the most universally liked of all stations now broadcasting," a judgment he based on hundreds of conversations with "farmers in Kansas, Nebraska, Oklahoma and Texas." Milwaukee police patrolman G. H. Briddle wrote to Zion to say that "you surely would be surprised to know how many families on my beat listen to your broadcasting." Of all of the volunteer pollsters laboring on behalf of WCBD, the prize surely goes to the telephone operator in Marine, Illinois, who in 1927 took it upon herself to conduct a telephone survey of all the rural exchanges within her reach. Her research indicated that some three thousand inhabitants of Madison County had "equipped their homes with expensive radios for the express purpose of enjoying WCBD."[13]

A significant percentage of the fan mail published in *Leaves of Healing* came from major urban centers such as New York, Philadelphia, and Los

Angeles. Most of the letters, however, bore the postmarks of obscure rural hamlets, for example, Sleepy Eye, Minnesota; Shamokin, Pennsylvania; and Schaller, Iowa.

On the air four nights a week (Monday, Wednesday, Friday, and Sunday), WCBD mixed about one part Voliva to three parts music. The Zion station plied what might be termed a Victorian oldies format, heavily dependent on what its musical director, Apostle John D. Thomas, called "sacred music, wholesome secular, and old-time favorites."[14] In practice this entailed a steady diet of sentimental parlor songs from the post-Civil War, preragtime era ("Tenting on the Old Camp Ground," "Where Is My Wandering Boy Tonight?," "A Flower from Mother's Grave," "The Convict and the Bird") and dulcet low-church hymns of similar vintage ("The Little Brown Church in the Vale," "Lead, Kindly Light," "In the Sweet Bye and Bye," "Softly and Tenderly").

This music clearly held a special appeal for older listeners. Correspondents to *Leaves of Healing* often referred to the particular pleasure that WCBD's musical programs brought to the most senior members of their households: "an old lady, past ninety-one years"; "a grandmother almost blind and past seventy-six"; "my dear old mother who is almost eighty-two years of age." Even when not stated, the general maturity of WCBD's audience is underscored by the listener correspondence, much of which throbs with decades-deep nostalgia for what one fan called the "old time favorites of the musical world of bygone days." A Minnesota listener wrote, "The tears trickled down my cheeks as I listened to the wonderful music as I had never expected to hear these songs again. I surely was carried beyond the realms of the earth. . . . In all the world, there never was and never will be anything so thrilling to me." Another fan, from Salem, North Dakota, wrote, "Continue to give us the good old songs our mothers sang in the sweet days of our childhood"; and a party from Burlington, Iowa, wrote, "Your splendid program took me back over a flight of fifty years."[15]

Unlike other stations popular in the countryside, WCBD made frequent musical forays onto higher cultural ground, programming choral and orchestral works by Saint-Saens, Verdi, Rossini, Beethoven, Liszt, and Handel. There is no sign that any rural listeners were put off by these deviations from farmer-station norms. It may have been WCBD's lack of pretension that made the difference: fans often wrote to praise the station's announcers as "the best and plainest" on the air—"so clear and plain that a child could understand every word."[16] Zion's strict avoidance of opera likely also helped to minimize the offense: in 1928 Mr. and Mrs. A. G. Nye of Blomhead, Michigan, wrote to explain that they found "good music" acceptable when it came from WCBD but that they still did "not like the operatic stuff that comes over the chain."[17]

If they accepted highbrow music when it came from Zion, WCBD listeners still did not care for corporate broadcasting. According to the station manager J. H. DePew, antipathy toward the chain stations and their programs was a perpetual theme of the listener correspondence that crossed his desk.[18] Letters published in *Leaves of Healing* reflect even greater contempt for cabaret broadcasting of the WHN school. Indeed, WCBD fans were virtually incapable of putting pen to paper without taking a shot at "hated jazz"; "dastardly jazz"; "New York jazz"; "night hawk jazz"; "rotten jazz"; "crazy jazz"; "terrible jazz"; "worldly jazz"; "dry, silly jazz"; "cheap jazz"; "tin pan jazz"; "razzy, jazzy jazz"; or just "jazz! jazz!! jazz!!!" A related thread of complaint reflected a somber rural impatience with the vaudevillian comedy of the lowbrow stations, with their "frolic and jokesters," "suggestive nonsense," "parodies and superficial stuff," "foolish programs," "trashy shallow things," and "silly dialogue." A listener in early 1926 wrote, "One would think that the whole continent were being drowned in jazz and jokes." Amid this clamor, WCBD's fans tuned their receivers to Zion as "an oasis," "a spring of living water in a desert," "a rose among many thorns," "a bright morning star in the cloudy sky of broadcasting."[19]

Although music was clearly WCBD's biggest draw, it is likely that many listeners also tuned in for its evangelical content. Judging from the rudimentary program schedules in *Leaves of Healing*, between a quarter and a third of WCBD's 14.5 hours of weekly airtime was consecrated to sermons and other discourses, sometimes given by a church elder but usually by Voliva, who was regarded as a master of the hellfire-and-brimstone idiom. "His invective," as a biographical sketch in *Leaves of Healing* put it, "is as a scorpion's sting. . . . He rebukes sin in low and high places with a verbiage calculated to arouse the sinner and make him repent." Expressions of enthusiasm for this aspect of WCBD's schedule, while less common than praise for its musical offerings, were also a routine feature of the station's fan mail. Often listeners wrote to applaud the general overseer's condemnation of a given symptom of the nation's moral decline. A party from Lafayette, Indiana, wrote to say that Voliva's "speaking of bobbed-haired women as possessed of many devils was appreciated"; a listener from Lindley, New York, wrote to say ,"You express our sentiments with every word you speak on the subjects of tobacco, drink, and movies." A righteous soul in Walhalla, South Carolina wrote, "We are writing to commend your position on present-day amusements. If the preachers were not tender-footed and would proclaim the truth in its simplicity, there would be hope of checking this carnival of crime."[20]

Assessing the returns that Zion reaped from broadcasting is a difficult matter; in fact, the pragmatic intent behind the community's mammoth investment in radio is not entirely obvious. Although Zion's economy was based on the manufacture and sale of consumer goods, the station never went in for the direct marketing tactics of the farmer stations, and the closest it came to direct advertising was to single out a segment of its weekly schedule and call it *The Zion Fig Bar Hour* after the Fig Newton-like candy bar made by the town's confectionery. Listener letters sometimes included references to the enclosure of sums of money—two, five, ten or fifteen dollars—sent in gratitude for programs received, though there is no sign that WCBD solicited such donations on the air

At least a few listeners were moved to action by Voliva's broadcast exhortations to "come out of Babylon, and get into Zion." Arthur Moon emigrated from Wisconsin with his wife and children and was soon made a member of Voliva's uniformed security corps, the Zion Guard; Laura C. Moriarty of Columbus, Ohio, was called to Zion after hearing the White Robed Choir sing her favorite hymn, "The Ninety and the Nine." In the estimate of Chicago radio listener A. J. Anselm, migrations like these were the true purpose of the station. "We can readily understand why Voliva wants 5,000 watts," wrote Anselm to the Commerce Department in 1925: "He needs recruits to keep his industrial units fully manned with cheap labor. He must have distance to advertise, because no one in nearby towns takes Voliva's bunk seriously."[21]

If Anselm was right and WCBD was intended as a migratory beacon, then it was a dud: the population of Zion remained rock steady throughout the 1920s. The station seems to have had slightly more success at winning long-distance converts to the CCC. From places as far away as Caddoa, Colorado; Spencer, West Virginia; and Glen Aubrey, New York, radio congregants faithfully paid tithes and purchased prescribed dietary items such as Zion-made "beef bacon" and pork-free shortening through the mail.[22] But most WCBD fans seem to have been ecumenicists who accepted those aspects of Zion's religious agenda that conformed to their own ideas of Christianity while overlooking the aberrant bits, such as Voliva's enduring obsession with "globular astronomy." One such fan was Harry K. Goodall of Elmhurst, Illinois, who wrote to the Commerce Department in early 1924 to defend the station against its detractors: "I read that some people had complained about Voliva's sermons. I don't believe all he says, but let him preach by radio. Those that don't like it, why do they listen? The poor boobs! We get some splendid music from WCBD."[23] Similar flexibility was demonstrated by a listener in Antioch, Illinois, who wrote to WCBD to vouch that "while we may differ in minor matters with Brother Voliva, yet in the main we agree, and congratulate him on the great work of spreading the Gospel of our Savior."[24]

From the time of Dowie, Zion had worked hard to promote itself as a tourist destination, and in this respect WCBD clearly succeeded. Encouraged by invitations renewed with every broadcast, fans came from Indiana, Kansas, Wisconsin, Ohio, Kentucky, Mississippi, Pennsylvania, and New York to tour the station's studios, participate in services in the Shiloh Tabernacle, and shop in Zion's large retail arcade. In 1928 station manager DePew credited WCBD with bringing "hundreds of visitors to the Tabernacle each Lord's day, year after year," an effect he called "the chief good that this station has done for Zion." On returning home, listener-pilgrims frequently wrote back to Zion to applaud all they had seen: "the wonderful Christian atmosphere," as a couple from Kansas put it, "the clean-cut young men, and the kindness and friendliness shown to us."[25]

In addition to attracting travelers to Zion, WCBD made it easier for Zion's own travelers to make their way through Babylon. Like any such commercial concern of the day, Zion Industries Inc. relied on a legion of traveling salesmen to develop and service distant markets for its products. According to DePew, the burden of representing Zion to the world was substantially reduced with the advent of its broadcasting. "Whereas our traveling men used to meet rebuffs," declared DePew in the summer of 1928, "they are now greeted in a friendly way, and I believe all of them will tell you that the people are glad to see them, and that they have a good word to say for the radio station."[26]

All things considered, WCBD was a good thing for a lot of people. General Overseer Voliva commanded the bulliest of bully pulpits; the musicians of Zion enjoyed an outlet for their gifts; traveling representatives of Zion Industries Inc. got a warm welcome wherever they went; and a lot of farm families enjoyed listening to a bracing hellfire sermon followed by gentle, beautiful music four nights a week. This all came to an abrupt halt on 11 November 1928, when the Federal Radio Commission's reallocation plan for the midwestern states took effect. Promulgated one month earlier, the plan entailed the relocation of WCBD from its accustomed, charmed wavelength to a marginal piece of the spectrum located off the dials of many receivers. Even more calamitous for Zion, the reallocation plan limited WCBD's schedule to daylight hours, a ruling that, in tandem with the unforgiving laws of signal propagation, reduced the international superstation to a humble service radius of a few hundred miles.

In the weeks before the reallocation plan was to take effect, WCBD fans poured out their hearts to their favorite station. A devoted Milwaukee listener wrote to declare that news of the impending separation "has aroused in me a feeling of regret such as one would experience upon the loss of an old and faithful friend." "It's like losing one of our family," concurred a fan in Oshkosh, Wisconsin. Particularly afflicted listeners retreated into a state of denial. A fan in Rockford wrote, "I do not believe that God will let such a good station go off the air." Another Milwaukee fan wrote, "My, how fearful. When my son John came in after you had signed off Lord's Day evening, I could scarcely tell him about it, I felt so badly; and he said, 'Mother, that is only for the time being. They would not stop a Station such as Zion's from broadcasting their programs.' I sincerely hope such may be the case." Others denounced the ruling as "criminal," "an outrage," "almost murder." Wrathful and heartbroken listeners alike expressed bafflement that, of all the stations on the air, one so uniquely and consistently "uplifting," "inspiring," "soothing," and "sensible" should be singled out for suppression. "I cannot," protested a Wisconsin listener, "think of a single just reason for this strange ruling." A fan from Elmwood, Illinois, wrote, "If these men would just sit down and let their minds drink in some of the good that comes from WCBD, they would give a different order. If only they would take off the air some of these wild radio stations, these commercial hounds that broadcast for the sake of gold and think nothing of the poor public that has to suffer and listen to their rotten messages!"[27]

The indignation and disbelief of its fans notwithstanding, the disadvantageous treatment WCBD suffered at the hands of the FRC was more or less inevitable. As a class, religious broadcasters fared poorly with the commission, which in its *Third Annual Report of 1929* had enunciated as a guiding principle the sentiment that there was "not room in the broadcast band for every school of thought, religious, political, social, and economic, each to have its separate broadcasting station, its mouthpiece in the ether."[28]

In practice, this principle of selection was selectively applied. Independent political broadcasters such as station WEVD of New York, operated by the American Socialist Party, and WCFL of Chicago, licensed to the Chicago Federation of Labor, managed to mount effective campaigns of defense against this regulatory prejudice and hold on to their licenses and wavelengths. As a rule, minority religious sects fared much worse. The Jehovah's Witnesses, for example, received crippling wavelength reassignments comparable to WCBD's during the reallocation period, even though their two stations, WBBR of Staten Island and WORD of Batavia, Illinois, were, like WCBD, well financed and technically above reproach.

Another strike against WCBD was the fact that it never sought to expand service past its original 1923 schedule of 14.5 hours of programming over four nights a week. The FRC expressly favored a broader continuity of service—50 or 60 hours a week—in assessing "public interest, convenience and necessity."

In 1929 Voliva appealed the FRC's reallocation ruling in Washington,

D.C. He might have had a chance of succeeding if he had stood on his First Amendment right of free speech and sought the help of the American Civil Liberties Union, which was searching for disfranchised broadcasters to defend against the government's new power of censorship. Instead, Voliva clumsily cited the Fifth rather than the First Amendment, arguing that his rights to property had been negated when the commission took away his original wavelength of 870 kilocycles. The appeals court easily rebuffed this appeal, ruling that "there is no property right, as against the regulatory power of the United States, to engage in broadcasting."[29]

The loss of its international radio audience was just the first in a series of setbacks for the city that Dowie built. Though the autocratic Voliva had worked wonders in restoring Zion's economy to health in the wake of Dowie's mismanagement, the Great Depression hit the utopian community like a thunderbolt. By 1933 the assets of Zion Industries Inc. had been placed in receivership. Voliva's loss of financial control weakened his political authority, enabling a coalition of dissidents calling themselves the Independent Party to seize political control of the town from his Theocratic Party and to disarm his personal police force, the Zion Guard. Voliva swore to the press that he would regain control of the city and drive his enemies out, but after 1935 he began spending less time in Zion. He settled into a peevish semiretirement in Florida, where he would die from diabetic complications in 1942.

With Voliva out of the way, the Independent Party quickly set about repealing most of the blue laws for which Zion had been famous. Soon cigarettes, pork, shellfish, baseball, motion pictures, card playing, lipstick, medicine, and other previously forbidden commodities and activities were legal in Zion. In a related reform, the Independents reoriented the science curriculum taught in Zion's schools to conform with the precepts of modern "globular astronomy."

On its new wavelength, WCBD continued to provide local daytime service to a drastically reduced audience until 1934, when Voliva sold the station and its license to a secular concern, Oak Leaves Broadcasting Inc., for ten thousand dollars. Resituated in Chicago and given the call sign WAIT, the new station pursued a conventional line of commercial broadcasting and was later affiliated with the Don Lee Network. In 1937 a fire set by the teenage son of one of Voliva's disaffected followers destroyed the Shiloh Tabernacle and its derelict radio studio.

\*    \*    \*

The reprieve that WCBD's audience prayed for never materialized, and so they ceased to exist as a constituency when their favorite station was taken off the night-time airwaves. Individually, however, WCBD's bereaved fans may have taken solace in certain emerging trends in network programming after 1930. Part of the genius of the chain system was its willingness to pick up program formats and cultural styles from the independents and adapt them for commercial purposes—which always entailed knocking the rougher edges off the original article. A prime example is NBC's hit program *Seth Parker*, inaugurated in 1930. A weekly thirty-minute dose of "hymn singing, homey philosophy and cheerfulness," the program centered on the life of its eponym, a yeoman farmer and lay minister living in the fictional hamlet of Jonesport, Maine. To the extent that it was driven by plot, *Seth Parker* dealt sentimentally or humorously with the trials and tribulations of small-town life, but its minimal narrative elements were essentially setups for concerts—conducted in the imaginary parlor of the Parker family home—of old-fashioned hymns such as "Lead, Kindly Light" and secular chestnuts such as "My Old Kentucky Home." A studio simulacrum assembled out of the sweetest components of the farmer-station tradition, the program was pleasing to rural and urban sensibilities alike, and spawned equally benign, nondenominational imitators: *The Heart of Home Hour, Old Songs of the Church, The Old-Fashioned Revival Hour, The Joyful Hour, The Heaven and Home Hour, The Church by the Side of the Road, Remember with Joy*, for example. But to the extent that the fiery old-time religion preached by the likes of Voliva would have a presence on the airwaves during the Golden Age of Radio, it would be confined almost exclusively to small independent stations and border-blasting pirates on the Mexican border.[30]

*Chapter 7*

# The Dawn of the Golden Age

The plain fact is that educated people are becoming heartily and increasingly sick of the radio. The broadcaster has not merely underestimated his public, he has failed altogether to take it into account. He has consistently, and on a rapidly increasing scale, catered to those who possess neither brains nor education.

—*Marshall Kernochan, journalist, 1931* [1]

"Do you remember, a few years ago," the journalist Jack Woodford asked the readership of the cultural review *The Forum* in early 1929, "how we all felt a vague sort of elation when the radio first came to our attention? Ah, at last, we said, here is something . . . something . . . we were not quite sure what. Something overwhelming that was going to bring peace on earth and goodwill to men. Something that was going to do everything but change the actual physical outline of North America. Do you think I exaggerate? Get out the papers of a few years back and read the editorials." Woodford continued, "Now we know definitely what we have got in radio—just another disintegrating toy. Just another medium—like the newspapers, the magazines, the billboards, and the mail box—for advertisers to use in pestering us." Warming to his subject, Woodford testified that he had lately "searched the ether hopelessly trying to find something with some sense in it," a quest that had yielded nothing better than "the rattle and bang of incredibly frightful 'jazz' music. . . . a prolonged jungle beat, monotonous and meaningless." Listening in to allegedly informational programs had proven equally futile for Woodford: "I have gleaned information concerning the thug who slew a cop, the man who scattered his votes in every precinct, the organist who eloped with his sister-in-law, the man who bit the dog." But "intelligent men," complained Woodford, were nowhere to be heard on the air "for the obvious reason that a radio audience which enjoys what it is now getting would not know what such men were talking about, nor be interested if they did." American radio, he concluded, "has been made safe for democracy."[2]

While he was slightly ahead of the pack, opinions like Woodford's would soon be ubiquitous in the middle-class periodical press—the very forums where utopian radio dreams had reached their previous peaks of optimism. Bearing titles such as "Station B-U-N-K," "Abuses of Radio Broadcasting," "Saving the Radio," "Can Radio Be Rescued?," and "Why Isn't Radio Better?," the new literature of disenchantment was as homogeneous as the utopian discourse it supplanted.[3] Summarizing the charges against radio for *Harper's* in 1933, the composer and critic Deems Taylor distilled the grievances of "the more literate and intelligent radio listeners" down to two essential themes: "first, that there is too much vulgar material, particularly vulgar music, in today's programs; and, second, that there is far too much blatant advertising and selling talk connected with radio."[4]

The extinction of radio's utopian aura followed the ongoing consolidation of the commercial network system, a development begun in earnest in 1926. In that year AT&T came to the conclusion that there was no rational place in the operations of a telephone company for broadcasting and the problems it entailed. After a series of quiet negotiations with RCA, AT&T sold off WEAF and its assets of reputation to the radio trust for a million dollars. The sale of WEAF did not mean an end to AT&T's involvement in the radio business, however. The plan hatched between AT&T and RCA called for the creation of a permanent radio chain, the National Broadcasting Company. While the new network was to be a wholly owned subsidiary of RCA, AT&T would still earn profits from the arrangement by leasing to NBC the dedicated long distance telephone lines that would link the network's affiliated stations to its metropolitan anchor stations, WJZ and WEAF, of Newark and New York, respectively.

Publicity for the new network pledged that it would be an "instrument of great public service," a "semi-philanthropic" enterprise. Programming standards, promised NBC spokesmen, were to be kept on the highest cultural plain with the help of the network's "Advisory Council," a body composed of prominent civic leaders, statesmen, philanthropists, and cultural authorities. Advertising would adhere to the standards of discretion traditionally in force at WEAF. NBC sponsors, testified network president Merlin Aylesworth before Congress in early 1928, were paying to "keep their names before the public," not to impose on listeners with annoying hard-sell pitches and vulgar price quotations. Manifesting pride in the fact that NBC had lost five hundred thousand dollars in its first year of operation, Aylesworth further voiced doubts that the network "should ever make any money," although he did allow for the possibility "that within another year we will have enough sponsors of our fine entertainment programs, or that we will find some individuals or institutions that will endow our educational features, in order that we may break even." "Please remember," Aylesworth implored Congress, "that the NBC has a very definite editorial policy. We carry definitely the things that are recommended by our advisory council, or that we think that we ought to carry for the enlightening and uplift of the public."[5]

There is nothing to indicate that NBC's vaunted Advisory Council was created in bad faith or that Aylesworth consciously perjured himself before Congress. Still, the Advisory Council was not the network's only source of guidance. In early 1928 NBC hired the pollster Daniel Starch to conduct a survey of radio-equipped households east of the Rocky Mountains. Starch's statistical tables confirmed what the independents, urban and rural, had known all along. The superiority of genteel cultural goods was not, after all, self-evident to anyone who heard them. Opera, classics, and jazz appealed primarily to the city markets. Farm families preferred old-time music to uplift.[6]

Although criticized by later radio pollsters for methodological shortcomings, the Starch survey was a landmark of rigor compared to all that had come before and much of what would follow in the way of audience research. A window on the traditional way of doing things at the big metropolitan stations is provided by a 1924 article in *The Wireless Age*. Asked to explain their system of determining what listeners desired, the programmers at the Big Four stations outlined their vision of the global radio public as a three-tiered structure: a "purely cultured class" at the top; a middle tier consisting of "people of education and breeding who apparently favor the less subtle renditions, but still hold themselves aloof from strictly popular features"; and, at the bottom, "a great mass that includes several groups ranging from indifferent patrons of the muses down to illiterates." Weighing the importance of these social strata, explained the programmers, entailed a careful triage of listener correspondence. "Such letters," reported *The Wireless Age*, "can be classified according to the letterhead, quality of the stationery, the composition, or even the grammar of the writers. Extreme care is exercised in discounting the natural tendency of some classes to write prolifically. That precaution is necessary to accurately gauge the representation of the class to which the writers belong." Removing any doubt as to class of listener whose opinions might be harmfully overrepresented, the article stated that "philharmonic concerts and classics never receive the volume of applause accorded to popular and jazz numbers" but reassuringly added that "the enthusiasm rings with the same genuine approbation in either case."[7]

Circular though it was in its reasoning, the Big Four's early approach to audience research looks like empiricism itself when compared to a widely cited 1933 survey conducted by the *Literary Digest*, which proved that listeners overwhelmingly preferred classical music to jazz and were subject to turn off their radios at the first hint of a sales pitch.[8] The poll belonged to a long lineage of newspaper and magazine surveys dating back to 1925, all demonstrating the unpopularity of popular culture and the unfeasibility of broadcast advertising.[9] All were what present-day pollsters call SLOPs: self-selecting listener opinion polls. The *Literary Digest* poll may have reflected the sentiments of the readership of the *Literary Digest*, but a cross-section of vox populi it was not. (In 1936 the *Digest* published a similarly flawed poll that predicted a landslide for Republican presidential candidate Alf Landon, an error that helped put the magazine out of business.)

The Starch poll and subsequent NBC-backed audience research were part of the network's ongoing campaign to break down the national advertising industry's resistance to radio with irrefutable audience numbers—circulation being an issue just as important to the admen as were their ethical reservations about radio advertising. In promoting radio to the advertisers, NBC's commercial development staff still had their work cut out for them: *Printers' Ink* remained rigidly opposed to radio advertising into the 1930s, frequently reiterating as fact the opinion that "broadcasting is not an advertising medium" and reminding its readers to ask themselves, "What would be my own reaction to the programs I contemplate putting on the air as advertising or publicity?"[10]

The first sign of a shift in the party line at *Printers' Ink* would not appear until 1934; it took the form of an iconoclastic opinion piece by the New York advertising executive Frank Finney. Titled "Grand Opera, Symphonies and Cigarettes," Finney's essay forthrightly posed the question whether "high hat" programs were worth a sponsor's consideration. Rejecting the notion that "the handful of consumers who can understand, appreciate and enjoy classical music" represented a market worth courting, Finney held up as an industry ideal an advertising executive of his acquaintance whose campaigns were written with "an audience of one person" in mind: "the humble woman who cleans up his office after hours."[11]

Finney's challenge to the advertising industry's accustomed definition of consumer citizenship provoked a flurry of dissenting responses. One such, emanating from the eminent New York firm of Henri, Hurst, and McDonald, fell back on the *Literary Digest* survey of the previous year as proof positive that the genteel radio public outnumbered the charwoman demographic by one hundred to one and that the discreetly sponsored presentation of an operatic or symphonic program was still the best advertising bet on the airwaves.[12]

By this time, however, the discipline of audience research was progressing into a new phase of maturity and authority. Paving the way for the future science of broadcast ratings, in 1929 Archibald Crossley established his Cooperative Analysis of Broadcasting service, a telephone survey service supported by subscribing broadcasters and advertisers. Joining the fray in 1934 was a similar research firm created by C. F. Hooper. The findings of these new agencies, noted Roy S. Durstine of Batten, Burton, Durstine and Osborne in early 1935, brought consistently discouraging news "to the advertising man who feels that taste and restraint should have their rewards." To the contrary, he added, "many radio programs which carry the most relentless and insistent advertising are the most successful." Grappling with this conundrum, Durstine advanced a decidedly bleak reading of the inner lives of the American masses. "The typical listening audience for a radio program," he wrote "is a tired, bored, middle-aged man and woman whose lives are empty and who have exhausted their sources of outside amusement when they have taken a quick look at the evening paper. They are utterly unlike those who are most vocal in their criticisms of radio programs—people with full lives, with books to read, with parties to attend, with theaters to visit, with friends whose conversational powers are stimulating. Radio provides a vast source of delight and entertainment for the barren lives of the millions." Durstine continued, "It is small wonder that the millions do not complain, and that the unhappiness and sensitiveness about over-commercialism and other objectionable features is confined to the top layer." This depressing evaluation of American life notwithstanding, Durstine concluded his essay with the conventional appeal for "reform from within," calling for renewed industry restraint in radio advertising, an emulation of British standards of cultural taste, and the imposition of limits on repetitive song plugging.[13]

Again the weekly reverted for several issues to its traditional antiradio stance, cautioning the industry that "radio has been getting away with murder" where advertising was concerned and affirming the necessity to "maintain dignity and good taste" and to ignore "the minor percentage of the listening audience that enjoys inane or risqué comedy, and other inferior entertainment."[14] Then, in September 1935, the gloves came off for good at *Printers' Ink*. Responding to a recent report issued by the Women's National Radio Committee, an affiliate body of the General Federation of Women's Clubs, the adman Harold Clark picked up where Frank Finney had left off two years earlier and carried Finney's argument to its logical end. In previous issues *Printers' Ink* had respectfully deferred to the committee as an authoritative moral voice. Now, however, Clark dismissed the committee as just "another worthy endeavor on the part of a small cultured group to express the opinions, likes and dislikes of the masses of the people." Clark proceeded to offer the watch-dog group a crash course in aesthetic relativism. The committee, he wrote, had spoken "very unkindly" about NBC's *Rudy Vallee Hour* and the direct advertising for Fleischmann's Yeast that supported it. Also singled out for condemnation by the body was an old-time musical revue called *Home on the Range*—"the worst musical program on the air," in its estimate. In arriving at these judgments, wrote Clark, the committee had made "the mistake which is made so often of judging what the people like by our own cultural and educational standards." The Vallee program commanded between one-fourth and one-third of the national radio audience and ranked third among all programs on the air, whereas *Home on the Range* was attracting "better than 10 per cent of the listeners." Clark continued remorselessly, "It would seem logical that the people do not resent the commercials to a degree which interferes with their listening habits."[15]

Were there only the editorial content of *Printers' Ink* to go by, one might assume that most of Madison Avenue was still remaining true to the chaste ideals of indirect sponsorship through 1935. In practice, however, the corruption of the advertising industry at the hands of the American masses was all but complete by the time Harold Clark published his dismissal of the Women's National Radio Committee. As the historian Erik Barnouw observes, "the years 1929–32 were a period of an almost spectacular retreat from previous standards" where broadcast advertising was concerned, both nationally and locally.[16] Perhaps the retreat of the networks and the national advertisers from the path of propriety would not have been quite so abrupt were it not for two accelerative factors: the rise of a second national network, CBS, and the onset of the Great Depression.

At the time of the sickly debut of the Columbia Broadcasting System in September 1927, the notion that it would ever challenge NBC would have seemed risible. Abandoned before its first broadcast by the backer to whom it owed its name—the Columbia Phonograph Company—CBS was undercapitalized and understaffed. The new network was also obliged to recruit its affiliates from among the lesser stations on the map, the cream of the crop having already been picked over by NBC. But in late 1928 a rescuer appeared in the form of William S. Paley. A twenty-six-year-old executive in his father's business, the Congress Cigar Company of Philadelphia, Paley was testing the advertising potential of a local "cheap" station, WCAU, when the latter became a CBS affiliate. His interest piqued by a 100 percent surge in cigar profits within WCAU's service area, Paley sat down with CBS executives and came away as the network's controlling shareholder and president. With Paley on board, the start-up network began to look like a legitimate venture, and investment capital began to pour in from other sources, including the Paramount Pictures corporation.

Coming up from behind NBC, CBS displayed a distinct willingness to try harder in the realm of commerce, affording a freer hand to its sponsors than did its senior, semi-philanthropic rival. It was CBS, for example, that led the way in breaking down the taboo against KFNF-style price quotation at the national level in 1932. In order to remain competitive with sponsors, NBC was obliged to follow suit within a matter of months.[17]

The networks' race to the bottom in advertising practices was no doubt hastened by the Depression. The market crash had been particularly hurtful to the less substantial CBS, whose corporate culture was already far less influenced by the public service ethos that defined NBC's corporate self-image. But standards were slipping at every level of the radio business—among sponsors, programmers, and advertisers. As profits slid, listener surveys took on increasing importance, and the pragmatic equation of "best" with "most popular" in programming became less and less controversial.

"As 1933 began," writes Erik Barnouw, "the networks were experiencing a vaudeville boom. The collapse of vaudeville and the slump in the theater had brought to radio a barrage of comedy and variety programs which now dominated the schedule."[18] Another way of putting this is to say that the networks were rapidly moving toward what had once been the distinct cultural condition of the lowbrow independents. No better index of this transition could be imagined than the fact that Nils Thor Granlund, erstwhile master of ceremonies at WHN and living symbol of lowbrow broadcasting circa 1925, had by 1935 infiltrated the studios of WEAF, where he served as host of *NTG and His Girls*. Sponsored by the Emerson Drug Company and broadcast nationally by NBC's Blue Network, the program was a showcase for Granlund's wisecracks and the talents of Broadway dancers and chorus girls.

\* \* \*

Circa 1930 America's cultivated classes began loudly declaring themselves to be the big losers in the war for control of the American airwaves, but their claims of neglect are not necessarily to be taken at face value. Consider national network programming after 1930 to represent a confluence of three previously separate cultural tributaries: the highbrow, as exemplified by WEAF; the lowbrow, as exemplified by WHN; and the rural, exemplified by KFNF. The vitality of each in the 1920s compels recognition of the existence of three corresponding listening publics, more or less discrete. Of these three, the urban lowbrow audience surely had the least to complain about in the 1930s and 1940s. In fact, class-based griping about the prevalence of genteel programming, abundant throughout the 1920s, dwindled into inaudibility by the 1930s.

If any part of the radio audience had reason to complain of neglect during the Golden Age, it was the country folk, who had seen a disproportionate number of their favorite stations suppressed or absorbed into the networks, which gave low priority to rural cultural preferences. Prior to 1945 there were only three barn dance-style revues carried nationally by the major networks: *The National Barn Dance, The Grand Ole Opry*, and *Gene Autry's Melody Ranch*; and all of them were weekly. It was left to low-power independent stations scattered throughout the Midwest and the South to meet the daily hunger for old-time music—although Brinkley's mighty border blaster, XERA, greatly helped to augment the supply of protocountry music on the national airwaves for much of this period.

The relative disfranchisement of the rural audience is that much more striking when considered in proportion to the lip service paid to the special needs of the countryside by powerful broadcasting interests and federal regulators. Solicitude for rural needs was the rationale for the Federal Radio Commission's creation in 1930 of a privileged category of broadcaster, the clear-channel stations, each entitled to maximum signal power and the exclusive use of their assigned wavelengths, the better (in theory) to extend program service to remote and underserved areas. These advantages made the forty "clears" a major force in U.S. broadcasting between 1930 and 1950, their big voices dominating the national airwaves at night, when sky waves ricochet off the upper atmosphere and carry AM signals maximal distances. But the clear-channel interests did virtually nothing to discharge their responsibilities to the constituency they were created to serve: making only desultory efforts to discover and meet the particular desires of the rural audience, they put greater energy into simulating grassroots support by wooing the top leadership of agricultural lobby groups. These campaigns of courtship were not consistently successful, and certain agricultural groups, notably the National Farmers' Union, remained outspoken opponents of the clear-channel interests throughout the period of their dominance.[19]

"Highbrow" cultural values, in comparison, were scarcely neglected by the networks. America's senior network was intensely conscious of the political necessity of maintaining a substantial margin of "uplifting" programs in order to legitimate private stewardship of the airwaves and forestall a middle-class revolt against the still-controversial commercial order. "Good music" constituted the single most potent signifier of

NBC's dedication to the ideals of public service; Shakespeare was another high-yield source of prestige.[20]

In the 1930s NBC executives felt, perhaps not without justification, that they alone were holding up the sky where the defensive discharge of radio's higher responsibilities was concerned. "RCA-NBC inaugurated public service broadcasting in all the various fields," grieved NBC vice president Frank M. Russell in a private house memorandum (marked "Please destroy"), "because we wanted to demonstrate beyond any question of doubt that radio should remain in the hands of private interests. . . . Obviously, therefore, we were protecting and benefiting radio as a whole."[21] In other words, tyro concerns such as CBS and the Mutual Broadcasting System (the distant-third placer among the national networks) were not pulling their own cultural weight.

However, in the later 1930s CBS, having nursed itself to adequate size and strength with WHN-style cultural and commercial tactics, began to compete with NBC for cultural plaudits. At this juncture a "marquee war" broke out between the two chains, who began pitting their finest concert and dramatic offerings against each other in their respective schedules.[22] This rivalry was pushed to potlatchlike intensities by the artificial economic conditions that obtained during the American involvement in World War II. Responding to residual populist outrage over corporate profiteering during World War I, Congress had imposed upon the industrial sector an excess-profits tax of up to 90 percent. But gaping loopholes in the wartime tax code permitted manufacturers to mitigate the penalty by plowing excess profits into their advertising budgets. The consequence was a massive boom in advertising—especially radio advertising—despite the fact that many of the consumer goods being promoted were in short supply. Although such surplus advertising was criticized as wasteful, sponsors and advertisers justified it on the grounds that many national brand-name products had fatally slipped from public consciousness while advertising was suspended during World War I. Under these extraordinary conditions, writes Erik Barnouw, sponsors were "delighted with prestige programs of less than maximum audience," including an unprecedented bounty of top-drawer classical and operatic music performances, literate and original dramas, and world affairs programs.[23] Thus the advertising industry would, at least for a few years, happily and profitably shoulder a burden of responsibility it had once sworn to avoid: that of serving as "the philanthropist of radio."[24]

Radio during the Golden Age—the interval between the rise of the networks and the advent of television—was predominantly vaudevillian, dominated by popular song, comedy, and melodrama. But compared to the currents of vaudeville locally mediated by the lowbrow independent stations of the 1920s, the network version of vaudeville was conspicuously clean, conforming to the moral strictures of the Keith-Albee circuit, whose demure standards had made vaudeville safe for middle-class family consumption. Indeed, NBC's founding director of program policy, John Royal, was a former Keith-Albee executive hired by RCA largely on the basis of his reputation as a master of the blue pencil. Throughout Royal's long watch at NBC, scripts and routines were assiduously vetted for anything that might offend. Double entendres; borderline profanity ("hell" and "damn"); sexual innuendo, however tame or oblique; the utterance of the name of "God" outside contexts of worship—all these were proscribed.[25] Popular song lyrics were routinely bowdlerized by the networks' continuity officials.

In sum, the consolidation of the commercial network system, with its gimlet-eyed censors and timorous corporate sponsors, brought the equivalent of the Hays Code, the self-imposed system of censorship that guided the motion picture industry, to the airwaves. It would be several decades before American broadcasting again approached the standards of freedom of expression practiced by the likes of WHN and KWKH in the 1920s.

The sanitizing, pacifying effects of the commercial imperative on the airwaves were not limited to the censorship policies of the major networks. The commercial climate also generally disfavored the uglier, more socially divisive currents of American radio in the 1920s. A case in point is the story of a radio station operated by the Ku Klux Klan.

In 1927 the Independent Publishing Company, publishers of a Klan weekly called *The Fellowship Forum*, applied for and acquired permission from the Commerce Department Radio Division to take over the license of a failing Brooklyn independent station, WTRC, and to relocate its transmitter to Mount Vernon Hills, Virginia, on the southern outskirts of Washington, D.C. Precisely why the Commerce Department assented to this controversial acquisition is unclear. The regional radio supervisor assigned to evaluate the proposed transfer predicted that the purpose of the new station would be to attack the Catholic Church and deemed it "questionable whether such a station would be in the interest of public convenience, interest and necessity."[26] Regardless, the deal went ahead. Under its new call sign of WTFF, Washington's new Klan station was even granted permission to boost the inherited signal strength of the defunct WTRC from fifty to ten-thousand watts.[27]

Then, within months of its opening, the proprietor of WTFF, James S. Vance, decided that there would be more profit in ecumenical commercialism than in the dissemination of sectarian hatred. Vance wrote to the Federal Radio Commission in the autumn of 1928:

Carefully scrutinizing the public interest in programs being broadcasted [*sic*] from WTFF as manifested and revealed in thousands of letters received from "listeners-in," and recognizing that a super power station of ten thousand watts owes the public the very best programs obtainable, it is our purpose, on and after November 11 to change the policy and improve the quality of all programs flowing through the microphone of WTFF. In order, therefore, to make this change complete and for the purpose of reparating [*sic*] the past from the future, The Independent Publishing Company respectfully wishes that its call letters be changed from WTFF to WJSV. When this change of call letters has been approved by your honorable body, it is our intention and purpose to emphasize religious programs on Sundays and devote the remainder of our time to talent of a varied character, laying particular stress upon education and agriculture.[28]

Judging from a 1930 WJSV program schedule preserved in the FRC files, Vance was true to his word: under its new call sign the erstwhile Klan station worked the rural end of the cultural spectrum, offering programs such as *The Old Fashioned Gospel Song Service*, *The Blue Ridge Mountaineers*, and *Big Ed and Pa Brown's Boys* with no detectable residue of a Klan-style political agenda. The severance of the station from its Klan roots was completed in the summer of 1932, when WJSV became a full-time affiliate of the CBS network.[29]

\*    \*    \*

The creation of hundreds of stations in lieu of a single centralized system of broadcasting entailed a fateful chain of consequences for American broadcasting. It virtually guaranteed the presence of a freebooting entrepreneurial element among the pioneering generation of broadcasters, station owners determined to pursue a nakedly commercial agenda no matter who disapproved or why. In pursuit of profits, these stations flooded the airwaves with popular cultural fare that, under other circumstances, would likely have been far less prevalent or, in some cases, not heard at all.

Although the hopeful partisans of broadcast uplift long contrived not to notice, the prosperity of these entrepreneurial independents represented concrete proof against two cherished tenets of the middle-class utopian ideology: the belief that broadcast advertising was untenable—that it was ultimately liable to "kill" radio; and the assumption that the self-evident superiority of "good" culture would lead to its inevitable triumph over the "bad." What is odd about these twinned doctrines is that they contravene the customary logic of cultural hierarchy, which, as Lawrence Levine observes, more typically adheres to "a Gresham's Law of Culture," the default assumption of the cultivated being that, in the absence of eternal vigilance, the bad inevitably drives out the good.[30] Precisely why the normal logic of cultural competition should have been in abeyance in this particular set of circumstances is difficult to say. The uplifters in charge of British broadcasting at this time certainly manifested no such confidence in the power of the good to dispel the bad. Perhaps this is an example of the fabled American tendency toward optimism.

Whatever its etiology, this blindness was to have momentous ramifications. Had the partisans of uplift been able to shed their complacent illusions in time—say by 1925 or 1926—they might have been moved to organize earlier and militate more effectively for noncommercial alternatives, at a moment when the utopian mood and hostility to advertising were at their peak and the laws governing radio had yet to be rewritten. Instead, the doctrine that commercialism equaled death for radio provided a rationale for political inaction until very late in the day. Even after 1930 many pundits and critics were still predicting the imminent collapse of American radio under the weight of advertising, after which breakdown they imagined that they would have a chance to start over and build anew, this time along the lines of the BBC.

Overall, it seems safe to say that the evolutionary odds for a noncommercial outcome in American radio look better the further back in time one looks. As was suggested in Chapter 1, the chances for the creation of an American BBC would have been much improved if only the federal and corporate architects of the Radio Corporation of America had anticipated broadcasting back in 1919. Armed with that foreknowledge, they would almost certainly have reserved the broadcasting privilege to RCA and constructed a single, centralized network for the nation, thus avoiding the fateful proliferation of private stations and the ensuing competitive conditions favoring the erosion of genteel standards.

Exactly what such a monopoly might have come to, culturally and commercially, is impossible to say, but this scenario would have afforded the urban middle classes a better chance at asserting control over the airwaves and putting their own cultural agenda to the forefront. Philanthropic and/or listener-support schemes for the finance of programming that failed to thrive in the fragmented and competitive broadcasting environment of the 1920s would likewise have stood far better odds of success. Self-interested champions of "free" broadcasting such as George Schubel and Henry Field would never have attained their fateful footholds in the ether. Never having heard them, rural and urban "lowbrow" audiences would not have missed the commercial independent stations they came to cherish. Everything might have been different. The fact that it was not stems less from corporate hegemony than from corporate impotence during the critical period at the dawn of the broadcasting age.

# Notes

*Preface*

1.  Michele Hilmes, *Radio Voices: American Broadcasting, 1922–1952* (Minneapolis, 1997), xvi.

*Prelude*

1.  "Wireless Music Fails to Connect," *New York Herald,* 23 December 1921, in George H. Clark Radioana Collection, Series 8, Box 188, Archives Center, National Museum of American History, Smithsonian Institution, Washington, D.C.

*Chapter 1*

1.  Elmer Douglas, "Lines from a Listener," in *Chicago Tribune Picture Book of Radio* (Chicago, 1928), 67.
2.  Frank Bannister, *The Education of a Broadcaster* (New York, 1965), 11–13.
3.  Ibid., 14–16.
4.  Ibid., 16.
5.  Ibid., 22–23.
6.  Ibid., 22, 47, 74, 76–77.
7.  Newton Minow, "The Vast Wasteland" (address to the thirty-ninth annual convention of the National Association of Broadcasters, Washington, D.C., 9 May 1961).
8.  Bannister, *Education,* 323–25.
9.  Ibid., 324.
10. Ibid., 51–52.
11. Edgar H. Felix, *Using Radio in Sales Promotion* (New York, 1927), 85.
12. "Who Shall Judge the Quality of Our Broadcasting Stations?," *Radio Broadcast* 10 (December 1926): 180–81.
13. Robert W. McChesney, *Telecommunications, Mass Media, and Democracy* (New York, 1993), 15.
14. Hilmes, *Radio Voices,* 17.
15. Bannister, *Education,* 12.
16. "Bootlegger Clears Slain Radio Orator," *New York Times,* 27 July 1930, 17.
17. See Cash Asher, *Sacred Cows: A Story of the Recall of Mayor Bowles* (Detroit, 1931), and Cash Asher, *The Real Buckley Tragedy: Political Gravediggers Use the Dead to Rob the Citizens of Detroit* (Detroit, 1931).
18. Coughlin began broadcasting in 1926, two years before Buckley did, but

for the first four years of his radio career he was simply a moderately popular children's entertainer and religious instructor. Only after 1930 did Coughlin gradually begin to incorporate political themes into his broadcasts, emerging as a full-time political gadfly in late 1931. The tabloid journalist Ruth Mugglebee, the author of a slapdash 1933 biography of Coughlin written for the newsstand trade, noted that the resemblance between the new Father Coughlin and the deceased Jerry Buckley was not lost on the citizens of Detroit. According to Mugglebee, the "cry went around town in 1931" that "Coughlin has taken his cue from Buckley. . . . He had better watch out. They'll be giving him the works if he doesn't watch out" (Ruth Mugglebee, *Father Coughlin, the Radio Priest of the Shrine of the Little Flower* [New York: 1933], 268–69).

19. Robert L. Kent, "Jerry Buckley Radio's First Martyr," *Radio Digest* 25 (October 1930): 24–25, 108.

20. The transfer of data from one decade back to another is, of course, no one's ideal of historical method. Still, imperfect evidence is better than none at all. Moreover, one would assume that generalizations about class and taste that were true for the 1930s and 1940s would also be generally valid for the 1920s unless there were some compelling reason to embrace a contrary assumption. In the particular case of broadcasting, often said to promote the homogenization of thought and sensibility, logic would seem to favor the assumption that patterns of stratification manifest in the 1930s and 1940s would have been more and not less pronounced in the 1920s.

21. Clifford Kilpatrick, *Report of a Research into the Attitudes and Listening Habits of Radio Listeners* (St. Paul, Minn., 1933), 39–44; Jeanette Sayre, "A Comparison of Three Indices of Attitude Toward Radio Advertising," *The Journal of Applied Psychology* 23 (February 1939): 161.

22. Paul Lazarsfeld and Harold Field, *The People Look at Radio* (Chapel Hill, N.C., 1946), 20–21, 67. See also H. H. Maynard and Kenneth Dameron, *A Broadcasting Survey of Columbus, Ohio* (Columbus, Ohio, 1931).

23. H. M. Beville, Jr., *Social Stratification of the Radio Audience* (Princeton, N.J., 1939), v; Isabelle F. Wagner and Margaret Erb, "Program Preferences of Different Groups," *Journal of Applied Psychology* 23 (February 1939): 189. Note that in employing the words "serious" and "good," Beville was, in accordance with contemporary convention, denoting specific genres of music. Generically speaking, "good" and "serious" meant the European classical orchestral music tradition, chamber music, grand opera, and contemporary semiclassical works. Excluded always from the canon of the good and the serious were popular commercial forms like jazz and Tin Pan Alley pop.

24. Lazarsfeld and Field, *People Look at Radio*, 25.

25. Alvin Meyrowitz and Marjorie Fiske, "The Relative Preference of Low Income Groups for Small Stations," *The Journal of Applied Psychology* 23 (February 1939): 158–61.

26. "KDKA," *The Wireless Age* 9 (August 1922): 40.

27. Charles D. Isaacson, "Radio and Fine Music," *The Wireless Age* 10 (February 1923): 38.

28. Erik Barnouw, *A Tower in Babel: A History of Broadcasting in the United States to 1933* (New York, 1966), 126.

29. "One Wave for the Chain," *Radio Digest*, 1 April 1927, 8.

30. "The Listener's Voice," *Radio Digest*, 15 June 1927, 22. John McCormack was an internationally famous Irish tenor. In 1925 McCormack and Lucrezia Bori, lead soprano of the New York Metropolitan Opera Company, were fea-

tured performers of a special broadcast program produced at AT&T's New York flagship station, WEAF. On this widely publicized occasion thirteen specially chosen metropolitan broadcasting stations (including WWJ, Detroit) were linked by long-distance telephone lines to WEAF in order to relay the program to the widest possible audience. This special event played a crucial role in welding the participating stations into the NBC network the following year. Marion Talley was a famous operatic soprano of the day, routinely featured on WEAF in the 1920s.

31. "The March of Radio," *Radio Broadcast* 11 (July 1927): 139.

32. H. V. Kaltenborn, "Radio: Dollars and Nonsense," *Scribner's* 88 (May 1931): 490.

33. On the utopian response to early radio, see Mary S. Mander, "Utopian Dimensions in the Public Debate on Broadcasting in the Twenties," *Journal of Communication Inquiry* 12 (summer 1988):71–88; Clayton R. Koppes, "The Social Destiny of Radio: Hope and Disillusionment in the 1920s," *South Atlantic Quarterly* 68 (Summer 1969): 368; Daniel Czitrom, *Media and the American Mind:From Morse to McCluhan* (Chapel Hill, N.C., 1982).

34. Waldemar Kaempffert, "The Social Destiny of Radio," *The Forum* 71 (June 1924): 768.

35. William H. P. Faunce, "Will the Radio Create a 'Mob Mind' In America?," *California Christian Advocate*, 3 July 1924, 14, 23.

36. Koppes, "Social Destiny," 368.

37. Gleason Archer, *Big Business and Radio* (New York, 1939), 51–52.

38. James True, "What the Public Thinks About Advertising Over the Radio," *Printers' Ink*, 2 April 1925, 116.

39. Marshall Beuick, "Broadcast Advertising Losing Its Force," *New York Herald Tribune Radio Magazine*, 21 September 1924, 4.

40. "Westinghouse Warns Advertising against Use of Radio," *Printers' Ink*, 1 March 1923, 103.

41. Roland Marchand, *Advertising the American Dream: Making Way for Modernity, 1920–1949* (Berkeley, Calif., 1985 ), 8, 32–38. See also Richard Ohmann, *Selling Culture: Magazines, Markets and Class at the Turn of the Century* (New York, 1996), chap. 6.

42. Howard Angus, "Radio Needs Showmanship," *Printers' Ink*, 30 June 1932, 46.

43. Marchand, *Advertising*, 38.

44. "Radio Listeners Still Protest against Broadcast Advertising," *Printers' Ink*, 6 May 1926, 137.

45. "Why Radio Advertising is Impracticable," *Printers' Ink*, 15 November 1923, 137; "Broadcasting Doesn't Belong in Advertising Account," ibid., 6 August 1925, 125.

46. Albert E. Haase, "How to Remove Advertising as the Philanthropist of Broadcasting," *Printers' Ink*, 5 March 1925, 140.

47. Albert E. Haase, "Should Advertising Shoulder the Cost of Radio Broadcasting?," *Printers' Ink*, 5 February 1925, 2; "How to Remove Advertising," 140.

48. McChesney, *Telecommunications*, 4.

49. Susan Smulyan, *Selling Radio: The Commercialization of American Broadcasting, 1920–1934* (Washington, D.C., 1994), 3–4.

50. Hilmes, *Radio Voices*, xvii.

51. For an exploration of the social world of the wireless amateurs, see Susan J. Douglas, *Inventing American Broadcasting: 1899–1922* (Baltimore, Md., 1987), 187–215.

52. "NAWA Monthly Service Bulletin," *The Wireless Age* 2 (February 1922): 41; Clinton B. DeSoto, *Two Hundred Meters and Down: The Story of Amateur Radio* (West Hartford, Conn., 1936), 75.

53. For a concise history of the early BBC, see R. H. Coase, *British Broadcasting: A Study in Monopoly* (Cambridge, Mass.,1950).

*Chapter 2*

1. William Ellis of Oak Park, Illinois, to Herbert Hoover, U.S. Commerce Secretary, Washington, D.C., 27 December 1924, WBCN Station File, Correspondence Relating to Applications for Broadcast Licenses, 1928–32, Records of the Federal Communications Commission, Record Group 173, National Archives II, College Park, Maryland (hereafter cited as Radio Division Correspondence). An earlier version of this chapter was published as "Serving the Masses, Not the Classes: Station WHN, Pioneer of Commercial Broadcasting in the 1920s," in *The Journal of Radio Studies* 6 (winter 1999): 81–100.

2. F. William Boettcher, "Memories," typewritten manuscript, 1980, Schubel Papers. The Schubel Papers are property of the *Times Newsweekly*, Ridgewood, New York.

3. Ibid.

4. WHN Studio Log for May 1922 through February 1923, Schubel Papers.

5. I am extremely grateful to Maureen Walthers, editor and publisher of the *Times Newsweekly*, for preserving these papers and for letting me borrow them.

6. "Wireless Advertising," n.d., Schubel Papers.

7. Letter of contract between Williamsburgh Savings Bank and Associated Broadcasters, 8 November 1922, Schubel Papers.

8. Nils T. Granlund, with Sid Feder and Ralph Hancock, *Blondes, Brunettes, and Bullets* (New York, 1957), 86–89.

9. Ibid.

10. Ibid.

11. Robert W. Snyder, *Voice of the City: Vaudeville and Popular Culture in New York* (New York, 1989), 37, 93–97.

12. Granlund, *Blondes*, 89.

13. "Radio's Possibilities Draw Showmen's Notice through Circulation," *Clipper*, 3 August 1923, 3, 14; "Loew's Radio Sort of Freaky," ibid., 2 November 1923, 21; "WHN up to 500 Watts," ibid., 24 August 1923, 17; unidentified newspaper clippings, 5 August through 9 August 1923, WHN Scrapbook, Schubel Papers. George Schubel kept a scrapbook of newspaper clippings about WHN. Many of these clippings are sparsely identified; I will identify them in accordance with Schubel's handwritten notations.

14. Granlund, *Blondes*, 90, 92; "NTG's Medal," *Variety*, 1 October 1924, 27; "Wise Cracks Draw, Granlund Has Daily Audience Back Stage at Studio," ibid., 17 August 1923, 13; "WHN's Special Guard," *Clipper*, 6 March 1924, 12.

15. Raymond Francis Yates, "The Perfect Announcer: Where Is He?," *Popular Radio* 9 (January 1926): 176; Thomas J. Stephens, "Popularity of Broadcasting Station Depends on Personality of Announcer," *New York Herald Tribune Radio Magazine*, 2 March 1927, 7; Carl Dreher, "The High and Mighty Place of the Announcer," *Radio Broadcast* 8 (January 1926): 181.

16. "Abel's Comment," *Clipper*, 24 April 1924, 16

17. "Last Night on the Radio—by Pioneer," *New York Herald Tribune* (hereaf-

ter cited as "Pioneer"), 6 July 1925, 9. C. A. Hughes's sketch does not identify a station or announcer by name, but the inclusion of NTG's signature phrases "Oh boy!" and "Let 'er go!" identify the object of the parody as Granlund.

18. "Keep Radio Clean," *Radio Dealer* 2 (September 1923): 56.

19. "Abel's Comment, "Fans Prefer Humorous Announcing System," *Clipper,* 7 September 1923, 21; "Loew Studio Bans Spice," ibid., 25 January 1924, 25; "Stay-at-Homes Find Radio's Value," ibid., 3 April 1924, 14.

20. Raymond Francis Yates, "Rating the Announcers," *Popular Radio* 8 (August 1925): 181.

21. Felix, *Using Radio,* 173.

22. "Advertising on the Radio," *Variety,* 18 March 1925, 41.

23. "WHN, Target of WEAF in Air Battle, Is Station of Pep," *Jersey Journal,* 12 March 1924, WHN Scrapbook, Schubel Papers.

24. Goldman, "N.T.G. Speaking," *The Wireless Age* 12 (May 1925): 5.

25. William K. Randle, "Payola," *American Speech* 36 (May 1961): 105–6. On preelectronic payola see David Ewen, *The Life and Death of Tin Pan Alley* (New York, 1964); and Kerry Segrave, *Payola in the Music Industry: A History, 1880–1991* (Jefferson, N.C., 1994).

26. Harry Richman, with Richard Gehman, *A Hell of a Life* (New York, 1966), 97–98.

27. "Radio's Chance in Newspaper Strike," *Clipper,* 21 September 1923, 20; "Beaucoup Dance Music on Radio Programs," *Variety,* 4 February 1925, 35.

28. "Fair Evening before Receiving Set, Listening to Pluggers and Others," *Clipper,* 9 November 1923, 21. See also "'Song Plugging' Predominates in Radio's Night Concerts," ibid., 2 November 1923, 21; "Much Ether Band Music Along with Song Pluggers," ibid., 23 November 1923, 20.

29. "Radio 'Plugging' and Suggestions," *Clipper,* 11 January 1924, 20; "Gimbel's New Station to Equal City's Best; Song Pluggers Out," *Variety,* 15 October 1924, 37; "Singers Tied Up to Single Music Publishers Barred From WEAF or WJZ," ibid., 31 August 1927, 55; "'Lifting' on Radio," ibid., 3 September 1924, 36. "August 1927, 55; "'Lifting' On Radio," ibid., 3 September 1924, 36.

30. "WOR, Bamberger Station, Licenses from Music Men," *Clipper,* 7 September 1923, 21; "Radio 'Plugging' and Suggestions," ibid., 11 January 1924, 20.

31. "Watch Out for Program Directors," *Radio Digest,* 23 February 1924, 5.

32. "Radio Plug Worth More than Royalties, Firm Quits Society," *Clipper,* 21 December 1923, 20; "Value of Radio as Music Plug," ibid., 7 December 1923, 20; "Music Firm Wants to Rejoin Society Ranks," ibid., 24 April 1924, 16; "American Society's Binding Pact Stops Publishers from Releasing," *Clipper,* 15 February 1924, 12; "Broadcasting Subterfuge Explosion," ibid., 20 March 1924, 12; "Say Music Men Use Dummies for Radio," ibid., 27 March 1924, 19; "Weekly Comment by Abel," ibid., 10 April 1924, 14; "Waterson, Berlin & Snyder Suing American Society, Alleges Music Monopoly," ibid., 13; "Music Angle on Radio Song-Plugging," ibid., 24 April 1924, 15.

33. Duncan MacDougald Jr., "The Popular Music Industry," in Paul Lazarsfeld and Frank Stanton, eds., *Radio Research 1941* (New York, 1941), 71–72; John Gray Peatman, "Radio and Popular Music," in Paul Lazarsfeld and Frank Stanton, eds., *Radio Research 1942* (New York, 1942), 363–64.

34. "Cabarets Bid for Plug Via Radio Music," *Clipper,* 14 September 1923, 21; "WHN Charges $50 a Week to Cabarets," ibid., 6 May 1924, 18.

35. "Kidding Radio," *Clipper,* 29 February 1924, 12.

36. "Radio's Advertising Stunt," *Variety*, 19 November 1924, 32.

37. Goldman, "N.T.G. Speaking"; "Loew's Radio Charging All Cabarets," *Clipper*, 14 June 1924, 16; "Advertising on the Radio," *Variety*, 18 March 1925, 41; "Same Old Stuff—Radio Plugs," ibid., 2 December 1925, 48.

38. Lewis A. Erenberg, *Steppin' Out: New York Nightlife and the Transformation of American Culture, 1890–1930* (Chicago, 1981).

39. "Daily Broadcast Programs," *New York Herald Tribune Radio Magazine*, 1923–26; "Cabarets Bid for Plug Via Radio," *Clipper*, 14 September 1923, 21; "Suggestions for Henderson's Orchestra," ibid.; "Plugging and Advertising Mainly on Radio Evenings," ibid., 15 February 1925, 12; " 'One Helluva Night' Thursday," *Variety*, 24 December 1924, 35; "Pioneer," 7 October 1924, 15.

40. Granlund, *Blondes*, 139.

41. Richman, *Hell*, 103–8; "N.T.G. on Radio for 1-Nighters," *Variety*, 4 March 1925, 40.

42. Granlund, *Blondes*, 100–101.

43. "Giant Battery of Stills Bared by Own Radio," *New York Herald Tribune*, 11 April 1926, 21; Janet A. Dublon, "Million Dollar Rum Ring," *Radio Digest*, 23 (December 1930):14–18, 120; "Stations Give Bootleggers Aid," *Radio World*, 23 May 1931, 17; "W5NE Ousted for Aiding in Rum Running," ibid.; "Seize Three Bootleg Transmitters, 7 Men," *Radio World*, 9 August 1930, 21; Harry Mack, "Radio Rackets," *Radio Digest* 23 (April 1930): 112; Radio and Rum," *Variety*, 4 March 1925, 40.

44. "Pioneer," 23 March 1924, 11; ibid., 5 March 1925, 17; "Before Long They Will Protest," *New York Times*, 8 October 1924, 18.

45. "Pioneer," 28 February 1925, 15; "1st Squawk on Radio Concert," *Variety*, 4 March 1925, 1, 6.

46. E. L. Harrison, New York, to Department of Commerce Radio Division, Washington, D.C., 5 March 1925, WHN Station File, Radio Division Correspondence.

47. James A. Cruikshank, New York, to the Office of Herbert Hoover, Secretary of Commerce, 10 March 1925, WHN Station File, Radio Division Correspondence.

48. Justice Joseph Callahan, City Court of New York City Hall, to the Office of Herbert Hoover, Secretary of Commerce, 5 February 1925, WHN Station File; Radio Division Correspondence.

49. George Chauncey, *Gay New York: Gender, Urban Culture, and the Making of the Gay Male World* (New York, 1994), 257–58, 309–21.

50. Arthur Batchellor, New York City Radio Supervisor, to the Office of the Commissioner of Navigation, 21 April 1925, WHN Station File, Radio Division Correspondence.

51. William Peck Banning, *Commercial Broadcasting Pioneer: The WEAF Experiment, 1922–1926* (Cambridge, Mass., 1946), 56.

52. Quoted in "Mistake to Broadcast Advertising," *The Radio Dealer* 1 (November 1922): 55.

53. Banning, *Commercial Broadcasting Pioneer*, 153.

54. Gleason Archer, *History of Radio to 1926* (New York, 1938), 321; Banning, *Commercial Broadcasting Pioneer*, 112–13.

55. " 'Lifting' on Radio Comes Up in Evening's Review of the Air," *Variety*, 3 September 1924, 36.

56. Deems Taylor, "Music," in Harold E. Stearns, ed., *Civilization in the United States* (London, 1922), 212–13; "Bringing the Classics to Motion Picture Audi-

ences," *Musical America*, 23 June 1923, 5; "Roxy Denounced," *Variety*, 1 April 1925, 40; Kingsley Welles, "The Listener's Point of View," *Radio Broadcast* 7 (October 1925): 758; "The Music That Is In Every Man," *The Etude* 45 (December 1927): 903–4.

57. "The March of Radio," *Radio Broadcast* 9 (October 1926): 475.

58. "Radio 'Monopoly' Position Outlined in New York Area," *Clipper*, 13 March 1924, 12.

59. "WHN, Target of WEAF in Air War, Is Station of Pep," *Jersey Journal*, 13 March 1924, WHN Scrapbook, Schubel Papers.

60. F. H. Keefe, Newburgh, N.Y., to George Schubel, 19 July 1922, Schubel Papers.

61. T. B. Hatfield, Indianapolis, to George Schubel, 22 June 1922, Schubel Papers.

62. Schubel to Caldwell, n.d., Schubel Papers.

63. William Harkness, "Reminiscences," 1951, Radio Pioneers Project, Columbia Oral History Collection, Columbia University, New York, N.Y.; "Radio Suit Seeks to Close Up WHN," *New York Herald*, 6 March 1924, WHN Scrapbook; "Loew Station Under Attack," *New York American*, 6 March 1924, WHN Scrapbook; "WEAF Sues to Silence Stations," *Evening Journal*, 6 March 1924, WHN Scrapbook; "Big Radio Society Joins in Battle against AT&T," newspaper clipping marked "World," n.d., WHN Scrapbook; Untitled typewritten radio script, n.d., Schubel Papers.

64. "AT&T's Air Grab Has Radio Fans Gasping Angrily," newspaper clipping marked "News," 6 March 1924, WHN Scrapbook; untitled typewritten radio script, n.d.; "Series III: Shall the Public Pay for Listening?," typewritten radio script, n.d., Schubel Papers.

65. "Radio Battle in Air over Broadcasting Monopoly Planned," *Brooklyn Eagle*, 7 March 1924, WHN Scrapbook; "War Dept. Opposes Radio Control Bill," ibid., Schubel Papers

66. "Whalen Asks U.S. Sift Radio 'Trust' He Lays to AT&T," unidentified newspaper clipping, 3 March 1924, WHN Scrapbook; "Broadcasters Dodge Patent Issue in Suit," *New York Herald Tribune*, 12 March 1924, WHN Scrapbook, Schubel Papers.

67. "Radio Battle in Air"; "Number One Release for Broadcast or Publication from WHN Station," handwritten script, n.d., Schubel Papers.

68. "Furniture on Installments," *Clipper*, 29 February 1924, 12; "Unusual Radio Features," ibid., 13 March 1924, 13.

69. "Protest Suit of WEAF," *Evening Journal*, n.d., WHN Scrapbook; "Public's Cash for Radio War," *New York American*, 14 March 1924, WHN Scrapbook, Schubel Papers; Harkness, "Reminiscences."

70. "Public's Cash for Radio War; "Protest Suit of WEAF," *Evening Journal*, n.d., WHN Scrapbook, Schubel Papers.

71. "Committee Postpones Raising Fund," *New York Herald Tribune*, 13 March 1924, WHN Scrapbook, Schubel Papers.

72. "Series III: Shall the Public Pay for Listening?," typewritten radio script, n.d., Schubel Papers.

73. "Committee Postpones," ibid.

74. "WHN Will Not Settle Suit on Radio Patents," newspaper clipping marked "World," 14 March 1924, WHN Scrapbook, Schubel Papers, "Points Regarding Question Raised by American Telephone & Telegraph Co.," typewritten manuscript, n.d., Schubel Papers.

75. "Radio Combine Grasps at City," *New York Herald Tribune*, 12 March 1924, WHN Scrapbook; "Will the City Tackle WEAF?," *Brooklyn Eagle*, 8 March 1924, WHN Scrapbook; "Whalen Bobs Up for Air in Radio Fight with AT&T," newspaper clipping marked "News," 8 March 1924, WHN Scrapbook; "Whalen Attacks AT&T; Demands Federal Probe," *Brooklyn Eagle*, 6 March 1924, WHN Scrapbook; "Whalen Asks U.S. Investigate AT&T," unidentified newspaper clipping, n.d., WHN Scrapbook, Schubel Papers.

76. Unidentified newspaper clipping, headline missing, n.d., WHN Scrapbook, Schubel Papers.

77. "City's Radio Station Ready in Convention Week, Says Whalen," newspaper clipping marked "Union," 16 March 1924, WHN Scrapbook, Schubel Papers; Banning, *Commercial Broadcasting Pioneer*, 213.

78. "Outlaw Stations to Be Closed," *Radio Broadcast* 5 (July 1924): 132.

79. "WHN Charges $50 a Week to Cabarets," *Clipper*, 8 May 1924, 14.

80. Banning, *Commercial Broadcasting Pioneer*, 212, 214.

81. "See AT&T Yielding to Radio 'Grab' Protests," *Brooklyn Eagle*, 12 March 1924, WHN Scrapbook, Schubel Papers.

82. "Pioneer," 23 September 1924, 11; ibid., 28 October 1924, 13; ibid., 5 May 1925, 13; ibid., 13 November 1925, 13; "Two at Radio," *Variety*, 1 October 1924, 27; "Radio Advertising's Cost," ibid., 25 March 1925, 40; "Ads on Radio— Little Else," ibid., 9 September 1925, 37.

83. "Pioneer," 10 November 1925, 17; ibid., 13 November 1925, 13; "Committees Report to the Radio Conference," *New York Herald Tribune Radio Magazine*, 15 November 1925, 7.

84. "The Month in Radio," *Radio Broadcast* 7 (July 1925): 341.

85. "Radio Advertising's Cost," *Variety*, 25 March 1925, 40.

86. Associated Broadcasters Incorporated pamphlet, date-stamped 25 February 1925, WMCA Station File, Radio Division Correspondence.

87. "New 'Advertising' Radio Station is WMCA," *Variety*, 18 February 1925, 35; Stephen L. Coles, "Bloops and Static," *New York Herald Tribune Radio Magazine*, 1 March 1925, 17; "Pioneer," 15 April 1926, 17; ibid., 10 March 1926, 19.

88. Granlund, *Blondes*, 90; J .P. White, Brooklyn, N.Y., to Department of Commerce, 6 May 1927, WBBC Station File, Radio Division Correspondence; Arthur E. Morris, New York, N.Y., to Federal Radio Commission, 26 June 1929, WKBQ Station File, Radio Division Correspondence; Felix, *Using Radio*, 103.

89. Listener letters, WBCN Station File, Radio Division Correspondence; "Radio Advertising's Cost," *Variety*, 25 March 1925, 40.

90. "Bomb Damages Radio and Newspaper Plant," *Washington Post*, 5 August 1924, WBCN Station File, Radio Division Correspondence.

91. "The Yes and No Man," *Popular Radio* 10 (September 1926): 458; John Wallace, "The Listener's Point of View," *Radio Broadcast* 8 (March 1926): 579; "Broadcast Miscellany," ibid., September 1926, 393.

92. Richard Crabb, *Radio's Beautiful Day* (Aberdeen, S.D., 1983), 122; *Who's Who in Radio* (Chicago, 1925), 7.

93. Wallace, "Listener's Point of View," (March 1926): 579; "Chicago Broadcasters Ready to Yield on Music License," *Clipper*, 21 December 1923, 20; "Radio Advertising's Cost," *Variety*, 25 March 1925, 40; "$1 Radio Show Not Worth It," ibid., 29 April 1925, 38.

94. John Wallace, "The Listener's Point of View," *Radio Broadcast* 10 (February 1927): 375; ibid. (May 1927): 31; "Chicago's New Station," *Variety*, 11 February 1925, 33; William Howland Kenney, *Chicago Jazz: A Cultural History* (New York, 1993), 156.

95. "Radio Advertising's Cost," *Variety*, 25 March 1925, 40; "In Re: WKBI," Docket no. 102, Docketed Case Files of the Federal Communications Commission, Record Group 173, National Archives II, College Park, Maryland (hereafter cited as FRC Dockets).

96. Clippings from *Minneapolis Journal*, October–November 1925, WDGY Station File, Radio Division Correspondence.

97. Clippings from the *Rochester Times-Union*, March 1927, WOKO Station File, Box 468, Radio Division Correspondence.

98. Felix, *Using Radio*, 84; Mrs. H. C. Devraux, Detroit, to Radio Division, 20 January 1926, WXYZ Station File, Radio Division Correspondence.

99. Postcard circular, n.d., KWKC Station File, Radio Division Correspondence.

100. H. F. Engle, Pittsburgh, to Radio Division, 25 May 1927, WJAS Station File, Radio Division Correspondence.

101. R. E. Edwards, Miami, to Herbert Hoover, Secretary of Commerce, 8 January 1926, WQAM Station File, Radio Division Correspondence.

102. J. M. Harsch, Cincinnati, to Herbert Hoover, Secretary of Commerce, 12 February 1925, Hugh W. Cobbert, Cincinnati, to Radio Division, 13 February 1925, WLW Station File, Radio Division Correspondence.

103. Notarized petition of Mrs. J. G. Schreiner, St. Louis, Mo., 10 February 1931, 2; assorted letters of listener grievance, WIL Station File, Radio Division Correspondence.

104. KXA Station File; KXL Station File;WAAT Station File; WADC Station File; WBMS Station File; WKBG Station File; WMAK Station File; Listener correspondence, 1924–28, Radio Division Correspondence.

*Chapter 3*

1. "John Warren Erb Urges Curb on Trashy Radio Music," *The Musician* 32 (October 1927): 35.

2. J. B. Schuyler, "Tune in on WHAP!," *The Country Editor* (Bogota, N.J.), January 1926, WFAB Station File, Radio Division Correspondence. Although these words appeared under the byline of the *Country Editor*'s editor, J. B. Schuyler, I am certain that their real author was WHAP announcer Franklin Ford, who likely paid Schuyler to insert them in his paper. I base this judgment on familiarity with Ford's prose style. The clincher is the palpable disgust associated with the word "lips," a recurrent trope in Ford's writing.

3. "WHAP, New York City's Latest Broadcaster, to Have Formal Opening Tomorrow," *New York Herald Tribune Radio Magazine*, 29 November 1925, 4–5.

4. "New Radio Station Opens," *New York Times*, 1 December 1925, sec. 8, p. 2.

5. Intelligence gathered by agents of the Christian Science Mother Church indicates that WHAP's physical plant cost seventy-five-thousand dollars, a figure that placed the station among the top 2 percent of contemporary stations for initial capital outlay. See Memorandum, Mr. Munro to Christian Science Board, n.d.; anonymous memorandum to Christian Science Board, 8 February 1926, WHAP File, Christian Science Historical Archive, Boston, Mass.

6. "Pioneer," 4 December 1925, 24.

7. "WHAP, New York City's Latest Broadcaster," 12.

8. "Symphonic Sextet, Weekly Feature, to Give Program," *New York Herald Tribune Radio Magazine*, 27 December 1925, 11.

9. "Radio Has Advanced Civilization," *New York Herald Tribune*, 28 March 1926, 29.

10. "Pioneer," 7 January 1926, 19; ibid., 4 May 1926, 19; ibid., 3 December 1925, 19.

11. C. P. Smith to Christian Science Board of Directors, 18 December 1925, WHAP File, Christian Science Historical Archive, Boston, Mass.

12. "Pioneer," 6 March 1926, 11; ibid., 20 May 1926, 19; ibid., 9 March 1926, 20; ibid., 17 April 1926, 14; ibid., 13 May 1926, 17; ibid., 2 September 1926, 15; ibid., 3 September 1926, 13; ibid., 4 January 1927, 13.

13. "Station WHAP to Move," *New York Herald Tribune*, 28 March 1926, WHAP File, Christian Science Historical Archive, Boston, Mass.; "New Location for Station WHAP's Studios, Offices," *New York Times*, 28 March 1926, 29.

14. On Stetson's life and career in Christian Science, see Alton K. Swihart, *Since Mrs. Eddy* (New York,1925). Other biographical sources include Sarah Gardner Cunningham, "A New Order: Augusta Stetson and the Origins of Christian Science in New York, 1886–1910" (Ph.D. diss., Union Theological Seminary, 1994); Edwin Dakin, *Mrs. Eddy: The Biography of a Virginal Mind* (New York,1929); James B.P. Hyndman, *New York City Christian Science Institute, Augusta Stetson, C.S.D., Principal: Historical Review, 1891 to 1928* (Washington, D.C., 1928).

15. Swihart, *Since Mrs. Eddy*, 125–32, 138–41.

16. Many of Stetson's newspaper announcements can be found in her *Sermons Which Spiritually Interpret the Scriptures and Other Writings on Christian Science* (New York, 1924).

17. Augusta E. Stetson, *Correspondence with a Jewish Leader Regarding the Broadcasting Policy of Radio Station WHAP* (New York, 1927), 19.

18. Swihart, *Since Mrs. Eddy*, 140–41.

19. "The *American Standard*'s Program for America," *American Standard*, 1 November 1924, 4.

20. Swihart, *Since Mrs. Eddy*, 168–70; C. P Smith, New York, to Christian Science Board of Directors, 19 May 1924, WHAP File, Christian Science Historical Archive, Boston, Mass.

21. "A Letter from the Editor to Mrs. Stetson, and Her Reply," *American Standard*, 15 April 1924, 16–17.

22. "Radio Uncovering Jesuit Hypnotic Methods," *American Standard*, 1 January 1925, 304–05; "Secret Hypnotism by the Jesuits," ibid., 1 November 1924, 5–7; "Jesuit Hypnotism of Protestants Thwarted," ibid., 1 May 1925, 197–98.

23. Swihart, *Since Mrs. Eddy*, 154–59; "Mrs. Stetson Discusses Her Musical Beliefs," *Musical America*, 14 July 1917, 11–12.

24. Stetson, *Sermons*, 1123.

25. "Mrs. Stetson Discusses Her Musical Beliefs," 11. In disallowing opera as high culture, Stetson was perpetuating a position once standard among purist elements of the nineteenth-century concert-going elite, who disdained opera's theatrical and visual dimension as vulgar distractions incommensurable with a truly spiritual listening experience, and who condemned the narrative content of operatic libretti as implausible and frequently immoral; Lawrence Levine, *Highbrow/Lowbrow: The Emergence of Cultural Hierarchy in America* (Cambridge, Mass., 1990), 220.

26. "John Warren Erb Urges Curb," 35.

27. Vida Milholland, "The Love of God," typewritten radio script delivered from WHAP, 1 December 1926, Christian Science Collection, Burke Library, Union Theological Seminary, New York City.

28. U.S. Department of Justice FOIPA Search No. 410965/190-HQ 1270756; documents in possession of the author; "War Records: Final Notice," Franklin Ford Alumnus File, Princeton University Archives, Mudd Library, Princeton, N.J.

29. Franklin Ford, *Tammany Hall's Roman Catholic Greeting to Colonel Lindbergh* (New York, 1927), 4–7.

30. "Pioneer," 3 August 1926, 13; ibid., 13 August 1926, 13; "Actor to Sue for Million," *New York Herald Tribune*, 25 March 1927, 20.

31. "Pioneer," 27 July 1926, 15; ibid., 9 January 1927, sec. 9, p. 2; listener letters, WFAB Station File, Radio Division Correspondence; "Dickstein Assails WHAP," *New York Times*, 1 March 1927, 28; "The March of Radio," *Radio Broadcast* 11 (August 1927): 205.

32. "Church Takes Issue with Mrs. Stetson," *New York Times*, 2 August 1927, 13; Vida Milholland, "Freedom Under God," typewritten radio script delivered from WHAP, 7 July 1926, Christian Science Collection, vol. 18, Burke Library, Union Theological Seminary, New York City.

33. Augusta Stetson to the Staff of WHAP, 27 May 1927, Christian Science Collection, vol. 21, Burke Library, Union Theological Seminary, New York City.

34. "Deny Wavelength to WHAP," *New York Times*, 18 August 1927, 18.

35. "Tells of Fighting Smith by Radio," *New York Times*, 23 June 1927, 11; "Plan Radio Drive on Smith," ibid., 25 October 1927, 8; "WHAP to Attack Smith," ibid., 25 August 1928, 18.

36. "Mrs. Stetson Quits Radio," *New York Times*, 30 August 1928, 14.

37. "In Re: Application of WOAX, Preliminary Statement and the Issues," Docket No. 1042, FRC Dockets.

38. Ted Husing, *Ten Years before the Mike* (New York, 1935), 193; Kathleen J. Smith, Counselor at Law, Park Avenue, New York, to Arthur Batchellor, U.S. Radio Supervisor, 5 March 1929, WLTH Station File, Radio Division Correspondence.

39. Circular letter, Franklin Ford, 7 September 1930, Christian Science Collection, vol. 19, Burke Library, Union Theological Seminary, New York.

40. "The Attack on WHAP," *American Standard* 4 (December 1931): 2.

41. Domenico Trombetta, *Pervertimento: L'Antifascismo di Carlo Fama* (New York, 1931), 87; "Fama Fights Censorship," *New York Telegram*, November 1931, in ACLU Papers, vol. 511, 192, Mudd Library, Princeton University.

42. Hatcher Hughes to FRC, 11 November 1931, ACLU Papers, vol. 511, 124–27, Mudd Library, Princeton University.

43. FRC Secretary James Baldwin to Hatcher Hughes, 17 November 1931, ACLU Papers, vol. 511, 127, Mudd Library, Princeton University.

44. Franklin Ford to Radio Division, 1 March 1932, WFAB Station File, Radio Division Correspondence.

45. Franklin Ford, *St. Peter Not the Founder of Romanism* (New York, 1926), back jacket copy; "The Catholic Church and the Radio," *Bob Shuler's Magazine* 12 (March 1933): 615.

46. *The 1913 Bull* 49 (1952), Princeton University Archives, Mudd Library, Princeton, N.J.

*Chapter 4*

1. C. H. W., Fulton, Arkansas, "People Voice Opinions," *Radio Digest*, 15 January 1927, 28.

2. C. Vincent, Vincent Grain Company, Omaha, Nebraska, to Radio Division, 23 March 1925, WAAW Station File, Radio Division Correspondence.

3. Richard Hofstader, *The Age of Reform* (New York, 1955 ), 175.

4. On contemporary hostilities between city and countryside, see William E. Leuchtenberg, *The Perils of Prosperity, 1914–1932*, 2nd ed. (Chicago, 1993); Don Kirschner, *City and Country: Rural Responses to Urbanization in the 1920s* (Westport, Conn., 1970).

5. "Radio and Farm Life," *The Literary Digest*, 23 September 1922, 28.

6. Mrs. Christine Frederick, "Exit the Jonas Hayseed of 1880," *The Wireless Age* 12 (November 1924): 34–35, 60.

7. William A. Hurd, "Harvest Time on the Air," *The Wireless Age* 12 (November 1924): 20.

8. John Wallace, "What the Farmer Listens To," *Radio Broadcast* 11 (August 1926): 316–17. The gist of the National Farm Radio Council survey was anticipated by the private researches of Elwood Washington, a radio fan who asked hundreds of farmers about their listening preferences while on an extended tour of the rural Midwest and South in 1924. "The barn dances by WLS were liked very well," Washington reported in a letter to *Radio News*, "although their orchestra music was criticized and not well liked. . . . The two things most condemned were soprano solos and technical lectures. The first would nearly always cause a listener to tune it out. . . . Jazz music was almost universally condemned. Old songs were the favorites" ("What the Rurals Like," *Radio News* 6 [ January 1925]: 1183).

9. Richard A. Petersen, *Creating Country Music: Fabricating Authenticity* (Chicago, 1997), passim.

10. James F. Evans, *Prairie Farmer and WLS: The Burridge D. Butler Years* (Chicago, 1969), 214–16; Michael Kammen, *The Lively Arts: Gilbert Seldes and the Transformation of Cultural Criticism in the United States* (New York, 1996), 251; Charles. K. Wolfe, *A Good-Natured Riot: The Birth of the Grand Ole Oprey* (Nashville, Tenn., 1999), 9.

11. Alfred Goldsmith and Austin Lescarboura, *This Thing Called Broadcasting* (New York, 1930), 76–77.

12. The oft-noted affection of the rural audience for Hawaiian music is an interesting enigma. From an urban perspective, Hawaiian pop clearly stood for some exotic vision of grass-skirted hedonism, a vision scarcely in tune with the predominant rural ethos. Conceivably, rural fans of Hawaiian music attached their own, separate set of meanings to it. It is worth noting that the Hawaiian pop genre bore certain tonal and instrumental similarities to rural folk music. The Hawaiian steel guitar, for example, shares its glissando sound with the fiddle and the bottleneck guitar, and by the 1930s it had become more or less indigenized.

13. Orson Stiles to Morris Sheppard, Nebraska senator, 10 November 1924, WOW Station File, Radio Division Correspondence.

14. Ernest F. Andrews Jr., "The Development of Amplitude Modulation Radio Broadcasting Stations in Iowa: A Selective History" (Ph.D. diss., State University of Iowa, 1956), 339.

15. W. W. Baker, "Friendly Philosophy of Henry Field Built on Garden Seeds and Radio," *Kansas City Times*, 24 October 1949, 33.

16. John M. Henry, "A Faith That Moves Merchandise," *The Nation's Business* 30 (April 1930 [offprint]), 3, KFNF Station File, Radio Division Correspondence.

17. Ibid., 3; Francis St. Austell, "Direct Selling by Radio," *Radio Broadcast* 11 (May 1928): 58; Kansas City *Better Business Bulletin*, 7 February 1927, KFNF Station File; Radio Division Correspondence.

18. Henry, "Faith," 3; "Studio and Broadcasting Station KFNF, The Friendly Farmer Station," Souvenir Program, 1926; "Advance Program Schedule of KFNF," 1927, KFNF Station File, Radio Division Correspondence.

19. "Midwest to Henry Field," *Radio Digest* 24 (June 1930): 103–4.

20. Jacob Rasmussen to Henry Field, 12 December 1925, KFNF Station File, Radio Division Correspondence.

21. "In Re: Application of Station KMA," 11 August 1927, sec. 3, p. 2, Docket 49a, FRC Dockets.

22. Andrews, "Development," 351.

23. "In Re: Application of Station KMA," sec. 3, p. 16.

24. "Communications," *Radio Broadcast* 11 (July 1927): 162.

25. "Shenandoah Stations Win Radio Popularity Contest," *Omaha Sunday World-Herald*, 13 March 1927, Docket 499, FRC Dockets.

26. Henry, "Faith," 2–3.

27. "Unpopular Broadcasting Stations," *Radio Broadcast* 11 (September 1927): 269; "Is Direct Advertising a Service?" ibid. (November 1927): 16; St. Austell, "Direct Selling," 58–60.

28. C. E. Crow to Secretary of Commerce Herbert Hoover, 27 January 1927, KFNF Station File, Radio Division Correspondence.

29. Andrews, "Development," 345.

30. Henry, "Faith," 3.

31. Henry Field to Herbert Hoover, 23 November 1925, KFNF Station File, Radio Division Correspondence.

32. In Re Application of Station KMA," 11 August 1927, sec. 3, p. 18.

33. "Voice of the Listener," *Radio Digest*, 1 July 1927, 11.

34. Ibid., 1 May 1927, 18.

35. Ibid., 1 March 1927, 29.

36. Ibid., 1 May 1927, 18.

37. Henry, "Faith," 1.

38. *Second Annual Report of the Federal Radio Commission* (Washington, D.C., 1928), 168–69.

39. St. Austell, "Direct Selling," 59.

40. D. J. Cowden to Henry Field, 15 December 1925, KFNF Station File, Radio Division Correspondence.

41. Gerald Carson, *The Roguish World of Doctor Brinkley* (New York, 1960), 17–18.

42. Carroll D. Clark, "Dr. John R. Brinkley: A Case Study in Collective Behavior," *Kansas Journal of Sociology* 2 (spring 1966): 58.

43. In Re: Application of KFKB," 11 June 1930, Docket Case File 835, 27–29, FRC Dockets.

44. Ansel Harlan Resler, "The Impact of John R. Brinkley on Broadcasting in the United States" (Ph.D diss., Northwestern University,1958), 91.

45. Clement Wood (Alvin G. Winston), *The Throttle: A Fact Story of Norman Baker* (Muscatine, Iowa, 1934), 98.

46. Norman Baker, "Gentlemen," circular letter, 11 April 1927, WOC Station File, Radio Division Correspondence.

47. Wood, *Throttle*, 127.

48. "Report of Investigation of Radio Station KTNT," 25 August 1930, Docket 83A, pp. 7–8, FRC Dockets.

49. "Ousted Station Gets Injunction," *Radio World,* 5 July 1930, 17.
50. Clement Wood, *The Life of a Man* (Kansas City, Mo., 1935), 273.
51. W. G. Clugston, *Rascals in Democracy* (New York, 1940), 157–58.
52. Duke Bettelton "The Listener's Voice," *Radio Digest* 23 (November 1929): 73.

*Chapter 5*

1. Louis MacCabe, "Report on KWKH," 3 February 1928, p. 3, KWKH Station File, Radio Division Correspondence.
2. Affidavit of M. R. Hueber, 12 February 1929; affidavit of Marietta Williams, 17 February 1929, Docket 356, FRC Dockets.
3. Louis McCabe, "Abstracts from broadcast programs of Station KWKH," 19 February 1928, p. 2, KWKH Station File, Radio Division Correspondence.
4. William K. Henderson to Commissioner of Navigation D. B. Carson, Washington, D.C., 3 February 1926, KWKH Station File, Radio Division Correspondence; Lillian Jones Hall, "A Historical Study of Programming Techniques and Practices of Radio Station KWKH, Shreveport, Louisiana: 1922–1950" (Ph.D. diss., Louisiana State University, 1959), 34–40.
5. William K. Henderson to Commissioner of Navigation D. B. Carson, Washington, D.C., 17 March 1925, KWKH Station File, Radio Division Correspondence.
6. William K. Henderson to U.S. Senator Joseph E. Ransdell, Washington, D.C., 18 January 1926, KWKH Station File, Radio Division Correspondence.
7. "KWKH Has Real Personality," *Radio Digest* 23 ( October 1929): 60.
8. A recording of this song is preserved on *Byways of Jazz,* an LP anthology of jazz rarities from the 1920s released in the 1960s on the Origin Jazz Library label.
9. Supervisor of Radio S. W. Edwards to Radio Division, 7 November 1928, KWKH Station File, Radio Division Correspondence.
10. "KWKH Has Real Personality," 60.
11. Supervisor of Radio O. R. Redfern to Radio Division, 16 September 1927; "Observation of KWKH's Transmission," 10 January 1930, pp. 3–4, 6, KWKH Station File, Radio Division Correspondence.
12. Ibid.
13. Affidavit of Louis Block, Davenport, Iowa, 17 November 1929, Docket 356, FRC Dockets.
14. Ibid.; Radio Supervisor Theodore G. Deiler to Radio Division, 19 February 1928, KWKH Station File, Radio Division Correspondence; affidavit of Chas. S. Fex, Natchez County, Texas, 15 February 1929, Docket 356, FRC Dockets.
15. Radio Supervisor Theodore G. Deiler to Radio Division, 19 February 1928, KWKH Station File, Radio Division Correspondence.
16. "Directory of the Musical Library, KWKH" (n.d.), Docket 65a, FRC Dockets; "KWKH Has Real Personality," 60; Hall, "Historical Study," 46; Gerald D. Bettelon, "Voice of the Listener," *Radio Digest* 25 ( July 1930): 70.
17. Radio Supervisor Louis McCabe to Radio Division, 3 February 1928, p. 2, 8 February 1928, p. 2, KWKH Station File, Radio Division Correspondence; Hall, "Historical Study," 64–65.
18. "Transmission of KWKH, Shreveport," 6 January 1929, KWKH Station File, Radio Division Correspondence.

19. "In Re: Application of Hello World Broadcasting Corporation," 22 September 1930, p. 25, Docket No. 889, FRC Dockets.

20. Ibid., 69.

21. Hall, "Historical Study," 51.

22. Louis McCabe to Radio Division, 3 February 1928; Carl Butman to Radio Division, 5 February 1928; McCabe to Radio Division, 6 February 1928; McCabe to Radio Division, 11 February 1928; McCabe to Radio Division, 15 February 1928; McCabe to Radio Division, 18 February 1928; McCabe to Radio Division, 23 February 1928; McCabe to Radio Division, 28 February 1928; William K. Henderson to U.S. Senators Morris Sheppard and Smith W. Brookhart, 20 January 1931, KWKH Station File, Radio Division Correspondence.

23. See Carl G. Ryant, "The South and the Movement against Chain Stores," *The Journal of Southern History* 39 (May 1973): 207–22.

24. "In Re: Application of Hello World Broadcasting Corporation, Statement of Facts," 4 December 1931, KWKH Station File, Radio Division Correspondence.

25. D. B. Carson to Radio Division, 18 May 1926, KWKH Station File, Radio Division Correspondence; Raymond Francis Yates, "Will 'Canned Music' Return?," *Popular Radio* 11 ( January 1927): 100; "General Order No. 16," in *Supplement to the Second Annual Report of the Federal Radio Commission* (Washington, D.C., 1928), 41.

26. Louis McCabe to Radio Division , 3 February 1928, p. 2, KWKH Station File, Radio Division Correspondence; Hall, "Historical Study," 57

27. A detailed account of the troubled relations between WWL and KWKH can be found in C. Joseph Pusateri, *Enterprise in Radio: WWL and the Business of Broadcasting in America* (Washington, D.C., 1980), passim.

28. *Third Annual Report of the Federal Radio Commission* (Washington, D.C., 1929), 196–97.

29. "In Re: Southwestern Sales," 10; O. R. Redfern to Radio Division, 4 October 1927, p. 1, KWKH Station File, Radio Division Correspondence.

30. Louis McCabe to Radio Division, 15 February 1928, p. 4; McCabe to Radio Division, 2 March 1928, p. 2, KWKH Station File, Radio Division Correspondence.

31. Theodore Deiler to Radio Division, 7 February 1928, KWKH Station File, Radio Division Correspondence.

32. "Observation of KWKH Transmission," 10 January 1930, p. 3, KWKH Station File, Radio Division Correspondence.

33. Pusateri, *Enterprise*, 74, 76; "In Re: Station KWKH," 10 January 1930, Docket 356, p. 13; "In Re: Station KWKH," 10 January 1930, Docket 356, p. 13; "Motion for a Re-Hearing," 28 December 1930, Docket 889, pp. 8–9; Affidavit of William K. Henderson, 29 April 1931, Docket 889, FRC Dockets; Louis McCabe to Theodore Deiler, 5 March 1928; Theodore Deiler to Radio Division, 22 January 1931, KWKH Station File, Radio Division Correspondence; Ernest G. Bormann, "This Is Huey P. Long Speaking," *Journal of Broadcasting* 2 (spring 1958): 114–15.

34. "Motion for a Re-Hearing," 10; "Exceptions to Report of Examiner," 7 February 1931, Docket 889, pp. 2–7; "Affidavit of W. K. Henderson," 28 April 1931, Docket 889, p. 12, FRC Dockets; "Observations of Station KWKH," 9 March 1932, p. 2, KWKH Station File, Radio Division Correspondence.

35. "Motion for a Re-Hearing," 8–10; "Affidavit of W. K. Henderson," 2, 13–16. In January 1931 Henderson admitted to listeners that he had used "much"

of the Modern Minute Men funds for the payment of personal debts; see "Statement of W.K. Henderson as Broadcast over Station KWKH," 26 January 1931, Docket 889, p. 3, FRC Dockets.
36. William K. Henderson to Senators Morris Sheppard and Smith W. Brookhart, 20 January 1931, Docket 889; Oscar U. Schlegel to FRC, 4 February 1929, Docket 356, FRC Dockets; Hall, "Historical Study," 95; Pusateri, *Enterprise,* 151.
37. Pusateri, *Enterprise,* 151.
38. Ibid.

*Chapter 6*

1. James L. Dwyer, "Elijah the Third," *American Mercury* 15 (July 1927): 299; "Religion," *News-week,* 13 April 1935, 26.
2. Grant Wacker, "Marching to Zion: Religion in a Modern Utopian Community," *Church History* 54 (December 1985): 497.
3. Theodore Forby, "Zion City—Religious Life," in John J. Halsey, ed., *A History of Lake County, Illinois* (Chicago, 1912), 774.
4. "A Brief Authentic Biography of the Rev. Wilbur Glenn Voliva," *Leaves of Healing,* 15 March 1924, 401–6.
5. John D. Thomas, "The Musical Organization of Zion," *Leaves of Healing,* 3 May 1924, 139.
6. Ibid.; "Report of the Mid-Week Prayer Meeting," *Leaves of Healing,* 9 June 1928, 199, 201; J. H. DePew, "Zion Radio Station WCBD," ibid., 28 November 1925, 167.
7. J. H. DePew, "Zion Radio Broadcasting Station," *Leaves of Healing,* 21 July 1923, 274; ibid., 3 May 1924, 137–38; ibid., 28 November 1925, 167.
8. "General Overseer Signs Contract for New Super-Power 5,000-Watt Radiocasting Station to Be Installed Early Next Year," *Leaves of Healing,* 9 August 1924, 424; "Radiophone Notes," ibid., 21 February 1925, 365.
9. "General Overseer Signs Contract," 424.
10. "Report of the Mid-Week Prayer Meeting," 201.
11. Dwyer, "Elijah the Third"; "Religion," 26.
12. Wilbur G. Voliva, "Whence Am I? and Whither Am I Going?," *Leaves of Healing,* 24 November 1923, 148; "Divine Healing Address," ibid., 14 October 1923, 453.
13. "Radiophone Notes," *Leaves of Healing,* 10 January 1925, 264; ibid., 28 May 1927, 173; ibid., 10 November 1928, 132.
14. Thomas, "Musical Organization," 139.
15. Radiophone Notes," *Leaves of Healing,* 31 January 1925, 314; ibid., 2 December 1923, 215; ibid., 14 December 1923, 303; ibid., 12 January 1924, 268; ibid., 26 January 1924, 300; ibid., 9 February 1924, 332; ibid., 23 February 1924, 284; ibid., 1 March 1924, 380; ibid., 27 December 1924, 235; ibid., 14 February 1925, 348; ibid., 17 November 1928, 148; ibid., 8 March 1924, 392; ibid., 26 January 1924, 300; ibid., 21 March 1925,13.; ibid., 15 December 1923, 203.
16. "Radiophone Notes," *Leaves of Healing,* 12 May 1928, 141; see also ibid., 7 November 1925, 121; ibid., 25 February 1925, 381.
17. A. G. Nye to WCBD, 26 October 1928, found in listener correspondence in possession of the Christian Community Church, Zion, Illinois; photocopies in possession of the author.

18. "Report of the Mid-Week Prayer Meeting," 199, 201.
19. "Radiophone Notes," *Leaves of Healing*, 22 December 1923, 215; ibid., 5 January 1924, 252; ibid., 23 February 1924, 363; ibid., 1 March 1924, 380; ibid., 12 April 1924, 97; ibid., 26 April 1924, 126–8; ibid., 5 July 1924, 349; ibid., 26 July 1924, 389; ibid., 9 August 1924, 420; ibid., 1 November 1924, 106; ibid., 6 September 1924, 485; ibid., 25 October 1924, 91; ibid., 3 January 1925, 252; ibid., 13 June 1925, 201; ibid., 7 November 1925, 121; ibid., 30 October 1926, 109; ibid., 10 November 1928, 132; ibid., 19 November 1928,134; ibid., 1 December 1928, 185; ibid., 8 December 1928, 199.
20. "Radiophone Notes," *Leaves of Healing*, 30 August 1924, 471; ibid., 29 December 1923, 235; ibid., 5 January 1924, 252.
21. A. J. Anselm to Radio Division, 12 February 1925, WCBD Station File, Radio Division Correspondence.
22. "Timely Truths Uttered by Wilbur Glenn Voliva," *Leaves of Healing*, 28 July 1923, 294; "Radiophone Notes," *Leaves of Healing* , 17 May 1924, 234; ibid., 15 November 1924, 140; ibid., 21 February 1925, 365; ibid., 5 September 1925, 396; ibid., 17 August 1926, 333.
23. Harry K. Goodall to Radio Division, 7 March 1924, WCBD Station File, Radio Division Correspondence.
24. "Radiophone Notes," *Leaves of Healing*, 29 March 1924, 20.
25. "Report of the Mid-Week Prayer Meeting," 201; "Radiophone Notes," *Leaves of Healing*, 29 March 1924, 20.
26. "Report of the Mid-Week Prayer Meeting," 201.
27. "Radiophone Notes," *Leaves of Healing*, 10 November 1928, 131; ibid., 29 October 1928, 132; ibid., 17 November 1928, 149; ibid., 1 December 1928, 184.
28. Federal Radio Commission, *Third Annual Report of the Federal Radio Commission to the Congress of the United States* (Washington, D.C., 1929),11.
29. Federal Radio Commission, *Wilbur Glenn Voliva, Appellant,* v. *Federal Radio Commission, Brief for the Federal Radio Commission, 1929*, 5, Publications of the Federal Government, Record Group 287, National Archives, Washington, D.C.
30. Philip Lord [Seth Parker], *Seth Parker's Album, by Seth Parker of Jonesport, Maine* (New York, 1930).

*Chapter 7*

1. Marshall Kernochan, "The Suicide of Radio," *Outlook*, 22 April 1931, 561–74.
2. Jack Woodford, "Radio–A Blessing or a Curse?," *The Forum* 79 (March 1929): 169–71.
3. H. L. Bercovici, "Station B-U-N-K," *American Mercury* 15 (February 1929): 233–40; Henry Volkening, "Abuses of Radio Broadcasting," *Current History* 83 (December 1930): 396–400; William Orton, "The Level of Thirteen-Year Olds," *Atlantic Monthly* 147 (January 1931): 1–10; "Saving the Radio," *Outlook*, 21 January 1931, 86; Johan Smertenko, "Noises on the Air," *Outlook*, 16 July 1930, 561; "Can Radio Be Rescued?," *New Republic*, 24 June 1931, 139–40; James Rorty, "The Impending Radio War," *Harper's* 61 (November 1931): 714–26; "In the Driftway," *Nation*, 5 October 1932, 309–10; Merrill Dennison, "Why Isn't Radio Better?" *Harper's* 168 (April 1934): 576–86.
4. Deems Taylor, "Radio: A Brief for the Defense," *Harper's* 166 (April 1933): 554.

5. "Broadcasting Advertising Is Sold at a Loss," *Printers' Ink*, 16 February 1928, 140.

6. Daniel Starch, *A Study of Radio Broadcasting in the United States East of the Rocky Mountains* (Cambridge, Mass., 1928), 24.

7. William Hurd, "Is It 'Who pays for broadcasting?' or 'How do we get the bill?,'" *The Wireless Age* 11 (April 1924): 26–28. Polled for the article were W. E. Harkness, assistant vice-president of AT&T; David Sarnoff, vice president and general manager of RCA; H. P. Davis, vice president of Westinghouse; Martin P. Rice, director of broadcasting for General Electric; Charles Popenoe, manager of station WJZ (Westinghouse); John Holman, manager of WEAF (AT&T); Paul Klugh, executive chairman of the National Association of Broadcasters; J. C. Rosenthal, general manager of the American Society of Composers, Authors and Publishers (ASCAP); and Austin Lescarboura, radio engineering authority and managing editor of *Scientific American*.

8. Bernard A Grimes, "'Digest' Poll of Radio Listeners," *Printers' Ink*, 21 December 1933, 64–66; Pauline Arnold, "Sizing Up the Audience," *Advertising and Selling*, 22 June 1933, 57–58.

9. "Radio Improves the Musical Taste of the Nation," *Popular Radio* 10 (August 1926): 385; "From Bananas to Bach in Radio Taste," ibid. (March 1928): 264; "Radio Giving Aid to Music Lovers Who Are Out to Kill 'Jazz,'" *Chicago Evening Post Radio Magazine*, 22 January 1925, 5; "Jazz Bows before Classical Music in KSD Contest," ibid., 9 April 1925, 3; "Prima Donna Says Radio Fans Want Classical Music," ibid., 16 July 1925, 12; "Radio Carries Good Music to Thousands Who Appreciate It," ibid., 24 December 1925, 2; "Classics Are in Lead over Jazz at WRC," ibid., 31 December 1925, 7; "Jazz Beaten By Classics in Contest," ibid., 5 May 1927, 5; "Big Applause For Jazzless Dance Music," ibid., 15 June 1927, 6; "Music Taste Elevated from Jazz to Bach," ibid., 16 February 1928, 7; "Radio Fans' Likes and Dislikes Revealed by Questionnaires," *New York Times*, 21 February 1926, sec. 10, p. 17; "Radio Opera Ousting Jazz," ibid., 1 April 1927, 28; "No Jazz Requests When Radio Fans Fix KDKA Program," *New York Herald Tribune*, 10 January 1926, sec. 2, p. 8; Jennie Irene Mix, "Good National Radio Programs Prove 'What the Public Wants,'" *Radio Broadcast* 7 (May 1925): 62–64; "Broadcasting as It Is Today," *New York Herald Tribune*, 22 February 1925, 13.

10. Silas Hopper, "Broadcasters Use Prize Contests Unfairly," *Printers' Ink*, 18 March 1926, 153; Harry P. Bridge, "If You Are Thinking of Broadcasting," ibid., 1 April 1926, 133; "Radio Listeners Still Protest against Broadcast Advertising," ibid., 6 May 1926, 137; Uriel Davis, "A Showman Looks at Radio Advertising," ibid., 24 February 1927, 135; "Radio Commission May Control Broadcast Advertising," ibid., 24 March 1927, 192; "Direct Advertising over the Air Is Showing a Decline," ibid., 26 May 1927, 50–52.

11. Frank Finney, "Grand Opera, Symphonies and Cigarettes," *Printers' Ink*, 25 January 1934, 13

12. "High Hats for Lowbrows," *Printers' Ink*, 8 February 1934, 61.

13. Roy S. Durstine, "Radio Advertising's Future in the United States," *Printers' Ink*, 24 January 1935, 41–45.

14. "Radio Cracks Down," *Printers' Ink*, 21 March 1935, 114; Yolanda Mero-Irion, "What the Women Like and Dislike About Radio," ibid., 21 March 1935, 66; "To Improve Radio," ibid., 23 May 1935, 24.

15. Harold Clark, "Women and Radio Programs," *Printers' Ink*, 12 September 1935, 63.

16. Barnouw, *Tower*, 237.

17. "Permits Price Mention on Radio," *Printers' Ink*, 15 September 1932, 33.

18. Barnouw, *Tower*, 273.

19. James C. Foust, *Big Voices of the Air: The Battle over Clear Channel Radio* (Ames, Iowa, 2000), 185–215.

20. Interviewed in his retirement, the founding head of NBC's programming department, John Royal, owned up to the prudential aspect of network's relationship to Shakespeare, admitting that NBC's frequent showcasing of the Bard occurred not "because we were great enthusiasts for Shakespeare. To be strictly honest, we put it on for exhibition, to show educators, etc., that we were adding something to culture" (quoted in Louis E. Carlat, "Sound Values: Radio Broadcasts of Symphonic Music and American Culture, 1922–1939" [Ph.D. diss., Johns Hopkins University, 1995], 108).

21. Quoted in Carlat, "Sound Values," 108.

22. Erik Barnouw, *The Golden Web* (New York, 1968), 70–73.

23. Ibid., 165–66.

24. Wartime conditions exerted an opposite effect on the British broadcasting system, vastly and permanently depressing its overall "brow level." Following the formal commencement of hostilities in 1939, the BBC divided itself into two separate services: the Home Service, providing regular domestic service; and the Forces Programme, dedicated to maintaining the morale of British expeditionary forces in Europe. At the insistence of the military authorities, the BBC dispensed with its usual, strenuous didacticism in designing the Forces Programme; instead, it obliged the young men and women in the field with the sort of programming that military survey data indicated they most preferred: undemanding light entertainment and plenty of popular dance music. The resulting program, which closely resembled the American-style commercial programs of prewar Radio Luxembourg, was also made available domestically as an alternative service on a separate frequency, and was soon discovered to be attracting more civilian listeners than the Home Service was. Further popular alternatives arrived with the American Forces Network (AFN), created in 1943 to provide American-style light entertainment and swing music to U.S. troops in Britain and on the Continent, but also popular with many Britons living within receiving range of the low-power AFN base transmitters. See Stephen Barnard, *On the Radio: Music Radio in Britain* (Philadelphia, 1989), 20–23, 28–29; Andrew Crisell, *An Introductory History of British Broadcasting* (London: 1997), 55.

25. Carlat, "Sound Values," 79–132.

26. Signature illegible, Acting Supervisor of Radio, Baltimore, Maryland, to Radio Division, 19 April 1927, WJSV Station File, Radio Division Correspondence.

27. "Pro-Klan Journal Buys Radio Station," *New York Times*, 27 July 1927, sec. 3, p. 26; "Klan Radio Station Seeks 50,000 Watts," ibid., 9 October 1927, 6; "Radio Board Seeks Klan Air Programs," ibid., 28 October 1927, 18; "Klan to Use High Power," ibid., 23 November 1927, 19.

28. James S. Vance to the Federal Radio Commission, 29 October 1928, WJSV Station File, Radio Division Correspondence.

29. "In Re: Application of WJSV," Docket 1653, 10 June 1932, WJSV Station File, Radio Division Correspondence.

30. Levine, *Highbrow/Lowbrow*, 218.

# Index

Adams, Hugh White, 59
advertising industry: as admirer of BBC,
15–16; embrace of broadcast advertis-
ing, 121–23; as opponent of broadcast
advertising, 13–16, 120–21; professional
pretensions of, 14. See also *Printers' Ink*
Allen, Steve, 69
American Civil Liberties Union (ACLU),
68, 115
American Jewish Committee, 65
American Marconi Corporation, 18
American Medical Association (AMA), 88
*American Mercury* (magazine), 72
American Protective League, 59
American Protestant Alliance, 59
American Socialist Party, 20, 114
American Society of Composers, Authors
and Publishers (ASCAP), 30–31
*American Standard* (magazine), 62, 67
American Telephone & Telegraph (AT&T),
vii, 10, 26, 29; asserts monopoly over "toll
broadcasting," 23, 36–37; attacked by
commissioner Grover Whalen, 42–43;
and creation of RCA, 18–19; in legal bat-
tle with George Schubel and WHN,
35–44; sells WEAF, 118; shut out of
receiver market, 35–36. *See also* WEAF
Anderson, William H., 59
Anglo-Israel, 61–62
Angus, Howard, 14
announcers: ideal conceptions of, 25; pop-
ularity contests among, 25, 80–81, 88
Anselm, A. J., 112
Armstrong, Louis, 33
Armstrong, LuEtta Minnick, 79
Associated Broadcasters Incorporated, 45
Atlass, Ralph and Leslie, 46
Atwood, Harry F., 59
audience research, 8–9, 119–21
Aylesworth, Merlin, 118–19

Bach, J. S., 63
Baker, Norman, vii, 86–88, 90–91, 101;
adopts direct sales model, 87; establishes
border station XENT, 90; establishes
cancer clinic, 88; establishes KTNT, 87;
madness of, 88; as public health cru-
sader, 87–88; runs for governor of Iowa,
90
Baldwin, James A., 68
Banning, William Peck, 36, 44
Bannister, Frank, 2–6, 16, 47
Barnouw, Erik, 10, 122, 123, 125
Barthelmess, Richard, 25
Batchellor, Arthur, 35
Batten, Burton, Durstine and Osborne, 121
Beethoven, Ludwig van, 12, 63, 110
Berlin, Irving, 25
Bettelton, Duke, 91
Better America Federation, 59
Beuick, Marshall, 13
Beville, H. M., Jr., 8
"Big Four" corporations, vii, 10, 16, 18–20,
35–36, 118–19
"Big Six" corporations (Britain), 18
Blake, Eubie, 33
Bloom, Solomon, 65
Boettcher, William, ix, 21–22, 23
Boissevain, Inez Milholland, 64
Bonanza, Cardinal, 65
Book of Revelation, 61
border radio, vii, 90–91,124; threatened
establishment of border blaster by Wil-
liam K. Henderson, 103. *See also* Baker,
Norman; Brinkley, John Romulus
Bori, Lucrezia, 37
Bosler, William, 59
Bowes, Charles, 7
Briddle, G. H., 109
Brinkley, John Romulus, vii, 68, 84–90,
101; broadcasting style of, 85; establishes

Henderson, William K. (*continued*)
  FRC and Radio Division personnel on
  air, 100; criticizes broadcast advertising,
  96; crusades against chain stores, 98;
  defends canned music, 99; dubious
  financial probity of, 102; establishes
  KWKH, 92; and Huey Long, 101; musical tastes of, 96; political cronies of, 99–
  101; as proto-disk jockey, 93, 95–96; as
  proto-shock jock, 93–95; pushes for
  greater signal power, 99–100; sells
  KWKH, 103; swears off profanity, 102;
  threatens to establish border blaster, 102
Henderson Iron Works and Supply Com-
  pany, 92, 103
Henri, Hurst, and McDonald Inc., 120
Henry, John M., 83
*Highbrow/Lowbrow: The Emergence of Cultural
  Hierarchy in America*, 69, 127. *See also* Lev-
  ine, Lawrence
Hilmes, Michele, vii-viii, 6, 16–17
Hofstader, Richard, 72
Hooper, C. F., 121
Hoover, Herbert, 13, 34, 45, 47, 82, 95
Hotel Alamac, 32
Hoxey, Harry, 88
Hughes, C. A., 26
Hughes, Hatcher, 68
hymns: from farmer stations, 10, 76; from
  networks, 116; from WCBD, 110, 112;
  "In the Sweet Bye and Bye," 110; "Lead,
  Kindly Light," 110, 116; "The Little
  Brown Church in the Vale," 110; "The
  Ninety and the Nine," 112; "Softly and
  Tenderly," 110

illustrated slide singers, 28
Iowa Radio Listeners' League, 81. *See also*
  St. Austell, Francis
Isaacson, Charles, 9

Janssen's Hofbrau, 32
jazz: highbrow disdain for, 11, 12, 34, 57,
  63; hot versus sweet, 33, 37; from
  KWKH, 96–97; as middle-class counter-
  culture, 32–33; polls predicting imminent death of, 120, 146 n.9; rural hatred
  of, 10–11, 74, 76, 79, 80, 84, 111; from
  WHN, 31–34, 48
Jefferson, Thomas, 72
Jehovah's Witnesses, 114
*Jersey Journal*, 27, 38

Johnson, Charlie, 33
Joy, Leslie, 59, 64
Juilliard, Frederic A., 42, 58

Kaempffert, Waldemar, 12
Kaltenborn, Hans V., 11
KDKA (Pittsburgh), 9, 74
Keefe, F. H., 38–39
Keith-Albee vaudeville circuit, 24, 37, 126
Kent, Robert L., 8
Kernochan, Marshall, 117
KFKB (Milford, Kans.), 68, 84–87, 89, 90.
  *See also* Brinkley, John Romulus
KFNF (Shenandoah, Iowa), 71, 78–84, 86,
  88, 91, 123. *See also* direct sales model of
  broadcasting; Field, Henry; May, Earl
KFNF Hawaiian Trio, 79
Kilpatrick, Clifford, 8
Kipling, Rudyard, 29, 33, 46
KMA (Shenandoah, Iowa), 71, 80–82, 84,
  86, 91. *See also* direct sales model of
  broadcasting; Field, Henry; May, Earl
KMMJ (Clay Center, Neb.), 84
Knights of Columbus, 65
Koppes, Clayton R., 13
KSO (Clarinda, Iowa), 84
KTFI (Twin Falls, Idaho), 84
KTNT (Muscatine, Iowa), vii, 84, 86–88,
  90–91, 101. *See also* Baker, Norman
Ku Klux Klan, 62–63, 64, 73, 102; broad-
  casting by, 126–27
KWKC (Kansas City, Mo.), 47
KWKH (Shreveport, La.), viii, 76, 92–104,
  126. *See also* Henderson, William K.
KXA (Seattle, Wash.), 47
KXL (Portland, Oreg.), 47

Landon, Alf, 120
Larkan, "Uncle" Bob, 85
Lazarsfeld, Paul, 8
*Leaves of Healing* (magazine), 109, 111
Leiber, Phillip, 98
Levine, Lawrence, 69, 127
Lindbergh, Charles, 64–65
Lindbergh, Evangeline, 65
Liszt, Franz, 110
*Literary Digest* (magazine), 73, 120
Loew, Marcus, 24, 43
Loew's Inc., 23–25, 29, 39
Loew's State Theatre, 25, 29
Long, Huey, 100
Loyola University, 99